Multinational
Enterprises

Multinational Enterprises

LEGAL AND MANAGEMENT STRUCTURES
AND INTERRELATIONSHIP WITH
OWNERSHIP, CONTROL, ANTITRUST, LABOR,
TAXATION AND DISCLOSURE

by ROBERT EMMETT TINDALL

1975

OCEANA PUBLICATIONS, INC., DOBBS FERRY, N.Y.

A.W. SIJTHOFF, LEIDEN

Library of Congress Cataloging in Publication Data

Tindall, Robert Emmett, 1934-
    Multinational enterprises.

    Originally presented as the author's thesis,
City University, London.
    1. International business enterprises. I. Title.
Law   341.7'53   75-14173
ISBN 0-379-00310-4   (Oceana)
ISBN 90 286 02453   (Sijthoff)

Manufactured in the United States of America

TABLE OF CONTENTS

TABLE OF CONTENTS

PREFACE

Much has been written about the organization of multinational enterprises from the managerial viewpoint. This is so because it was the managers of national business enterprises who provided the thrust for the internationalization of business. Within the framework of traditional national legal structures they have reorganized managerial structures to maximize global opportunities. As a consequence of these activities, pressures have developed for the design of new legal structures to facilitate business on a global scale. A limited number of such structures now exist in America, in some European countries, and in Japan. There are prospects for a European Company and even speculation about the possibility of a World Company.

Underlying this is the ever accelerating trend toward large scale global rationalization of business units, and an integrated world economy. The multinational enterprise is leading this course of events.

At times nation states have supported these trends, recognizing that extreme nationalism is economically indefensible. On the other hand, they have presented roadblocks when the direction of events threatened their legitimate national interests.

If nation states and multinational enterprises are to accommodate one another a variety of issues must be resolved. In part, the differences stem from the fact that industry and commerce have led governments in adjusting to new economic and technological realities. However, the specific problems center around certain legal, business and economic aspects. Among the crucial aspects are the concepts and institutions relating to Ownership, Control, Antitrust, Labor, Taxation and

Disclosure. These notions are based upon legal and managerial structures intended for business formerly conducted exclusively on a national scale. There is a need to modernize these notions to suit the current structure of multinational enterprise.

This book is a systematic description and analysis of the evolving legal and managerial structure of multinational enterprise and its impact upon and interrelationship with those concepts and institutions deemed most critical to the adaption of the multinational enterprise to the present global environment.

As representative of world multinational enterprises the work focuses upon the Ford Motor Company, Mitsubishi Group, the Royal Dutch/Shell Group, Unilever and the Dunlop Pirelli Union.

This book is the manuscript that was submitted as the thesis in fullfillment of the requirements for the degree of Doctor of Philosophy in Management Studies at the Graduate Business Centre of The City University in London.

There is no other person in the world today who surpasses Professor Clive M. Schmitthoff, of The City University and the University of Kent, in breadth of knowledge and insight in the field of study involved in this work. I am grateful for his indispensable guidance in our conversations, in his writings, and in our correspondence while I was in the Far East.

I am also thankful for the assistance and co-operation of Dr. Peter H. Grinyer and other members of the staff of the Graduate Business Centre, The City University. Thanks are likewise due to various faculty members and officers of the University of Arizona for their encouragement and for granting the necessary leaves of absence.

Part of the manuscript was researched and written while I was a visiting professor at the Graduate School of Law of Soochow University in the Republic of China. This was made possible by a generous grant from the Asia Foundation in San Francisco.

Acknowledgement is also given to the officers of Ford, Mitsubishi, Unilever, Royal Dutch Shell and Dunlop Pirelli who supplied company literature and instructive conversation.

The excellent services and facilities of the following libraries were vital: City of London Business Library, Graduate Business Centre Library of the City University, Institute of Advanced Legal Studies in London, London Business School, London School of Economics and Political Science, Soochow University in Tapei and the University of Arizona.

The book is dedicated to L.J.T., A.T., and R.E.T., Sr.

INTRODUCTION

Multinational enterprises are increasingly taking the center stage
in news media around the world. As each day passes leaders of business,
government, labor, and other social institutions are faced with new
policy issues engendered by the growth of multinational enterprise (MNE).
There has been an accompanying burst of scholarly research and writing
on the subject, the majority of it coming initially from Harvard Multinational Project group. Most of the studies have been undertaken by
business, management or economics scholars. And most have been limited
to one facet of the subject, such as organizational control or finance.

This study is comprehensive in nature and views the topic from a
legal as well as a business, managerial or economic standpoint. Existing
studies have often ignored fundamentals because they had as their goal
improved organization or operating efficiency, rather than a broader
attitude of understanding what multinationals are, and how they relate
to nations and world economic and social goals. Fundamentals were also
ignored becuse they lacked a legal understanding of the enterprise and
its interrelationship with existing national legal institutions. They
ignored the crucial fact that multinationals' economic relationship to
nations is necessarily entwined with its legal relationship.

To understand what multinationals are, five of the worlds' largest
were selected from the United States, Europe and Japan - Ford,

Unilever, Royal Dutch Shell, Dunlop Pirelli and Mitsubishi Group. Information was gathered from company publications and data, conversations with their executives, and from outside publications about them. The history of their organizational growth was reviewed, with special emphasis on their legal and managerial structures. As many detailed studies have already been done of the managerial organization of MNE, concentration was given to their legal structure and its relationship to the managerial structure.

Within those enterprises and throughout the study one basic idea emerged and repeated itself - the disparity between economic unity and legal unity. All five of the enterprises can be viewed as single economic units. Yet they are composed of separate legal units in many countries. Ford is the simplest. It consists of one legal parent company which owns its many domestic and foreign subsidiary legal units. The linkage is purely one of ownership. In the case of Mitsubishi there is no parent company. The linkage among the many legally separate companies is limited cross-holdings of shares, tradition, and voluntary co-operation. In the other three a single parent company is also absent. Two parents are joined by contract or special provisions in their articles of incorporation providing for common directors.

The economic/legal disparity exists because national corporate legal provisions were not designed with multinationals in mind. What has happened is that business leaders have organized their managerial enterprise structures on a multinational basis and have adjusted their

v

legal structures in various awkward ways. If there were a single
world corporation legal framework the awkwardness and disparities
would be reduced or eliminated. Theoretically, the legal and managerial structures could be the same. For the present, however,
these disparities are the basic source of difficulties requiring
adjustment on the part of all parties.

About a dozen other multinational enterprises were examined
in an attempt to arrive at a catalog of structures which are prototypes
of all multinationals now existing. These are organized in the order
of complexity and permanence of cohesion and unity. Their description
indicates the kinds of obstacles to unification that the structures were
intended to overcome.

It is apparent that there is an acceleration of mergers,
acquisitions and consolidations which has sprung across national
borders in attempts at greater rationalization, economies of scale,
global markets, and follow-the-leader strategies. In Europe, especially,
there is recognition that national and regional governments must take
steps to accommodate genuine multinational structures. Consequently,
a number of steps have been taken to harmonize European company law.
EEC directives on the subject are reviewed. The most progressive
step forward is the proposed European Company. If adopted, it will
supplement but not replace national company laws within EEC member
states. It is expressly intended for multinational companies and will
give the enterprise adopting it European nationality, thereby reducing
the psychological barriers to European cross border mergers. The
proposed European Company statute also introduces the concept of

worker participation in the managerial process, and makes a beginning recognition of legal unity of groups of companies comprising an economic unit. Successful use of the European Company concept would be the first step towards the possibility of a world company law.

As a consequence of the unique legal and managerial structures of MNE, national concepts of ownership, control, antitrust, labor, taxation and disclosure are rapidly being obsoleted. As they now stand these concepts influence the organization and conduct of MNE. These interrelations are explored and analyzed.

The separation of ownership and control has been recognized for some time. The implications of this are compounded when enterprises become multinational.

The enjoyment aspect of share ownership directs the ultimate profit or dividend flow towards the parent companies and shareholders. This has major significance for national balance of payments and capital accumulation. But it is the power or control aspect that is really the critical issue.

Although most multinationals retain 100 percent ownership of their foreign subsidiaries they are not reluctant to share their owner- ship if there are other means of retaining control. In this connection it is significant to note that host countries are sometimes more concerned with who appears to have control rather than who actually exercises effective control.

The truth of the ownership aspect is that virtually no enterprises that we call multinational enterprises are truly multi-national. If this fact were remedied it would reduce the overall tension between MNE and nation states. Mechanisms must be found to realize local participation in MNE subsidiaries or in the parent company. This can be accomplished by sharing ownership or by contractual rights in physical production as is done in some Eastern European countries.

Ownership implications have been exaggerated. Multinationals, regardless of their nationality of ownership, generally operate in response to a given institutional and economic setting in order to improve their economic position. In spite of opinionated criticism to the contrary, foreign-owned enterprises are often superior to local-owned enterprises in terms of employment conditions, export foreign exchange earnings, and other factors. The real issue is who controls MNE and towards what end. Even in those nations which have switched completely to state-owned enterprise, the control problems and policy difficulties still persist.

Internal control problems of managing and organizing the MNE are not fundamentally different whether privately owned or state owned. In both cases there is a constant tension between centralized and decentralized control.

Host and home countries of MNE have different control problems. The most progressive approach to this is for those problems to be resolved jointly and simultaneously by negotiation between equals, including government, enterprise and labor representatives. This was achieved in the Canadian American

Automobile Agreement of 1965. The dilemma is that home and host countries are far from equal in bargaining power. Some legal framework must provide this.

There is a benefit that has come from national reaction and possible desire to overcontrol MNE. That is that it awakens national governments to their proper role in the control of economic and enterprise developments which has been ineffective with its local enterprises, not to mention the more obvious threat from foreign enterprise. National control of MNE has been unsuccessful largely because enterprises are more flexible and can choose among more lenient nations for future investment. If nations cannot evolve rational and uniform regulations on a co-operative basis, it will either not be done, or be accomplished by new regional or international institutions.

Even at the national level corporate law, originally designed to control companies, has failed. A corporate charter is little more than an enabling document. It is this philosophy that has permitted MNE to approach the size and power that now offers a potential threat to the very bodies who were to control them. It is conceivable that this will be corrected at the international level before it is corrected at the national level. This is simply because MNE poses a greater threat than purely national enterprises.

The traditional method of controlling excessive economic power has been the antitrust concept. It is now impeded by the fact that many countries and regions are actually encouraging mergers and multinationalization as a defensive strategy against more powerful enterprises from other nations. What is slowly developing is competition among national and regional groupings with MNEs from each serving as the champions from each area. Unless the antitrust idea is applied at the global level MNEs may well become much more powerful before they are placed in check. At present European and other enterprises are building to the size of American MNEs. This will be a never-ending seesaw unless agreements are reached.

Although the United States professes to take the 'structural' approach to antitrust, in practice it and most of the developed countries seem to follow the 'conduct' approach. Size alone has never been a criteria to invite antitrust intervention. In world competition, size, financial power and diversification - factors characteristic of MNE - have become of primary significance. These factors are not generally taken into account in present antitrust criteria. Whether and to what extent they will be taken into account will have a decisive influence on multinationals.

While MNE structures have advanced to meet changing global conditions, labour organizations have not. Unless this changes there will be an increasing imbalance of power between labor and management, thereby eliminating labor as a balancing force or control. Trade unions were organized on a national basis and since jobs lost in one nation are gained in another, there is an inherent conflict of interest between national groups. Differing political and economic ideologies also separate them.

A roadblock to universal collective bargaining is that bargaining is presently done on many different levels depending on the company and the nation. In terms of global tactics the unions must decide between regional or global agreements involving all companies of a given industry or enterprise bargaining across all national boundaries. Varying national labor laws will affect either realization. As labor strategy does unfold, it will have a definite impact on MNE strategy of production organization.

European trends towards worker participation in enterprise governance may cast labor management relations in a new light. In any event, the International Labour Office should play a key role in the improvement of global working conditions. Two critical barriers to raising world labor standards are that there is no legal enforceability for potential international collective agreements, and upward harmonization may conflict with employment objectives in developing countries.

Tax planning is not the dominant influence in MNE strategy but MNE management does co-ordinate the work of its legally separate entities in attempt to optimize the international tax environment. The income tax problems related to them are similar to the treatment of multi-company enterprises within one nation. The latter may be called 'uninationals'. The difference is that several countries seek the income taxes from a multinational system of companies. The conflict is between the tax minimizing tactics of MNE and the tax maximizing policies of host nation states.

Variations in national taxing systems include differences in types of taxes, rates, definitions of income and expense, extraterritorial jurisdictional principles, and allowances for taxes paid. Unlike multi company 'uninationals' MNE may be subject to double taxation when their home country is a 'worldwide' taxing authority such as the US. By treaty or tax credit the double taxation can be avoided.

Where home country exchange controls and tax laws make it difficult for the parent company to act as a funnel for redistribution of profits throughout the MNE system, foreign holding or foreign base companies are created to perform that function.

There are dividend or profit avoiding devices designed to transfer resources to the parent with the least tax incidence, but the use of those tactics are exaggerated. When employed they generally do not reduce the overall long term tax bill of the MNE but merely shift the tax recipient nation. This has been deemed to be more of a political rather than ethical question.

The fact that some nations rely heavily on value-added tax (VAT) and others on income tax introduces unique implications for multinationals. It makes 'transfer pricing' less attractive and results in some tax discrimination depending upon the home country of the MNE.

Developing nations continue to forego tax revenues to which they are entitled, while multinationals are sometimes forced to use artificial structures and inefficient methods in order to minimize their total tax bill. To accomplish this the MNEs are beginning to employ computerized tax simulation models to find the optimal system. These models take into account factors such as the legal structure of the parent and subsidiaries, policies on internal movement of funds, home and host tax rates, currency convertibility, and devaluation probabilities.

Equitable tax revenue distribution among home country and host countries can only be fully achieved at the international level.

Since regulation of MNE on a grand international scale is unlikely for some time to come, data and information disclosure by MNE should be the immediate goal. It now seems probable that a permanent United Nations commission will be appointed to supervise this task. In the meantime traditional company disclosure techniques should be improved, expanded and harmonized across national boundaries. A complete national disclosure system is dependent upon legal requirements, stock market listing standards, professional and commercial tradition and the presence of qualified accountants and financial analysts.

Although harmonization of national accountancy standards is a long way off, internal MNE system accounts and reports are rapidly becoming standardized. This development could accelerate external accounting practices.

Failure to consolidate MNE accounts and reports is one of the chief shortcomings of present systems. As the need for simultaneous financing in many countries increases, this may be necessary to satisfy lenders or stock purchasers. Recognition and treatment of of MNE as a single legal unit is a significant aspect.

As a beginning, agreement might be reached among capital-exporting nations for worldwide consolidation and minimum disclosure by their MNEs in all cases where capital is sought outside of the home country.

In final conclusion, it is apparent that multinationals have outstripped the piecemeal national legal frameworks and that new legal frameworks are necessary. In the past it was an accepted reality that legal developments lagged behind social changes. However, recently in fields of technology such as nuclear energy and space vehicles it has been recognized that new legal rules must anticipate or precede scientific developments. This need should also be recognized with respect to the rapidly changing economic environment, led by the multinationals. If MNE is to grow in directions beneficial to society the law, national, regional and international, must take responsibility for it. Multinational enterprise is a political as well as an economic phenomenon. The dangerous lag presently existing is partly the result of the bulk of knowledgeable corporate lawyers being employed to pursue the efficiency of MNE. Others must be employed to create the necessary new legal frameworks to match the advances by business.

SYNOPSIS OF CHAPTERS

1.   Historical Perspective and Definitions

The multinational enterprise is a modern version of
the corporate concept fashioned hundreds of years ago. Since well
over half of the largest multinationals are American or British,
early corporate developments are traced within the context of
those two nations. At first it is difficult to distinguish between the
political and economic functions of early corporate forms. Clearly,
it was the nation state itself that took the initiative in forming the
early colonizing and trading companies. When purely private profit
companies were formed the state employed the chartering or
incorporation process as the means of maintaining control over
them. As businessmen made increasing contributions to national
interests governments relaxed their controls. Size, power, and
range of activities formerly limited, were expanded. The most
significant power given by the state was the power for one
corporation to own the stock of another. National networks of
corporations followed. Soon there were motivations for foreign
production and parent corporations, mostly American, in one
country extended their corporate networks overseas and became
the owners and managers of subsidiary corporations formed under
the laws of other nations. These networks have been named
multinational enterprises. They can be defined as a combination

of companies of different nationality, connected by means of share-holdings, managerial control or contract and constituting an economic unit. When a multinational has one parent company of a particular nationality then it is called a national multinational. When it has two or more controlling parent companies of different nationalities it is called an international multinational or, by some, a transnational. The various ways in which these networks are connected constitutes the legal structure of the enterprise.

2.   National Multinationals

     Ford Motor Company

     The Ford Motor Company was incorporated under the laws

of the State of Michigan in the U.S. in 1903. It was incorporated

in order to bring together in one controllable unit a dozen capital

contributors, the patents of Henry Ford, and mass production

know-how. In order to fully realize their resources the company

viewed the entire world as their market.

     Right from the start export agents and sales representatives

were appointed, and cars were shipped to numerous foreign countries.

In countries where sufficient volume justified it, a sales branch

office was opened. As volume climbed, sales branches developed

into assembly operations. When tax considerations warranted it,

branches were transformed into separate. foreign corporations.

Such corporations also insulated the Michigan parent company

from liability. Rising tariff barriers coupled with increasing foreign

governments' pressure for local manufactures impelled assembly

operations to expand to complete local manufacture. With the

coming of regional groups such as the Common Market, Ford

companies in different countries specialized in the manufacture of

certain components and exchanged those components among

themselves.

In the beginning foreign branches and corporations enjoyed considerable independence. Distances and communication difficulties left little choice in that regard. As that improved and as world automotive competition accelerated more and more managerial direction and coordination came from the parent company. At the present time Ford headquarters in the U.S. clearly decides overall Ford policy and plans. However it has coordinating headquarters in two of their major foreign areas - Europe, and Asia-Pacific. In both instances there are separately incorporated companies which house these facilities and activities. Both are incorporated in the U.S. although their headquarters are overseas.

Ford's present policy regarding ownership of foreign subsidiaries is for the parent company to directly hold full ownership where possible. This was not always the policy.

The Ford-Canada affiliate was the first foreign subsidiary and it was 51% owned. Over the years this has moved up towards 60% but never over. Because of British Empire tariff considerations it directly owned 100% interests in the subsidiaries located in Australia, South Africa, Malaya, and New Zealand. Since the late 1960's these have been directly and wholly owned by the American parent company.

The English and European subsidiaries began as wholly owned by Ford-U.S. In 1928 this was changed. Participation by local nationals was deemed advantageous. In the reorganization that followed Ford-England became 60% owned by Ford-U.S. and 40% owned by Englishmen. Ford-England was to coordinate European operations. It held 60% of the then existing nine European subsidiaries and local nationals held the remaining 40%

In the recentralization which followed World War II, Ford-U.S. reacquired direct ownership of the English and European subsidiaries. In almost all instances they became 100% owned or nearly so.

As of 1972 Ford's foreign production and distribution operations are housed in foreign corporations located in 30 different countries. Save for a few, all are directly owned. All but 10 are wholly owned. Of those 10, the parent company's interest is 70% or greater in all instances except in the 50/50 Japanese affiliate.

Mitsubishi Group

The Mitsubishi Group is a Japanese multinational enterprise. Although its worldwide sales have been substantial for a number of years, its overseas production facilities are of recent origin and, like Japan's, growing very rapidly.

Like Ford, it consists of about forty individual corporations. But, whereas the Ford corporations are owned by the single American parent company, the various Mitsubishi corporations each own portions of the shares of each other. It differs from Ford in that nearly all the corporations were formed and are headquartered in the home company, Japan. There is no single parent company having ownership control over the others. Instead, three of the corporations form a triumvirate of Group leadership. They are Mitsubishi Bank, Mitsubishi Corporation and Mitsubishi Heavy Industries.

The top executive of each of those companies are the chairman of the Kinyo-kai or Friday Conference. It consists of the presidents of 26 of the leading Mitsubishi companies. Policy decisions, coordination and cooperation among the Group depends upon the collective guidance exercised at those weekly conferences.

Mitsubishi Group cohesion is based on cross-holdings of shares, a community of interest, and a long cultural tradition of cooperation.

3.   International Multinationals (Transnationals)

   In describing these entities there is no need to describe
the pattern of connection between the individual parents and their
various foreign subsidiary corporations. In general, the pattern
of growth is much like that of Ford. The unique element is the legal
structure that ties the two parents, and their subsidiaries, together.
In each of the three entities the goal was to preserve the corporate
existence of each national parent company, and yet to link or
consolidate them so that they could function and be managed as if they
were a single economic unit.

   The Royal Dutch/Shell Group was probably the first to
accomplish such a unification in 1907. The Dutch parent company and
the British parent company each formed a wholly-owned holding
company in their home countries. Each parent then transferred
ownership of its operating subsidiaries to the holding company.
The parents then exchanged shares of the holding companies so
that the Dutch parent owned 60% of both holding companies and the
British parent owned 40% of both. Key directors of both holding
companies were appointed to be the Managing Directors of Royal
Dutch/Shell Group. They proceded to unify the management of the
Group and to conduct its operations as a single economic unit.

   In the case of Unilever the linkage of equal Dutch and British parent companies was achieved through an Equalization Agreement,

other unifying agreements, and an arrangement whereby the directors

of both companies would always be the same persons. These accords

were placed in the articles of association of each parent. The

Equalization Agreement guarantees equal rights to the shareholders

of each parent. It placed the shareholders of both companies in a

similar position to that which would exist if they held shares in a

single company. The result is that dividends paid to both sets of

shareholders must be the same. Equal distribution in the event

of liquidation is also secured. To insure identity of directors each

parent has a wholly owned subsidiary which holds one half of the

deferred shares carrying the right to nominate the directors of each

parent. The ordinary shareholders are not entitled to elect a director

who is not nominated by the deffered shareholders - the wholly owned

subsidiaries. These directors then supervised the consolidated

management of the enterprise.

The Dunlop Pirelli Union came into being in 1971. Oversimplified,

the ownership integration was accomplished by Dunlop giving Pirelli a

49% interest in all its subsidiaries in exchange for a 49% interest

in all Pirelli subsidiaries. In this way, each stockholder of the two

parents continues to hold the same shares, though they now represent

assets half in each parent rather than all in one parent. The same

method was employed in reaching the 60/40 ownership exchange in

the Royal Dutch/Shell Group. As complete managerial integration

was not immediately intended in the Union, and for other reasons,

the allocation of subsidiaries was done in a particular fashion. It

was done so that controlling interests in former Dunlop and Pirelli companies should remain with the original parent. Therefore, the former Dunlop interests are found in those jointly owned entities in which the British parent has a majority interest. The same is true of the former Pirelli interests. The result is that the companies originally owned by each parent are still controlled and managed by them. Movement toward management fusion has begun by joint purchasing, research and financing projects. This is accomplished by a Central Committee representing both parents.

In addition to the enterprises previously described in some detail there are a number of others that can be described as multinational enterprises. When these are analyzed according to their basic legal structure there are only about a half dozen different types.

A wide variety of enterprises first become multinational in nature by means of contract, without the formation of any new corporate structure. These linkages with foreign enterprises are prime contractor/sub contractor relationships, long term supply or distribution relationships, licensing and cross licensing arrangements, and temporary multinational consortium participations.

Moving up in terms of complexity and permanence of cohesion are connections based on cross-shareholdings and external non-legal committees, and other coordination devices. The Mitsubishi Group illustrates this.

There are frequent occasions when the joinder of companies of different nationalities are complicated for reasons of nationalistic pride or unwillingness to surrender control to a foreign company. This is particularly true when one company is considerably larger than the other. The Fiat/Citroen was such a situation. It was resolved by the creation of a jointly owned French holding company to hold 53% of the Citroen shares. The holding company itself is 51% owned by Citroen, thereby permitting it to retain control. The 49% Fiat ownership permits it, the larger, to justify substantial coordination of joint activities.

Panavia is an example of how satisfactory multinational

consortium operations can evolve into a permanent jointly owned

operating company. Its limitation, however, is that one of the

parents may develop competing products, or other conflicts of interest

may arise. On the other hand, when the relationship is successful,

additional joint operations can be transferred from the parents to

the joint company.

The national multinations, typified by Ford, are the most

prevalent category of multinations. They are simply large national

parent companies which own and coordinate the operations of subsidiary

companies in a number of foreign countries. In most instances the

subsidiaries are wholly owned to avoid local resistance to global

strategies. Some are jointly owned when required by local law, or in

instances when enterprise policy favours true partnerships.

Some giant multinationals are held together simply by

contract. The Equalization Agreement between the Dutch and British

parent companies of Unilever is such an example. This agreement

to treat the shareholders of each on an equal basis has permitted

complete managerial unification and production rationalization.

Unification is facilitated by special provisions inserted in the Articles

of both parents which results in identical directors. The

Scandanavian airline, SAS, is constructed similarly except that

the agreement between its three foreign parents is for the limited

time period of 25 years.

The technique of jointly owned operating companies and

coordinating management committees has been employed by the Dunlop

Pirelli Union. Oversimplified, each parent gave the other a 49% interest in its operating subsidiaries. This brought about an overall 50/50 split in ownership and profits. The parents, being of equal size, and desirous of retaining managerial control of their former operations, kept the majority interest in their former subsidiaries. Coordinating management committees are moving towards overall rationalization of operations.

Unification of the German/Belgian combine, Agfa-Gavaert is achieved by jointly owned holding companies with common directors. The German parent formed a holding company to hold its operating companies. The Dutch side did likewise. Each parent now owns half of both holding companies which have identical directors. In this enterprise a single holding company could not be utilized because it would have given overall control to the German chemical giant, Bayer, which owns Gavaert.

The Royal Dutch/Shell amalgamation also employs the structure of jointly owned holding companies. The Dutch parent created a Dutch holding company to hold its operating subsidiaries. The British parent did the same. Then the shares of both holding companies were split on a 60/40 basis, favouring Royal Dutch, between the parents. Key directors from each holding company are appointed Group Managing Directors and they oversee unified management of the combined entities.

A single jointly owned holding company is used in the VFW/ Fokker enterprise joining German and Dutch companies. The single holding company is thought to give formal legal recognition and permanence to the joint management of the enterprise. It is owned on a 50/50 basis and, in turn, owns 100% of the operating companies of the original parents.

Public transnationals such as Air Afrique, Saarlor, and a host of others are based on a special form of contract - treaties between the nations creating the enterprises. The resulting government controlled enterprises possess dual, treble, or wider nationality.

Virtually all existing multi national enterprises could be placed in one of the above classifications. In some instances the enterprise in the classification is the only model presently operating. In the future, new multinational enterprises will bear the characteristics of combinations of the above categories, as well as new characteristics. In addition, nations and international institutions will no doubt fashion new legal structures beyond the existing contractual and corporate concepts.

5.   Legal Structure of Future Enterprise - Harmonisation of

European Company Law, European Company, World Company

The United States. like other federal republics, has been
able to give birth to giant multinations even though it lacks a
nation-wide company law structure.   The company and merger laws
of each State are sufficiently similar to permit the linkage of groups
of companies.   The common law heritage at the root of each State's
legal system partly accounts for the near uniformity.

However, demand for increasing public control over
American companies in the U.S., has occasionally given rise to the
suggestion of national reform.   Proposals have been made for a
nationwide company law structure and federal rules for corporations,
especially the larger ones.   It is unlikely that this will come about
in the near future.

The prospect for a European Company is more immediate.
Motivation for its fruition is entirely opposite to that which suggests
a federal company structure in the U.S. Rather than being directed
at the control of enterprises, the European Company hopes to
encourage the crossborder formation of larger firms, in aid of
EEC economic integration.

The dearth of European crossborder concentration has been
due in part to a lack of harmonisation of the national company and
taxation laws of the EEC member states. A certain degree of
uniformity is a precondition to the overall success of the prosposed
European Company.

The EEC intends to achieve this harmonisation by the use of directives. They are drafted by the EEC Commission and are submitted to the Council of Ministers for its acceptance or rejection. Once accepted, each member state is obligated to change its national law to be consistent with the directive. At the present time there are about six directives in existence, all in various stages of realizing their purposes.

Although purely domestic mergers are recognised in nearly every EEC member state, there are a number of obstacles to cross-border mergers. The Commissions Third Draft Directive is the first major attempt to remedy this. It has been supplemented by the 1969 Draft Directive on Merger Taxation. A portion of the latter directive also deals with the problem of intercorporate dividend taxation between parent and subsidiary, and the tax status of foreign establishments or branches.

In 1970 the Commission submitted a Draft Statute for the European Company to the Council of Ministers. The proposed European Company (Societas Europa, SE) will not replace, but supplement the national company laws existing in the member states. The structure of the SE form is based upon the progressive aspects of corporate forms in operation among the member states. SE powers are divided between the general meeting, the supervisory board, the executive board, and the European works council. The most controversial aspect is the one-third workers representation on the supervisory board.

Since the purpose of the SE statute is to facilitate EEC integration, its application is restricted to those instances in which that result is likely to follow. Hence, the founders of an SE must be public companies of which at least two are incorporated under a different national law. Only public companies formed under the laws of one of the EEC member states can act as founders. However, since non-EEC companies can form subsidiaries within the EEC countries, those subsidiaries could qualify as founders.

Use of the SE form is envisioned when founders from different countries wish to merge, form a holding company, or a joint subsidiary. When a complete merger is intended 500,000 units of account (about U.S. $500,000) is the minimum required capital. In the other two instances it is 250,000 units. Thus, only the larger companies will be able to choose the SE form.

The SE Draft Statute contains significant provisions which concern "groups of companies". These provisions recognize that companies which are separate legal entities are often dominated, through ownership or other arrangements, by another company. The provisions are applicable to a group of related companies in which an SE is either directly or indirectly the controlled or controlling enterprise in the group. The provisions intend to safeguard the rights of creditors and minority shareholders. These provisions narrow the gap between economic realities and legal structures, and may be the beginning of a fully coordinated EEC policy toward all multinational enterprises.

xxx

If the European Company becomes a reality then the prospect for a "de jure" world company becomes more likely. Already, a number of world chartering and regulatory schemes have been suggested. The prospect is most tangibly evidenced by the recent conclusions of a United Nations panel. It concluded that there was a need for some coordinated government control over giant multinationals.

Whether the prospect materializes or not, it is plain that the present trend of mergers, acquisitions, and increased industrial concentration is rapidly leading to the "de facto" world company - one with genuine worldwide ownership, management, and operations. A giant world enterprise could presently come into existence by the combination of a Japanese company, a European company and an American company. The combined structure could take any of the forms previously described, combinations thereof, or entirely new structures.

6. OWNERSHIP AND CONTROL

The separation of ownership and control in large corporate enterprise has been recognized for some time. The resulting separation of the legal structure and the managerial structure is compounded when enterprises become multinational.

At the root of the friction between multinational enterprises and nation states are the concepts of ownership and control. This chapter takes the broadest possible view of the subject and relies heavily on the verbatim opinions of those commentators who are likely to influence resolution.

Ownership and control once confined to the boundaries of a single nation are now not only separated from one another but splintered among many nations. Absentee ownership has never been seen on the scale that is emerging. What has made the ownership/control problems especially complex is that the really significant economic resources are now technology and management. These assets enjoy the quality of global mobility as well as scarcity.

The free trade institutions have assumed that removal of trade barriers would produce maximum benefits for all countries. But according to some, the opposite has resulted. We see a world of nations increasingly dependent on infusions of foreign technology, management, capital and marketing skills - supplied principally by multinational enterprises. Production, owned and controlled by foreign-based corporations, is altering the pattern and composition of world trade.

The pursuit of economic efficiency has resulted in the ever-increasing size of the firm and the widening integration of its operations.

Multinational enterprises have been increasing their production and sales faster than most countries have expanded their gross national product.

The enjoyment aspect of share ownership directs the ultimate profit or dividend flow towards the parent companies and its shareholders. This has major significance for national balance of payments and capital accumulation. But it is the power or control aspect that is the critical issue.

The tendency has been towards 100% ownership of an enterprise's foreign subsidiaries. And many subsidiaries that began as joint ventures have evolved into wholly-owned status. The pattern of ownership policies is largely governed by overall enterprise strategy. Jointly-owned subsidiaries generally exist when capital investment is very large or where local law or realities require it. Multinational enterprises are not, however, reluctant to share their ownership of foreign subsidiaries if there are other means of retaining control. It is significant that host countries are sometimes more concerned with who appears to have control rather than who actually exercises effective control.

The truth of the ownership aspect is that virtually no enterprises that we call multinational enterprises are truly multi-national. This can be altered by local participation in subsidiaries or in the parent company. At the subsidiary level schemes are now coming into existence calling for gradual disinvestment by the parent company. At the parent level it has been suggested that a special class of blocked stock be created that could be traded only in a limited geographical area and not be allowed to return to the parent country. Such certificates would be negotiable only in the country for which it was issued or in a limited surrounding

region.

Another view of ownership is that it is not really significant

who owns multinational enterprises in so far as their behaviour is concerned.

Furthermore, host country criticism of foreign-owned enterprise is

often unjustified.   Studies demonstrate that they often surpass local

enterprise in wages and exports.   The quality of a firm's technology

and management is more significant than the nationality of its ownership.

In countries with a high proportion of MNE subsidiaries such as

Canada, the question is raised whether they would behave differently

if they were Canadian-owned.   It is suggested that enterprises,

regardless of their nationality of ownership, generally operate in

response to a given institutional and economic setting in order to improve

their economic position - that the enterprise is free of the bounds of

ownership and functions as an independent self-seeking entity.

Increasing state ownership of enterprise is one trend.   An

opposite trend in Eastern European countries, such as Yugoslavia, is the

accommodation of private Western enterprises.   This is accomplished

not by ownership participation but by contractual provisions.   The

Western multinationals insistence on attaching absolute ownership and

property rights to their capital is increasingly subject to criticism.   So

long as control is somehow tied to ownership, such criticism will grow.

The real issue is control - who controls the enterprise and towards what

end.   Even in those nations which have switched completely to state-owned

enterprise, the control problem persists.

Internal control problems of managing and organizing the MNE are not fundamentally different whether privately owned or state operated. The largest multinationals can be compared to centrally planned economies like Russia. Within each multinational there is a constant tension between centralized versus decentralized control. The advent of the computer and long-range corporate planning push in the direction of centralization, while local conditions and nationalistic pressures encourage decentralization. It is at least clear that there is an interrelationship between external governmental control measures and internal managerial control structures and devices.

Multinationals themselves could be looked upon as control or self-regulating mechanisms, especially if they begin to fulfil wider social demands and become politically responsive. Whether business enterprise control mechanisms are compatible with a broader role is open to speculation. For the present it is clear that enterprises without external control have a greater latitude for profiteering.

The multinational is a system operating in numerous economic environments with varying tax rates, costs of money and currency values. Plant location and inter-subsidiary pricing adjustments permit them to optimize profits, sometimes at the expense of particular nations.

National governments feel compelled to control MNE but if they overcontrol then desirable foreign investment is discouraged. As nations are competing for international investment there has been a distinct lack of control or any uniformity of control.

Rising instability in the international economic environment has forced nations to take regulatory measures. The interesting aspect of this is that nations seem to be more concerned with controlling the extent, direction and practices of a limited number of foreign enterprises than with controlling domestic enterprise. In many instances, it is questionable whether nation-states have ever really controlled domestic industry. It is the nation-state's liberal policy toward private capital movements and mergers that resulted in MNE.

There are control problems for both host and investing countries. The United States government must cope with the consequences of capital outflow, job displacement, overseas taxation, foreign dependency, anti-trust practices and other problems. Regulations dealing with these matters often come into conflict with host country regulations. At present, however, the problem of control is much greater for the host countries.

Perhaps the most progressive approach yet is the Canadian-American Automobile Agreement of 1965. It was a negotiated compromise among both governments and private companies. It dealt with problems of production expansion, trade and monetary imbalance, employment and overall integration and rationalization of the North American automobile industry.

Regulation of foreign-owned investment has generally taken the simple form of complete exclusion, exclusion of select industries, screening of individual proposals, or exclusion unless jointly owned with local nationals. A complimentary but ineffectual approach has been the requirement for a minimum number of local nationals in the governing or managerial structure.

National control measures have been unsuccessful largely because enterprises can move existing or future investment to more lenient nations. If nations cannot evolve rational and uniform regulations on a co-operative basis, it will either not be done, or be accomplished by regional or international institutions.

If MNE/nation-state conflicts were resolved by a single global body a 'common law' of international investment might develop. The World Bank Centre for the Settlement of Investment Disputes offers such a potential.

Another tack is for nations to establish a new institution to control the size and power of MNE through the traditional antitrust mechanism.

At the regional level, the most progressive measures are those that have been adopted by the Andean Group in South America. Those countries have adopted a set of procedures and guidelines with respect to foreign investment, transfer of technology and disinvestment.

At the international level, it has been proposed that a MNE information centre be established at the United Nations to provide a common factual basis for the establishment of national controls. Other suggestions call for the registration and regulational of multinationals at the U.N. The proposed European Company for the E.E.C. gives some idea of how a global companies law might be provided. A number of commentators believe that any idea of a supranational companies law is unrealistic because it would place multinationals beyond the reach of national politics.

Even at the national level the law has yet to play its proper roll with respect to corporate control. The implications of expanding separation of 'control' from 'ownership' and international absentee ownership and control are yet to be fully recognized and acted upon by the law.

When the state emerged victorious over the church, nationalistic politics superseded religion as the basic world force. Economic power still remained diffused. The situation has steadily changed. Multinationals have created a concentration of economic power which can compete on equal terms with the state. The role of law has become more critical.

The original philosophy of company law envisioned a structure and rules giving control powers to shareholders and creditors. This has been steadily reinforced by an endless series of ad hoc legislation governing the various actions of the corporation. Power is now in the hands of self-perpetuating management groups and the corporate charter is little more than an enabling document.

What is needed is a new companies law providing a structure which places control in the hands of management, labor and the national communities affected. In Europe this is just beginning. Recognition is being given to labor and to the concept that groups of companies ought to be treated as one economic unit. Although there is much discussion of social and community responsibilities of the corporation, these notions have yet to be translated into the internal legal structure of company law.

There have been extensive efforts by management writers and practitioners to modernize the managerial structure to meet the 'control' needs of large and diversified corporations. These efforts are now being devoted to the complex problem of the control of multinational enterprises. In contrast, it does not appear that the same efforts have been devoted to the evolution of the corporate legal structure. Managerial structures have changed radically and continue to do, whereas fundamental changes in corporate legal structure have just begun. As is generally the case with legal change, there is a considerable 'lag' element.

At the present time, there is generally a distinct difference and separation between the managerial and legal structures of enterprises, especially multinationals. This gap is compounded by the divergent company law among nations. In addition. there is a tendency for the 'management' people to view the legal structure as an incidental necessity. The result is that for purposes of 'internal' and 'external' control the law has not fulfilled the role that it might or should. Certainly there is an aspect of the corporate legal structure which must, by virtue of its external control goals, come into conflict with the enterprise's drive toward absolute efficiency. But further study of the managerial and legal structure interrelationship should reveal ways to make the two more compatible and to reinforce each other.

The size and global mobility of MNE is shifting the balance of power away from national governments and towards these international enterprises. This has yet to be counterbalanced by multi-national labor unions or multi-national governments.   For purposes of multi-

national ownership and control, national company law is becoming an

outmoded frame of reference.   If this is to be corrected by some

international mechanism it must be one that represents a balance of

advantages and responsibilities for governments and enterprises alike.

Because public opinion plays such a significant role in this area,

the chapter relies almost exclusively on an organized series of verbatim

quotations of leading experts.

7.   ANTITRUST

In some respects this chapter is a continuation of the 'control'

aspects of the previous chapter since antitrust or competition law is one

method of controlling multinational enterprises.   The advent of MNE

has changed the environment of competition in the world.   In turn, the

new environment has accelerated the formation of additional MNEs.

Size of enterprise is said to be a major determinant of overseas

investment.   Nations desirous of increasing their share of expanding

world business are encouraging the growth and multinationalization of their

firms.   In practice antitrust laws have not presented any serious or

continuous obstacle to bigness.   Consequently more mergers are coming

and multinationalization of enterprises thunders on.   Even nations and

regional groups with antitrust laws are encouraging mergers, especially

cross-border mergers.   Whereas American law has kept mergers in

check. European laws have not.   In international mergers and acquisitions

this has presented some inconsistencies.   American multinationals have been able to gain easy entry into Europe.   But European MNEs

meet the resistance of American merger law.

The international dispersion of enterprises away from their

home countries is upsetting export-import patterns and raising conflicts

of interest between the enterprise and its home country as well as

foreign countries.   The factual situation with which national antitrust

policy must deal has become confused and constantly changing.   A national

competition policy can no longer be made to favor home enterprises largely

absent and home markets with foreign enterprises within.   Although

this may in the long run dilute nationalism, the short term result is

accelerating national competition.

The fact that enterprises from one country can join with

enterprises from another country as in the case of transnationals or in

the joint venture subsidiaries of national multinationals presents additional

complications for antitrust policy makers.   Enterprise blocks from pairs

or groups of nations may develop.   Ultimately the communist monopoly

block could be pitted against the non-communist competition-oriented

block.   It is possible to view the enterprises within each communist

country as one giant conglomerate enterprise directed at the top by

political-economic unity of command.   In Russia it could be called

the USSR enterprise.   And it is multinational in that its joint activities

dovetail with other communist country enterprises and, increasingly,

with Japanese Arab, African and other national enterprises.

In their drive towards efficiency and growth the multinationals

are impeded by diversity of antitrust regulations in different countries

and regional groupings.   Likewise antitrust law makers in each country
are in a difficult position because the effectiveness of what they do is also
dependent upon the antitrust laws of other countries.   Indeed, the
absence of such laws in some countries means that new investment may
go there rather than face restrictions elsewhere.   Lack of uniformity
is understandable since each nation's economy and enterprises are at
different stages of growth.   Obtaining jurisdiction over enterprises
outside a country, and the general clash of one country's laws with
another, also presents a problem. The laws of some nations do not have
extra-terrirorial effect and often prohibit compliance with foreign
antitrust laws.

In many respects antitrust law disparities merely reflect basic
underlying value differences.   One is the capitalist-communist split;
another sees individual freedon against economic efficiency.   A
fundamental conflict is developing between national planning by political
units and international planning by enterprises.   This is fundamental
to antitrust-political power opposed to industrial power.

The two leading antitrust camps today are the United States and
the EEC. Those laws that take the 'structural' as opposed to the 'conduct'
approach are pertinent to the future formation and growth of multinational enterprises.

Present antitrust laws in the world have not generally been
applied to practices between constituent parts of an enterprise.   In effect,
multinational enterprises have been treated as one legal entity even though
they consist of many domestic and foreign subsidiaries which are technically
separate legal entities.   If and when such giant enterprises were felt to

have become too powerful or detrimental, these anticompetitive 'internal' practices could be attacked just like those between completely separate corporate enterprises. Such a policy would have an unmistakeable impact on multinationals. There is disagreement over whether this intra-enterprise doctrine applies in the U.S. As a general proposition I do not believe that it does. However, in the general statutory language there is ample room for the courts to apply it should unfolding circumstances require it. There is similar uncertainty in the EEC. Although there are more indications against its applicability the door appears to be still open for the application. One difficulty with applying the doctrine is that certain conduct would be illegal if done by a subsidiary, but legal if done by a branch or division. This would work a special discrimination against MNE which must, for practical reasons, function through separately incorporated foreign subsidiaries. A proper interpretation of Article 85 (1) would seem to come from concentrating on the economic meaning rather than the legal form in which the situations present themselves. In the final analysis the applicability of the doctrine depends upon the factual determination of whether or not subsidiary companies are autonomous.

Joint venture foreign subsidiaries are generally an organizational component of multinationals. Both the Clayton and Sherman Acts of the U.S. have been applied to joint venture subsidiaries where there is a finding of a reasonable probability of reduced competition or a tendency towards a monopoly. If the parent companies are competitors or potential competitors then there is a likelihood that the venture will be unlawful.   However such joint ventures are not unlawful "per se".

Joint venture subsidiaries outside the U.S. with a U.S. parent often

reduce imports into the U.S. and are unlawful if they reduce or

eliminate competition in the U.S. market.

Under EEC law the joint venture subsidiary is in an altogether

different economic environment and the laws attitude toward it is likely

to be liberal for the forseeable future.   The reason for this is that the EEC

is desirous of accelerating the formation of larger, more competitive

enterprises in comparison with American and Japanese enterprises.

In addition, in those instances where EEC joint ventures are created

they seldom hold a very large percentage of the market and do not present

anticompetitive effects.   Where one of the joint venture partners already

has a 'dominant' position it could take improper advantage of the venture

and come in violation of the EEC's Article 86.

EEC and American laws take much the same attitude towards

outright mergers as towards joint ventures.   American laws have been

used to prevent mergers within and without the U.S. whether involving

American or European corporations.   In the past the European attitude

has been almost entirely passive.   This incongruity tends to favor

multinationalization in certain directions.   The justified European policy

of encouraging mergers would apparently prefer to encourage exclusively

European mergers and discriminate against non-European firms,

especially the larger American firms.   Since the EEC has viewed

monopolies as neither good nor bad in themselves it is inconsistent for

for its law to prevent mergers. However, it now appears that the
EEC is moving in the direction of the policy adopted in the 1965
English statute on mergers. The latest EEC proposals move toward
the prevention of concentration.

Size and economic power can almost be coincidental with
multinationality. Consequently, multinationals are especially exposed
to antitrust laws concerning dominance, market power or monopolization.
Another, and possibly conflicting outlook is that enterprises become
multi-national partly in attempt to expand without dominating any one
particular national market. This suggests the need for revised national
laws or co-ordinated or international regulatory schemes.

The idea of the Sherman and Clayton Acts in the U.S. was to
preserve competition in favor of the self-regulating mechanisms of the
market. In contrast EEC does not oppose the achievement or existence
of monopoly or market power. But once an enterprise reaches a
dominant position it then becomes subject to regulation for abusive conduct.
One assumption inherent in Article 86 is that monopolistic structure does
not lead inevitably to monopolistic performance. Some American
observers have expressed the fear that the 'conduct' or 'abuse' approach
could ultimately turn dominant firms into public utilities.

Size alone has never been enough to invoke the U.S. laws.
Monopoly power has been defined primarily in terms of market percentages.
The percentage required to establish monopoly power has been relatively
high, in no case less than 75%. It is significant that the market power which
may be deliberately acquired by a single firm is substantially higher than

that which may be achieved by a merger of firms. This appears to favor existing multinationals which have the financial resources and international borrowing power to expand from within or to merge in selective nations and markets avoiding the critical market percentages. Also pertinent is that the percentage where mergers are considered to be against public interest is in most cases lower in the U.S. than in other countries. This makes it easier for American multinationals to merge outside the U.S., and conversely more difficult for non-American multinationals to merge within the U.S. Similar national disparities affect the overall pattern of multinationalization of firms.

The EEC law and that of other countries with a 'conduct' approach defines the degree of market power deemed significant. The extent to which that degree varies among nations and regions will have some influence on the location of new plants and expansion of existing ones. A related aspect - defining the relevant market - generally takes into account foreign product alternatives (imports). As import barriers are further reduced this factor will assume more significance.

At the present time definition of the relevant geographic market does not extend outside the national or regional boundaries where the law is in effect. This policy is justified by the fact that foreign imports are taken into account. This is deficient, however, in that it fails to take into account potential import competition. In addition it ignores the fact that some national firms are also competing in markets outside the nation. Such national firms may be restricted in some way to preserve present competition in the national market at the expense of the ability of the national enterprise to compete overseas. Resolving this matter requires assessment of present and future trade barriers in relevant nations, determination of competitors as well as potential foreign competitors, multinationality of enterprises concerned and relevant time frames.

Some critics question whether the present antitrust concepts of market power are adequare to deal with modern forms of business power, especially oligopoly forms. At present they exist at the national level, but are rapidly shifting to the global level. The critics believe that size, financial power and diversification - factors characteristic of MNE - have become of primary significance. These factors are not generally taken into account. Whether and to what extent they will be taken into account will have a decisive influence on multinationals.

8.   LABOR

Legal and managerial structures of MNE have advanced to meet changing global conditions. In contrast, the labor union organizations have not kept up with the integrating world economic structure. Unless unions adopt their organizational structures and techniques there will be an increasing imbalance of power as between labor and management. If the balance could be equalized, labor could be a balancing force and serve as a MNE 'control' device not unlike antitrust.

There are a number of impediments to the international labor movement. Jobs lost in one country are gained in another, thereby presenting an inherent conflict of interest between national unions.

Differing political and economic idealogies also separate them. In negotiations with MNE subsidiaries they are hampered by inadequat e published subsidiary data and by uncertainty regarding the locus of MNE decision-making power. Another obstacle is that sympathy strikes and secondary boycotts are unlawful in some countries, thereby precluding global solidarity. Some advocate that such laws are not justified. They suggest that MNEs are allowed to organize and function on a global basis, and labor should be allowed to do so.

There is mounting pressure by labor for special regulation of MNE. Whether this is justified, legally or economically, is open to debate. The issue is partly whether it is the same or different than large national enterprises. An analogy in the United States is that there is separate regulation or interstate or national enterprises as opposed to purely local or state enterprises.

The trade union global counterforce envisions co-ordinated international support of local unions dealing with MNE, simultaneous multiple negotiation with all national subsidiaries of an MNE, and, ultimately, integrated negotiation for common demands in all segments of a MNE. As the last step may be complicated by varying national labor standards. the common demands may be in the form of uniform proportionate increases in various categories of benefits.

A roadblock to universal collective bargaining is that bargaining is presently done on many different levels depending on the company and the nation. In terms of global tactics the unions must decide between regional or global agreements involving all companies of a given industry or enterprise bargaining across all national boundaries.   Varying national labor laws will affect either realization.   To date some international trade union confederations have enjoyed a limited number of successes in co-ordinated, cross-border union support.

As labor's strategy unfolds, it will have an impact on MNE strategy of production organization.   If a product is produced in many countries there is protection against a labor stopage in one country.   If there is vertical organization with the output of one national subsidiary as the input of another, then a stopage in any one country stops all production output.   International specialization with unique products produced in each country avoids a total shutdown but does not provide production replacement when one country is involved in a stopage.

Increased worker participation in management resulting from German-type co-determination or proposals in the European Company may ease the movement into regional and global relations.

The International Labor Office should play a key role in this process as it has the advantage of a tripartite organization structure uniting representatives from labor, management, and government from virtually every nation.   The ILO could be the organization to establish minimum world labor standards for MNE.   Two critical barriers to raising world labor standards are that there is no legal enforceability of international collective agreements, and upward harmonization may conflict with employment objectives in developing countries.

9.   Taxation

If there were no taxes in any nations of the world, and if there were freedom and stability in currency exchange, it would be of little importance to multinational corporations or to governments where, in a MNE system profits were shown. The facts being otherwise MNE management co-ordinate the work of legally separate entities in an attempt to optimize the international tax environment. Nevertheless, MNE tax planning does not play a preemptive role in overall enterprise policy strategy. Other considerations predominate. The conflict is between tax minimizing tactics of MNE and tax maximizing policies of nation states.

It should not be forgotten that MNE is not the only form of multi-company enterprise. Operating solely within the boundaries of a single nation there are multi-company enterprises that can be called 'uninationals'. If one understands the tax ramifications peculiar to them, then one is on the road to comprehending taxation of multinationals. The obvious complication of the latter is the numerous interested national taxing authorities.

There are many tax minimizing devices that can be employed by MNE. All of them have an impact on managerial and legal structure. However, a structural or tactical change for tax purposes also has an effect upon other critical variables such as cash flow and inventory considerations. Uninationals are vulnerable to the arbitrary or onerous taxation of one particular nation. The advantage of multinationals, if any, is in flexibility. Their 'eggs' are not all in one basket.

Variations in national taxing systems include differences in types of taxes,

1

rates, definitions of income and expense, extraterritorial jurisdictional principles, and allowances for foreign taxes paid.

Unlike multi-company uninationals, MNE may be subject to double taxation when foreign subsidiary dividends are transmitted to the home country parent. In cases where the home country grants a tax credit, or where there is a treaty between home and host country, this can be avoided.

Multinationals from 'worldwide' taxing authorities such as the US, have employed foreign subsidiary tax havens as a funnel for redistribution of profits to other parts of the MNE system. This practice is also employed by non-US multinationals. It is particularly important where home country exchange controls make it difficult for the parent company to fulfil that function. In a uninational company group that role can be played without such complications.

There are dividend-avoiding procedures designed to transfer resources of the foreign subsidiary to the parent in a form that does not attract the taxation of host and home country. These transfers can take the form of royalties, interest on loan capital, management fees and similar items. A related method is called transfer pricing. Generally, these tactics are employed to reduce the foreign subsidiaries profit base. The alleged use of these techniques is probably exaggerated. Conflict over the practices has been said to be wholly a political question between nations, rather than ethical.

The fact that some nations rely heavily on value-added tax (VAT) and others on income taxes introduces unique implications for multinationals. It makes transfer pricing more difficult, and results in some discrimination depending upon the home country of the multi-national.

Tax treaties have begun to level the differences among tax systems but these are generally only bilateral. United Nations' expert panels have made a beginning at arriving at a consensus between developed and developing countries. Some have suggested that a MNE's aggregate worldwide profits be proportionately taxed by nations in accordance with each nation's percentage of payroll, sales or assets of the MNE.

What tax harmonization takes place within the EEC will be some indication of what might be achieved in other regions or on a global scale. But even tax harmonization may not be enough if there are still differences in national usage of revenue and national economic policies.

The need of both multinationals and nation states is certainty and stability in taxation. In their development efforts many developing nations continue to forego revenues to which they should be entitled, while MNE's are sometimes forced to use artificial structures and inefficient methods in order to minimize their total tax bill. To accomplish this the MNE's are beginning to employ computerized tax simulation models to find the optimal system for this. These models take into account factors such as the legal structure of parent and subsidiaries, policies on the movement of funds within the MNE system, home and host tax rates, tax treaties, currency convertibility and devaluation probabilities.

The changes brought about by the organization of legal and managerial structures on a multinational basis have been discussed in previous chapters. Changes within multinational enterprises and between it and national and international bodies have brought new problems, conflicts, and policy issues which must be resolved. As with all such matters, the first step is to assemble the facts. Hence, the importance of the subject of disclosure by multinationals. And since there is no present consensus for MNE regulation on a grand international scale, information gathering should be the immediate goal. The information that is needed is not only the traditional company data required by shareholders and creditors. Nations themselves need to know about the flow of money, materials, and jobs in and out of their borders. Governments have spent lavishly on global political intelligence agencies, but little on global economic intelligence.

Disclosure varies from nation to nation and may come from laws, stock market listing requirements, administrative regulation, professional or commercial tradition. Those countries which have financed company growth through public shareholder equities seemed to have more developed systems of disclosure. The need for international financing should be the major force behind progressive MNE disclosure systems.

There is an interrelationship between disclosure and advances and uniformity in national accounting standards and practices, as well as in the existence of professional financial analysts and related institutions. Although effective disclosure is partly dependent on enlightened, understandable, and harmonized accounting, it appears that it is much easier, internationally, to evolve standards of financial disclosure than it is to evolve harmonized accounting principles.

The emphasis of accounting in many countries has been, and still is, on fulfilling external information requirements and tax determination. This has shifted attention unduly away from internal firm considerations. A large proportion of MNEs have made some formal effort to standardize internal accounting practices and systems to facilitate financial reporting between parent headquarters and foreign subsidiaries. These advances may accelerate similar advances in the external environment.

Failure to consolidate financial reports of subsidiaries with parents is one procedure that makes the reports of enterprises less meaningful. This is particularly true when the parent companies are holding companies as well as operating companies, which is the case for many European multinationals. A beginning approach to this is the multiple statement system requiring that reports of the subsidiaries accompany that of the parent. However, it does not eliminate double counting of inter-company transactions as does consolidation. Although consolidation is practiced to some extent in Great Britain, Germany and the United States, foreign subsidiaries are not normally eligible for consolidation. This is the area that needs attention. It is likely that worldwide consolidation will develop out of the need for MNE to supply meaningful financial statements for the raising of capital in several national jurisdictions. Difficulties in cross-border consolidation are partly being resolved by its achievment in increasing cross-border mergers.

Attention is already being given to the matter of striking a balance between treating MNE subsidiaries as separate legal entities or as treating the overall enterprise as a single legal unit. Attention must also be given to inter-enterprise transactions, and to the recognition that a company can be an affiliate of another through contract as well as stock ownership.

As a beginning, agreement might be reached among capital exporting nations for worldwide consolidation and minimum disclosure by their MNEs in all cases where capital is sought outside of the home country. In time that might be expanded to cover annual reporting on the same basis, possibly including a form of social responsibility accounting so much in need.

1.   <u>HISTORICAL PERSPECTIVE AND DEFINITIONS</u>

There has always been a need for men to act together, in unison, as a single group or in some form of unity. In England, long before men had authorization from King or Parliament, they organised boroughs for defence, and guilds for trade. In so doing, they built functioning entities out of experience rather than from official license.[1]

Official government license first became important when boroughs or trade guilds sought special privileges from national law-makers. But such grants did not create legal entities; they bestowed particular privileges on entities already existing in fact and accepted by law as legitimate. In the Tudor period boroughs and guilds did commonly obtain royal charters declaring their entity character. This association with the new central government authority increased their prestige. [2]

Not until the early 1600's was it firmly established that royal authorization was necessary to create a new entity or corporation. The major impetus derived from the need for the national authority to assert itself and to establish its legal superiority over dirisive local governments and interest groups. The purpose was not economic but political - to secure political power at the head of the state. [3]

However, the corporate device did have great functional possibilities for aiding business enterprise. From the late sixteenth and on into the seventeenth century royal chartering of companies to develop foreign trade and colonies was a prominent feature of

national policy. Royal charters were essential to such ventures

and merchants who combined for a foreign venture without it risked

prosecution for a criminal conspiracy against the national interest.

An additional purpose of the royal charter was to legitimize

a range of public functions performed by such trading companies in

organizing terms of trade, establishing local governments, controlling

customs, and, in effect, making foreign policy in their areas of

operation. Thus, in the early stages, the role of the corporation

was both political and economic. (4)

These early chartered trading and colonizing companies

can be viewed as predecessors of the multinational corporation. (5)

There are some interesting parallels, especially if multinational

enterprise is regarded as reshaping political and economic nationalism

into a world economic order. The chartered companies were a vital

force in the expansion and development of the nation states which

succeeded the city-dominated economy of the middle ages. This

resembled the earlier influence of the merchant guild, another

antecedent of the business corporation, on the medieval city economy.

The trading companies, acting in the interests, and often

backed by the military support, of their home governments, searched

the world for resources and colonies which would advance the economy

of the European countries, often at the expense of overseas areas.

Critics of the multinational enterprise (MNE) like to make this

analogy - one which is unfair. In any event, the impact on overseas

areas was such that the companies did require the approval and

cooperation of the governing authorities within the host country.
Among those cited as resembling MNE predecessors were the
Company of Merchant Adventurers, the Russia Company, the
Levant Company, the East India Company, the Virginia Company,
and the Plymouth Company.

In time, larger numbers of trading companies were
chartered at the request of merchants rather than being the result
of royal initiative, thus beginning the private incorporation pattern
that prevails today. The greatest of the trading companies, the
East India Company, was begun by the efforts of private merchants,
many of whom were already associated with other trading companies.
The English Crown was not itself an active force in the company's
formation nor a participant in the ongoing enterprise. In fact when
James I sought membership in the Company, fears of royal encroachment
and interference led to effective resistance by the Company. (6)
Nevertheless, the Crown used the Company for its own purposes,
exacting loans and other favours in return for its concessions of charter
and monopoly. This stands in contrast to subsequent governmental
attitudes against monopolies.

The East India Company, not only exported English products
but imported and then exported products from many other parts of the
world. One criticism from home was that its export activities
failed to stimulate English industries and that it competed with
domestic industry by its importation of Indian calicoes. The
inevitable result was a clash with the vested interests of the woolen

industry. This conflict with national interests was described as
stemming from "the peculiar position occupied by the Company which
can only be described as international".[7] As regards the current
debate about multinationals, this should illustrate that the multinational enterprise does not inherently favour the home country. It
is an instrument, like any other, that can be used to produce varying
results on differently situated parties.

Early trading companies differed from modern multinationals
in that the former saw the function of trade itself as the sole source
of profit. They had little interest in the production function and,
aside from portfolio-type investments, they did not engage in the
production of the goods they traded.

Yet, in certain respects, colonizing companies such as the
Virginia Company did resemble some of the subsidiary operations
of the present multinationals. The business portion of their activities
was   grounded upon the direct development of foreign economic
resources and the actual production of goods abroad. In addition,
the membership of those companies was multi-national to the extent
that it consisted of investors in England as well as the producing
colonists of the new world. This identity of interest between
investor and producer was comparable to the present joint venture
subsidiaries of multinationals.

In time, lawmakers and businessmen came to regard the
corporation mainly as a structure useful to private trading operations,
and public responsibilities receded into the background. The shift

in English policy from concern for political considerations to a focus upon economic utility resulted in a considerable blurring of corporate public policy. The new economic emphasis represented different goals and presented different tensions of interest from those that had determined prior attitudes toward corporate organisation. Policy toward the business corporation was confused by the earlier political context. It helped generate a general distrust of the corporate form and blurred the distinction between issues of power and utility, thus forshadowing the present confrontation between multinationals and nation states. (8)

By the eighteenth century the accepted English doctrine was that only the King in Parliament might create a corporation. Despite several centuries of experience with the corporate concept, English law drew little distinction between governmental, eleemasynary, and business corporations. In fact, the first English treatise on Corporations (Kyd 1794) has little to say concerning the use of corporations for economic enterprise. (9)

In North America

Early corporate policy developments in North America followed those of England and so even by the end of the 18th century United States law had no separate policy or rules for business corporations. The same legislative committees handled applications for all types of corporate charters. When uncertainties arose, courts applied to business corporations, the same judge-made law that had developed out of ecclesiastical, philantropic, and municipal corporations. (10)

From 1780 onwards the U.S. began to shape its own corporate concepts and businessmen's use of the instrument far outstripped that in England.   (11)

In the beginning American jurists spoke of the law as if it not only gave life to the corporation but as if it created the entire working arrangements.   Borrowing from Coke and Blackstone, Marshall gave this classic opinion: "A corporation is an artificial being, invisible, intangible, and existing only in contemplation of law.   Being the mere creature of law, it possesses only those properties which the charter of its creation confers upon it, either expressly or as incidental to its very existence".   Such statements were exaggerated and led future jurists to believe that their job was done when it had only begun.   Nonetheless the basic concept itself was important and to that extent the words of Columbia's Nicholas Murray Butler are justified: "I weigh my words when I say that in my judgement the limited liability corporation is the greatest single discovery of modern times . . . . . Even steam and electricity are far less important than the limited liability corporation, and they would be reduced to comparative impotence without it".   (12)

As American businessmen learned how to organize capital and manpower, business corporations developed their own kind of social structure and internal politics.   Beginning around 1800 corporate business operations began to influence political power and the relative growth of different sectors of the economy and geographical areas.   Consequently, the business corporation began to present important public policy issues requiring resolution by natural forces or by legal processes.   (13)

Because of the earlier dominance of trading and colonizing
companies there was always fear of the breadth of corporate
ambition. This found expression in the charters of banks and
insurance corporations which expressly limited their operations in
other businesses. Likewise, courts ruled that one corporation might
not own the stock of another without explicit statutory authority.
To control corporate size, statutes set ceilings on the capitalization
and on the value of permissible assets. Limits were also set on the
number of years that a corporation might exist, thus requiring renewal
and scrutiny of the legislature. Although these laws placed definite
limits on the corporation, the law regarding formation of corporations
was improved. From the 1890's to the 1930's state statutes provided
enabling-acts which made corporate status available through simple
administrative procedures. This contrasted with the earlier necessity
for each new corporation to obtain legislative approval on a case
by case basis.   (14)

Growth in Size and Power

In 1875 the state of New Jersey launched the interstate
competition for the corporate chartering business by abolishing all
limitations on maximum capitalization. It took a more significant
step in 1888 when it authorized companies under its law to do all
of their business outside of New Jersey, and to hold stock in other
companies. Delaware and other states followed these moves and all
of the states' corporate law permitted their corporations to own the

stock of other corporations. Hence, competition between political units resulted in the corporate concept which permitted the rise of multinationals in the form of interlocking corporate structures.

Authorization of holding companies provided a ready instrument for increasing the size of business operations under central command. In this way, corporate law reinforced financial, entreprenurial, and technological pressures for an economy of larger firms.

Aside from the mechanics for raising large sums of capital, the prime contribution of the corporate concept was to provide a framework for central control, thus permitting large groups of men and resources to function in unity. (15)

The Beginning of Multinational Enterprise

In the second half of the 19th century, businessmen in one country began to establish production facilities in other countries. They were motivated by the prospect of new markets, lower production and transportation costs, the need for natural resources, higher import duties, exploitation of patents, and for reasons of competitive strategy.

In 1865, two years after Freidrich Bayer's German chemical plant was opened, he purchased an interest in an aniline plant in New York State. High import duties also prompted Bayer to establish dyestuff factories in Moscow in 1876, in France in 1882, and in Belgium in 1908. (16)

The Swedish industrialist, Alfred Nobel, founded his first foreign plant in Hamburg in 1866. Singer, a U.S, company, established a factory in Glasgow in 1867. Du Pont and Edison began producing in Canada in 1876 and 1883 respectively. William Lever explained the Lever Brothers philosophy in 1902: "When the duty exceeds the cost of separate managers and separate plants, then it will be an economy to erect works in the country that our customers can be more cheaply supplied from". Henry Ford entered Canada in 1903 and England in 1906. By 1914 the British Ford company was producing a quarter of the cars made in Britain. (17)

As companies from one nation began to produce and compete within foreign countries they soon collided with one another. Before long they remedied this by agreements among themselves, thereby commencing the first international cartels. Companies involved in these arrangements included Imperial Chemical, Du Pont, I.G. Farben, Allied Chemical, and Alcoa. In some respects the nature of the collusive activities was comparable to the lawful activities that now take place between the various foreign subsidiaries of a single multinational enterprise. (18)

The international cartels broke down because of legal restrictions in certain nations and because they lacked a unifying structure within which to enforce the agreements among themselves. The World Wars' damage in Europe also contributed to their demise.

The period since the end of the Second World War has witnessed an explosive expansion of international direct foreign investment fed, initially, by the Americans. In 1945 direct foreign

investment of U.S. firms stood at about $10 billion. It is expected

to hit $100 billion by 1975. (19)

In 1972 direct foreign investment of American firms was

approximately $75 billion. The direct foreign investment of all non-

American firms was the same approximate level, thereby making

world direct foreign investment about $150 billion. That is estimated

to produce an annual output of $375 billion, an amount in excess of

the GNP of all nations except the U.S. It is this output, growing at

the rate of 10% per year, and faster than most national growth, that

is revolutionizing the world economy. (20)

The chapters which follow are intended to give an analytical

description of just how these various multinational enterprises came

into being and how they organize their legal structures to bring

about this new state of affairs.

Definition

Before going ahead it is useful to give a better idea of what

is meant by a multinational enterprise and to justify the selection of

that particular term. (21)

The word "enterprise" was chosen instead of the words

"company" or "corporation" for a particular reason. None of the

entities which are the subject of this thesis is an individual company

or corporation. In all instances they are groups of companies linked

together in various ways. To refer to the Ford Motor Company as

a multinational company is to concentrate on the American parent
company. Whereas, what makes Ford multinational is the linkage
of the parent company to all its foreign subsidiary companies. It is
more meaningful to refer to the overall entity as a multinational
enterprise.

Although entities like Unilever are looked upon loosely as a
company or corporation, there is no such company as Unilever.
There is a British company called Unilever Limited, and a Dutch
company called Unilever N. V. These two companies are linked
together in a unique manner, and they and their foreign subsidiaries
comprise a single economic entity or enterprise called Unilever.

From a legal viewpoint these enterprises are multi-national
because they own or control subsidiary companies incorporated or
headquartered in many different nations other than in the nation of
the parent company. Some writers refer to these entities as International
Corporations or Enterprises. The word "international" is not the
most appropriate. It suggests relationships between or among
nations, with emphasis upon the nations themselves as the actors.

Among economists, management theorists, and business
writers, the most prevalent term used to describe these entities
appears to be "multinational enterprise". However, many do not
permit the label to be applied to just any enterprise with multinational operations. They require that certain types of operations
take place in a specified minimum number of different nations;
and that foreign operations constitute at least a certain minimum
percentage of overall enterprise operations. For our purposes

it is sufficient to say that we are discussing the largest of the world's enterprises which produce and sell in many different nations.

A more technical, but brief, definition is that a multinational enterprise is a combination of companies of different nationality, connected by means of shareholdings, managerial control or contract and constituting an economic entity.   (22)

For purposes of brevity it has become common for multinational enterprises to be referred to as "multinationals". At least one writer has suggested that multinationals can be classified into "national" multinationals and "international" multinationals. (23)   A multinational enterprise is of national character if its central brain of direction clearly operates in one country, the home country, and its subsidiaries and associated companies in the host countries have to take orders from that central seat of management and are only the limbs of the corporate body. The Ford Motor Company is an American multinational because the parent company, which is the central brain, is incorporated and headquartered in the U.S. and most of its shareholders are U.S. citizens and residents.

An international multinational is one which has two or more parent companies from different nations. In the case of Unilever there are two parent companies. One was formed, and has its headquarters and the bulk of its shareholders in The Netherlands. The other was formed, and has its headquarters and the bulk of its shareholders in the United Kingdom. Although it functions as one ecomomic unit, it is fair to say that its central seat of management is Anglo-Dutch, or international. Some refer to these enterprises as "transnationals".

At present most multinationals are national in character. Not more than a dozen are international.

Something further should be said about the nationality of enterprises. Although we call the Ford Motor Company an American multinational, there are those who do not see it as multinational at all, but simply as American. They ignore the fact that its foreign subsidiaries were formed under the laws of different nations, and concentrate on the fact that Ford's overall control and ownership is American in character. Taking another viewpoint, let us suppose that on paper Ford terminates its American parent company and forms a parent company under the laws of the United Kingdom, and that it physically moves its headquarters personnel from the U.S. to the U.K. Neither of these changes would completely change the American character because no change will have taken place with respect to the ownership and control factors. Yet Ford will have become somewhat less American and somewhat more British. If more English persons purchase Ford parent company shares, and more Englishmen are appointed managers and directors, then the national character will change even further.

Therefore any one multinational takes on different nationalities depending upon whether one focuses on the place of incorporation of the parent company or companies, the location of its central headquarters, the location and place of incorporation of its subsidiaries, and the nationality of its managers, directors and shareholders. Some multinationals will remain clearly national in character, while with others the nationality of the above factors will be so diverse as to be truly multi-national.

2.   NATIONAL MULTINATIONALS

2.1   FORD MOTOR COMPANY

The Ford Motor Company is the third largest industrial
enterprise in the world. But for its overseas multinational activities
its ranking would be considerably lower. In 1972 approximately
37% of its vehicles were sold outside its home country, the United
States. It supplies 16% of the free-world car market and 20% of the
truck market. In addition to agents, dealers and dealer assemblers
in 180 countries and territories, it has manufacturing facilities in
10 countries and assembly plants in 10 more. Nearly half of its
employees work outside the U.S. (1)

Continental Europe had been the mother of the automobile
with the creation of crude models as early as 1875. In England there
was no incentive to produce motor cars before the passage of the
Highway Act of 1896. This repealed earlier absurd restrictions,
such as a four mile speed limit, advocated by hostile railroad and
carriage interests.   (2)

When Henry Ford began the manufacture of cars in 1903,
European production was well ahead of that in America. French
producers led all other countries, specializing in expensive, hand-
finished models for the aristocracy, and exporting the world over.
Ford's idea was to make an inexpensive, high volume model for the
average person. He intended to use machine tools, many suppliers,
and interchangeable parts.   (3)

What follows is a description of the evolvement of Ford's interlocking corporate legal structure. It provides the framework for the Company's worldwide activities. The description concentrates on those geographical areas which now account for the bulk of overseas sales and production. Those areas are Canada, Australia, Britain, Brazil, Germany, and Europe in general. The account includes business developments and the management organizational aspects connected with the corporate structure.

The Ford Motor Company was incorporated in June, 1903 under the laws of the state of Michigan in the U.S. Its initial authorized capital was $150,000. Henry Ford and a dozen other men were the beginning stockholders. From the start these men envisioned a world wide market for their automobiles. One of them, a Canadian by birth, appointed a Canadian distributor in July, and in August the sixth Ford-built car was shipped to that agent. The following month a New York export agent was named to handle foreign sales outside of Canada. Within the next few years a network of sales agents and branches covered the globe. Often these overseas sales operations undertook the assembly function and then later the manufacture of the American-designed product. (4)

Canada

Early in 1904 an enterprising Canadian wagon builder came from Windsor, Canada just across from the Ford Company's plant on the Detroit River. He proposed to organize a Canadian company

to manufacture Ford cars. His reasoning was based upon the 35%
tariff on American cars entering Canada. That same year Ford
Motor Company of Canada, Ltd. was formed with 51% of the shares
owned by the Ford Motor Company of Michigan. (5)

Ford-U.S. was to furnish it with patents, drawings, and
specifications needed to build Ford automobiles. Ford-U.S. would
also render the necessary technical assistance to assure proper
mechanical construction, and would be paid a fee for this service.
In return, Ford Canada received the sale and exclusive right to
manufacture and sell Fords in Canada and the British colonies,
possessions, and dependencies. Thus, from the outset India, Malaya,
South Africa, and Australia came under the authority of Ford-Canada.
What motivated Ford-U.S. in its assignment of Empire rights was
the future probability of a reciprocal preferential tariff within the
Empire. Rights to England and Ireland were not given because sales
rights to those areas had been previously granted until 1907. (6)

Ford-Canada began as an assembly operation and then
progressed to the complete manufacture of all parts. By 1913 it
built its own engines, axles and controls, and had plans to produce
transmissions and all other parts. Meanwhile, sales were expanding
through the efforts of its Canadian and Empire distributors. A third
or more of its production was being shipped overseas. As its
production capacity increased, new markets were required. (7)

By the 1920's foreign sales had so increased that Ford-
Canada began to give more attention to overseas areas. South Africa

received first scrutiny. It first reflected on how some of the profits of its distributors might be realized. It was also concerned with excessive pricing practices of some dealers. Also five dealers had erected assembly facilities which could have been consolidated into one single more efficient operation for the entire area. In addition, some dealers were also representing other car makers. Further, it was questionable whether overall area expansion plans should be left in the hands of a group of uncoordinated distributors.

All this could only be corrected and improved if put under the control of Ford-Canada. It was decided to form an African Corporation and to establish a single, centrally located assembly plant. A branch operation was ruled out because it would make it possible for South Africa to tax Ford-Canada.

Ford-South Africa, wholly owned by Ford-Canada was formed in that country in 1923. The coastal city of Port Elizabeth was then chosen as the warehousing, assembly and distribution center. Ford-South Africa then reorganized the dealer and sub-dealer network. (8)

The following year attention turned to Australia. During World War I the Australian government had considered banning all imports of automobiles to save vital shipping space, but had accepted a compromise which prohibited the admission of car bodies. As a result, the country developed a body-building industry which, following the War, was protected by a high tariff. All five Ford distributors manufactured the bodies of their vehicles. The bodies differed widely and so did the price. As in Africa, this had to be corrected. It was decided to do all body building at the seaport of

Geelong, Victoria, and to have assembly units in each of the vast Australian states.

For tax purposes, two separate entities were incorporated though they functioned together as if they were one unit. Ford Manufacturing Company of Australia was to operate only in Victoria, constructing bodies. The other, Ford Motor Company of Australia, Proprietary, Ltd., would manage the assembly plants and the marketing throughout Australia. Both corporations, created in 1925, shall later be referred to as Ford-Australia. (9)

By the end of 1926 additional wholly-owned companies were established in India and Malaya, and Ford-Canada found itself the largest automotive manufacturer in Canada and the British Empire. (10) Foreign, wholly-owned, corporations were used to own and contol its facilities and operations according to geographical location. The payoff began in the depression-riden 1930's when it was the dividends of these distant subsidiaries that made Ford-Canada a profitable enterprise. During that decade between 30 and 61 percent of Ford-Canada's output each year was sent abroad. (11)

A significant development occured at Ford-Canada head-quarters in 1942. In a labor representation election the employees chose to be represented by the UAW-C10. The company signed an agreement with the union regarding hourly pay and working conditions. Ford-Canada was the first foreign Ford plant to be unionized. (12)

By 1950 the rise in Ford-Canada foreign sales had faltered. Its overseas markets were demanding the smaller European cars rather than the larger North American models. At the same time

Australian and Indian governments were now insisting on local

manufacture. In India, Ford decided not to manufacture and,

because of government rulings, could not import. Other national

import restirctions, including quotas and limitations on foreign

exchange, also acted against Ford-Canada overseas sales. (13)

Because Ford-Canada's domestic sales had steadily

increased, expansion was planned at home. Toronto, with a

population ten times that of Windsor's, was selected for a new

manufacturing site. Being the center of highest sales potential,

Ford-Canada corporate headquarters was transferred there. An

additional motivating factor was that on three earlier occasions

corporate officials at Windsor were unable to get to their offices

due to UAW strikes.   (14)

Ford-Australia responded to local government pressure and

in 1951 expanded its Victoria assembly operation towards complete

manufacture of both North American cars and the smaller British-

Ford designed models. (15)

Ford's internationalization hence began with emphasis upon

contractual sales dealership arrangements, and by taking a controlling

shareholder's interest in a Canadian affiliate. And the pattern was

then repeated by the affiliate. Unlike the later European expansion,

the initiative for Ford-Canada's formation came from Canada and not

from the U.S. The working capital for the Windsor plant was obtained

mainly from Canadians.

Ford-Canada called upon Ford-U.S. for engineering and

manufacturing guidance but otherwise charted an independent course of its own. And this was true even though Ford-U.S. had voting control and, on paper, its officers were the top officers of Ford-Canada. Control was not exercised so long as the affiliate was profitable and expanding. Ford-Canada's expansion proceeded by the establishment of wholly-owned foreign corporations through which it governed activities in the Empire. This remained the state of organization and control until after World War II when overall Ford international operations were reorganized. (16)

England and Europe

Ford-U.S. had opportunities to sell to England and Europe because its standard high volume, low priced car undersold the flamboyant hand made European cars. Its European efforts began in England, it being the sole European country without duties on automobiles. No doubt the common language was also influencial. The Central Motor Car Company, formed in England, was the first to sell Ford-U.S. cars in Britain. It was incorporated and owned by Englishmen in London.(17)

Increasing English sales moved Ford-U.S. officials to open a London branch in 1909. At the same time Ford- Canada passed a corporate resolution waiving its rights in Great Britain and Ireland in favor of Ford-U.S. The waiver was influenced by the fact that the anticipated English tariff with imperial preference had not come into effect. The London branch served to strengthen the foreign trade network of Ford-U.S. (18)

By 1911 the level of British sales justified the erection of
an assembly plant. For reasons of status, tax advantage, and
English identity, Ford Motor Company (England) Ltd. was formed.
It was wholly owned by the stockholders of the American parent
Ford-U.S. Assembly operations began the same year at the plant
in Manchester. As time passed the proportion of locally manufactured
content increased. The year 1913 saw Ford-England responsible
for a quarter of British car production. (19)

The English Finance Act of 1921 was a blow to Ford. It
provided for a tax on passenger cars which was to be calculated by
horsepower. The other English car makers at once began to adapt
their engines to the provisions of the Act. The larger Ford-U.S.-
designed vehicles had considerably higher horsepower. Its price
rose and sales immediately declined. Since no change seemed likely
in the horsepower tax, Ford-England pressured Ford-U.S. for a
car with a smaller engine. It also urged for a completely new car
to be produced in England in high volume for distribution throughout
Europe. It was not until much later when these proposals coincided
with Ford-U.S. European reorganization plans, that action was taken. (20)

In the meantime Ford-U.S. formed wholly owned corporations
in a number of European countries. Each was responsible for sales
and assembly operations within their respective countries. These
national corporations were controlled by Ford-U.S. and, in effect,
operated as branches. Consequently, they received the same
communications about accounting, sales, production, and purchasing

as did U.S. domestic operations. The basis of Ford-U.S. control was its shareholdings, patents, growing technical knowledge, and its managerial appointees.

In addition to new operating corporations, the 1920's saw the creation of separate credit companies to facilitate Ford sales. At least five of these were formed in different European countries, all wholly owned by Ford-U.S. (21)

English and European reorganization began in 1928. A new English company with a larger capitalization was formed called Ford Motor Company (England) Ltd. It acquired all English assets including the new site at Dagenham which was planned to be the largest automobile factory in the world outside of the U.S. Vehicles coming from Dagenham would be sold in the U.K., continental Europe, Asia Minor, and parts of Africa.

Ford-U.S. became the owner of 60% of the shares of the new Ford-England and therefore retained control over policy. The remaining 40% was sold to the British public in small lots so as to obtain the widest possible distribution.

In order to centralize control over the then existing nine European companies 60% of their shares were given to Ford-England. The other 40% of the nine companies were sold to the public in each of the respective countries. It was hoped that national participation in ownership would reduce any feeling that Ford was a foreign company. National image was also enhanced by the appointment of some local directors and managers. (22)

By 1930 one defect in the restructuring became apparent.
Taxes threatened to devour the profits flowing to Ford-England,
for each continental nation taxed its Ford affiliate, and England
proposed to tax again the profit transmitted to the parent, Ford-England.
To remedy this a holding company was formed in the tax-haven state
of Liechtenstein. For reasons not clear, later in 1930 the holding
company was changed to one formed in Luxembourg. This company
acquired Ford-England's stock in six of the continental subsidiaries,
and accumulated their dividends. In 1939 the holding company was
again shifted to one in Guernsey where it was believed it would be
safer from World War II enemy action.   (23)

Latin America

In order to ride the boom of economic expansion following
World War I, Ford-U.S. considered it necessary to establish new
sales and assembly branches in South America. Its pattern of
expansion in Brazil closely resembled that which was taking place
in Argentina, Uruguay, Venezuela, and Chile.

In 1919 a branch was started in Sao Paulo, Brazil replacing
the distributors who handled Brazilian sales up to that time. The
officials of the branch, selected from the earlier-established
Argentine branch, began the creation of an assembly plant.
Although, in theory, the Brazilian branch was treated the same as
any domestic branch, the great distance and irregular communications
resulted in far more independence.

Since Latin America had no indigenous automotive industry, Ford encountered no local competition or government discrimination on behalf of native manufacturers. Such conditions were in contrast with those encountered in industrial Europe, where there was a traditional pride in national products and procedures.

Ford branch sales grew rapidly and the branch claimed to have the largest sales organization among all industries in Brazil.

Tax considerations made Ford incorporate Ford Motor Company of Brazil, a Delaware corporation, to own all Ford-Brazil assets. This was the first time a separately incorporated domestic corporation was used by Ford to hold foreign assets. This took place in 1923, and the same practice was later to be repeated for other foreign operations.

In 1925 the Brazil branch protested to Ford-U.S. that its sales could no longer be handled by the single assembly unit in Sao Paulo. Three new assembly plants were opened within two years. (24)

By 1950 Latin American sales reached the point where Ford-U.S. considered the establishment of complete production facilities. Consideration was given to a manufacturing plant in Brazil. However, economies of scale could not be reached unless the plant was used to export as well as to supply the domestic market. For the present this was impossible. Other Latin American countries could buy from Ford-U.S. or Ford-England cheaper than from Ford-Brazil. Transportation, tariffs, and exchange procedures were not so arranged to permit Ford-Brazil to supply its neighbouring countries easily, and nationalistic sentiment meant that the others would prefer to manufacture for themselves than to import from neighbours.

Soon, however, Brazil itself increased automobile tariffs and exchange controls, and moved to require nearly full local manufacture. Ford then had no choice but to increase its local investment or abandon operations in Brazil. It decided to manufacture only trucks and began an extensive expansion program towards that end. By 1960 its trucks were more than 90% Brazilian in content.

All of Ford operations in Brazil were wholly financed by Ford-U.S. with no local capital participation. (25)

Germany

A Hamburg branch was begun in 1912. It handled sales, spare parts, and repairs for Germany and neighbouring countries. Sales in Germany, which required an import license, rose steadily. Ford Motor Company A.G. was formed in 1925 and staffed with men from nearby Ford-Denmark. Its agents were increased and an assembly plant began outside of Berlin. Tariff increases in 1927 put pressure on the Ford assembly operation. In 1929 the City of Cologne offered favourable tax terms if Ford established a plant in that city. A large tract was acquired on the Rhine River. The following year the U.S. passed the notorious Smoot-Hawley bill erecting high tariffs against imports. Germany, along with most other countries, retaliated, and it became clear that Ford

must manufacture locally. The Cologne plant was begun. In

Germany, as well as throughout Europe, the role of the imported

car was ending, at least temporarily. (26)

Ford-England had been the primary source of Ford cars

for Germany and its German sales soon fell to nothing. Its only

compensation was through its 60% ownership of Ford-Germany.

As Ford-Germany investment expanded, Ford-U.S.

assumed the brunt of financing. Newly issued shares increased

Ford-U.S. holdings from zero to 34% and correspondingly reduced

Ford-England's and that of the German public.

In 1936 and thereafter the German policy of national growth

encouraged the export of autos and Ford-Germany vehicles began

to be exported. This was boosted by the Ford-U.S. policy of

purchasing Ford-Germany parts and its urging Ford-England to do

the same. A chronic German tyre shortage was met by an

agreement whereby Ford-U.S. supplied the rubber which the

Cologne plant paid for with exports of car parts. (27)

Increased sales justified the creation of a new factory in

Berlin in 1938. As a symbol of German identity Ford-Germany then

changed its name to Ford-Werke A.G. It expanded further after

World War II and further again when the prospect for the Common

Market became clear. Towards the end of the 1950's the smaller

European-built cars became popular in the U.S. Ford shared in

this turn of events through exports from Ford-Germany, as well as from Ford-England. (28)

Then in 1962 it purchased land in Belgium and built another factory. This Belgian branch plant expanded overall production by 50%. Ford-Germany went on to surpass all other Ford overseas operations in sales and production. (29)

International Consolidation

After World War II Ford-U.S. created an internal organizational unit called the International Division. It was to coordinate all overseas activities. The International Division preferred to direct European operations rather than do it through Ford-England. It also questioned the arrangement whereby Ford-U.S. owned 60% of Ford-England, which in turn owned 60% of Ford-Denmark, which owned 60% of Ford-Sweden, which owned 60% of Ford-Finland. This was the ownership pattern of Ford's European companies. Such a complex of relationships meant that Ford profits were being tapped at practically all levels of the pyramid. (30)

A related factor was American antitrust legislation and court decisions. Decisions in the postwar period indicated that a company might violate antitrust rules when it made certain arrangements with an affiliated firm, whereas the same action with a wholly owned subsidiary might not be vulnerable.

Furthermore, outside minority holdings did not always produce the desired result. Shareholders were often a few wealthy individualsor institutions, rather than the average member of the local foreign public. Frequently, no change in national image resulted. Ford had conducted a survey in Germany when its holdings in Ford-Germany were 52% and General Motor's holdings in Opel, its German subsidiary, were 100%. The findings showed that most Germans considered Opel a German firm, and thought of Ford-Werke as an American enterprise. . Stock ownership did not appear to determine national image. (31)

In 1948 all Ford managers around the world met together for the first time at Ford-U. S. headquarters. There were about 30 managers, all from different locations as dispersed as Buenos Aires, Singapore, Europe, and Bombay. They listened to Ford-U. S. executives who explained sound organization, teamwork, management by committee, and profit centers. Henry Ford II, dissatisfied with the loosely knit overseas organization, told them bluntly "... We are going to forumulate overseas policies right here ..... This is an American company and its going to be run from America". (32)

Two years later, in 1950, Ford-U. S. acquired direct shareholding control of the continental Ford companies and the Ford-England Guernsey holding company was liquidated. The acquisition by Ford-U. S. included stock holdings in Egypt (99%), Italy (100%), Belgium (57%), Holland (60%), Denmark (60%), Spain (60%), France (21%), and Germany (6%). Ford-U. S. already controlled most of the French and German, and by this purchase it increased its equity in the Franch and German Ford units to 55%

and 58%, respectively. It also acquired indirect holdings in Ford-
Sweden, Ford-Finland, and Ford-Portugal.

The balance of the shares in the Belgian, Dutch, Danish,
Spanish, Finnish, Swedish, Franch, and German firms continued
to be publicly owned, most of it by nationals within those countries.

All existing agreements among the Ford companies were
revised to ensure that the products of all Ford manufacturing
companies could be available in all markets. This change was based
in part on the recognition that the huge Dagenham Ford-England
plant had to export throughout the world to realize its potential.
It also brought Ford-U.S. policy in line with recent U.S. Supreme
Court antitrust rulings. Ford companies anywhere in the world were
free to compete in markets that had previously been the American
company's preserve. (33)

Shortly, car shipments from Ford-England Dagenham plant
reached a new high and exceeded exports from all other Ford
companies. The English-built cars went to markets that had
previously been served by American and Canadian Ford cars. A
shortage of dollars and the demand for a smaller, economical car
partly accounted for this shift. (34)

Ford-U.S. now held the majority of voting stock in all its
foreign affiliates. Its new policy, like that of its rival, General
Motors, was to move toward full ownership of all its foreign
activities. Ford executives believed that overseas operations had
previously gotten out of control by being directed from abroad.

With total ownership nothing could interfere with its being operated in the manner most profitable to Ford-U.S. Dividend and expansion policy could be shaped without deference to minority stockholders. Product planning and marketing could be based on international rather than national considerations. (35)

Throughout the 1950's Ford officials favoured greater financial, engineering, sales, and administrative coordination between the overseas companies and the parent company. At the same time, however, labour policies were left to the independent determination of each company. Overseas labour contracts were determined by local conditions. (36)

By the late 1950's the U.S. inflationary spiral raised the cost of raw materials and parts. The higher prices that followed, plus the trade barriers erected in foreign lands, sharply cut overseas sales of American Ford vehicles. For the first time in fifty years, in 1957, U.S car imports exceeded exports. English, German, French, and Italian manufacturers could now produce motor vehicles of worldwide appeal that sold at prices lower than those built in North America. European labour had always been cheaper, so this was not the decisive factor. European producers were now using Ford-pioneered mass production techniques and had achieved economies of scale. In 1958 Volkswagons, Anglias, Renaults, Fiats, and other small European-made cars took nearly 10% of the American car market. Ford-U.S. sales and profits declined and, for the same reasons, so did Ford-Canada's. (37)

There were other compensations for Ford-U.S., steming
from its multinational character. Ford-England's and Ford-
Germany's exports to the U.S surged upward. Ford could offer
17 foreign economy cars - the widest range available in America.
Ford foreign company sales rose to a record level. Moreover,
in practically every year since World War II Ford's overseas
profits had mounted, averaging 12% per year. Clearly, the
international operations of Ford were of crucial importance for
overall profits. (38)

In 1958 the Common Market came into being and in response
EFTA was created. Ford officials responded. The following
year Ford-England began construction of another large manufacturing
plant. This was located near Liverpool. Ford-England's
Engineering Department swelled from 270 men in 1950 to 1,830
men in 1960. It continued to design and produce a range of vehicles
entirely different from those made by Ford-U.S. The Ford-Germany
Belgian branch plant begun in 1952 would be dependent on supplies
from Cologne and was evidence that Ford-Germany strategy was
geared to its faith in the Common Market. At Cologne, where
labour was in short supply, Ford brought in Italian workmen -
acting in accord with the E.E.C. policy that goods, services, and
labour should move freely from one country to the next. (39)

Ford-U.S. planned a response to the foreign economy cars
by the design and production of a compact car called Falcon. Ford
enterprise cooperation was such that by 1960 the Falcon was being
manufactured by Ford plants in Canada, Argentina, and Australia.

Ford-U.S. drew the overseas companies into closer coordination by showing skills in management and production, by joint marketing studies, by common purchasing, and through increased investment and percentage of ownership of foreign companies. By 1962 nearly every foreign company or branch had an American general manager.   (40)

Ford-U.S.'s ownership in Ford-Canada was up to 75%, in Ford-Germany to 99%, in Ford-England 100%.[41] Ford-Brazil and Ford-Argentina were wholly owned. The only manufacturing company not directly controlled was Ford-Australia which remained a wholly owned subsidiary of Ford-Canada.   (42)

Control of the non-manufacturing companies followed, regardless of parent ownership, since they were dependent on the other companies for parts. This interdependence among all Ford companies was the desired goal.

By favouring total control, Ford-U.S went contrary to many American companies that preferred joint ventures with foreign firms. Ford believed that the advantages of full ownership far outweighed any merits of joint ventures. Its policy was now opposite to what it had been in the late 1920's and the 1930's.

Despite its huge foreign investments, in the eleven year period preceeding the end of 1961 Ford-U.S. contributed approximately $2 billion to the U.S. balance of payments. Foreign venture dividends had far surpassed investment. (43)

The 1960's and 70's

In 1965 Ford-built cars captured U.S. industry sales leadership in the world market outside of North America. For the first time it surpassed the mamouth General Motors. (44)

One of the chief assets of a multinational enterprise is its capacity to utilize the concept of complementation, which in the case of Ford means the interregional free trade of motor vehicles and components. Ford first used this during the 1960's in connection with tractor manufacture. Manufacturing was divided among three subsidiaries. Ford-England produced engines and hydraulic systems. Ford-Belgium made axels and four-speed, and eight-speed transmissions; Ford-U.S. provided ten-speed transmissions. Components were exchanged and assembled in all three locations and elsewhere. (45) This could also be called specialization within the enterprise.

The same concept was employed with the Ford Capri car introduced around 1970. Ford-England and Ford-Germany jointly designed and produced that model. Europewide acceptance suggested thatregional products might supplement or supplant nationally produced vehicles. Prior to the use of complementation or specialization, Ford cars produced in Germany, England and France had non-interchangeable parts, even though they were about the same size and performed the same functions. (46)

Complementation has been utilized outside of Europe. Ford-Mexico sends engines to Ford-Venezuela and engine blocks to Ford U.S. Ford-Brazil ships cams and chassis parts on a value basis for vehicles manufactured by Ford-Australia.

It is currently planning the use of complementation in the
Asia-Pacific area. ⁽⁴⁷⁾ This could come to complete fruition if

political and tariff agreements are reached by the participating

countries. Ideally, components would be exchanged and assembled

into vehicles in each country in the region. By tariff-free exchange

each country would pay for its imports through exports, and each

would assemble a finished product. This system would cut costs

by avoiding duplication in design, tooling, and manufacturing

facilities, while minimizing each country's outflow of funds.

Ford presently has seven automotive manufacturing or

assembly plants in the Asia-Pacific area. There are separate Ford

companies incorporated in Singapore, Thailand, Taiwan, Japan,

Malaysia, Australia, and the Philippines. Three are wholly owned,

Japan is 50% owned, and Taiwan is 70% owned. In the latter two

countries, 100% control was not possible.

As of 1972 Ford's foreign production and distribution

operations were housed in foreign companies located in 30

different countries. All but a few are directly owned by the U.S.

parent company. And all but ten are wholly owned. Of those ten

the parent company's interest is 70% or greater in all instances

except in the 50/50 Japanese affiliate.

In addition, there are Ford foreign credit companies to

assist overseas sales. They are located in Canada, England,

Germany, and Australia - the four leading countries in foreign

sales. Those companies are wholly and directly owned by the U.S.

parent. (48)

On the management side, Ford top level staff and advisory groups are organized by function, and each function serves worldwide Ford activities. There are three main operating units. Nonautomotive operations is organized on a worldwide basis by product. North American Automotive Operations manages manufacturing, assembly, and marketing in the U.S. and Canada, and is organized by function. International Automotive Operations directs production and sales by overseas areas. The areas are Latin America, Asia-Pacific, and Europe. The managers of these units oversee the activities of the affiliates within their areas. European management facilities and activities are housed within a separate corporation. It is Ford of Europe Incorporated which was formed under the laws of the state of Delaware in the U.S. It is headquartered in England and has a branch office in Germany. (49)

2.2   MITSUBISHI GROUP

Prior to 1970 there was little talk about Japanese companies as multinational enterprises. (50) None of them were very large by world standards and few of their production operations were located overseas. But these factors have been changing. (50.1)

The Fortune Directory of the 100 Largest Industrials Outside the U.S. which first appeared in 1957, contained only four Japanese Corporations. The Directory was since expanded to list the 200 largest non-U.S. corporations. Now the 1971 Directory lists 51 Japanese companies among the top 200, with 20 companies in the first 100. Japan now surpasses Great Britain as the country most heavily represented in the Directory. (51)

Japan was traditionally inclined to build industries located only in Japan. In the past Mitsubishi Group's production plants were heavily concentrated in Japan, and its limited overseas facilities were usually branches rather than locally incorporated foreign subsidiaries. Applying the usual multinational criteria, neither it nor any other Japanese company would have qualified. For reasons which follow, it is believed that the Mitsubishi Group should be considered a multinational enterprise.

In some respects the multinational criteria of foreign investment may not be appropriate in the case of Japanese companies. In the case of Mitsubishi, Group raw material requirements are usually secured by long term contracts like those for Australian ore; as opposed to foreign investment. Title to the ore mines is not held nor is there any foreign subsidiary. Yet the result is

the same with extended contract periods and immense requirements. (52)

However, the form and magnitude of its overseas investments

is rapidly changing. In addition to its already extensive overseas

manufacturing plants in Asia, it has ambitious plans for the

manufacture of heavy machinery, and for shipyard repair facilities,

in Singapore. In the U.S. negotiations have been in the air for the

possible construction of a container terminal on New York's Staten

Island. Its European headquarters in London is planning a vigorous

program in the EEC. (53)

During the 1970's Mitsubishi Group will take its share of

Japan's direct investment abroad, now standing at $7 billion and

expected to hit $30 billion by 1980. Limited land, yen revaluations,

skyrocketing currency reserves, and wages rates have accelerated

the multinationalization of all Japanese industrial companies. (54)

It is believed that the Mitsubishi Group is the largest

multinational enterprise not only in Japan but in the entire world.

Its annual sales now in excess of $40 billion are fity percent greater

than those of the mamouth auto producer General Motors. Outside

the U.S. its nearest rival is the Royal Dutch/Shell Group with a

sales volume one-third that of Mitsubishi. (55)

Nevertheless, the Mitsubishi Group (MG) is conspicuously

absent from the prestigous Fortune listings of the largest industrials

outside the U.S. , as well as from recent listings of the biggest

multinations. The explanation for this is directly related to the nature of its organizational structure. The Group is a family (56) of over forty interrelated but separate Japanese corporations. All but a few of them bear the "Mitsubishi" name and its "three diamonds" symbol. In the strictest legal sense MG is not a single juridic entity and therefore it is not listed in the Fortune Directory. Nonetheless, it is contended that MG is in fact a single economic entity and should be considered as such.

There are other enterprises, not separate legal entities, which are in fact listed. The Royal Dutch/Shell Group is one of them. It holds first place among the largest non-U.S. industrials. Yet its dual structure of British and Dutch corporations is not a single juridic entity. Nor is Unilever, in second place, a separate legal entity. Both are listed because of their unique unifying agreements and arrangements.

The factors that tie the Mitsubishi companies together are also unique.

In the Japanese industrial environment the concepts of "harmony" and "cooperation" are the cornerstones of managerial organization, and one of the bases for the phenomenal Japanese economic growth. So fundamental are these ideas that the relationship between business and government is the closest in the world except for the Communist-oriented nations. To grasp the depth of these inter-company and government bonds is to comprehend the extent of extra-legal integration in the Mitsubishi Group as well as in other industrial combines or zaibatsu such as Mitsui and Sumitomo. These three alone are reported to represent nearly 40 per cent of the capital of

all the firms listed in the first section of the Tokyo Stock

Exchange. (57)

Before examining the organizational structure of MG, it

is helpful to review portions of Japanese history and philosophy

(58)

in which these zaibatsu/found their roots. Mitsubishi and the

others are a combination of western technology and Japanese

traditional values. It is the latter that the West finds elusive.

Mitsubishi Origins

Japanese industrial might had its origins in the Tokugawa

Feudal Era which commenced at the beginning of the seventeenth

century and ended with the Meiji Restoration in 1868. It began

when Tokugawa Ieyasu conquered all rivals and established the

last in a series of feudal Shoganates or hereditary military

dictatorships. In descending order of group importance people

were classified as warriors, farmers, artisans, or merchants.

Feudal Japan was a collectively oriented society. The individual

hardly existed as a distinct entity. In every aspect of life he

was tightly bound to a group. Among farming communities

interfamily cooperation and interdependence reached the point

that the community took on the characteristics of one large

family. Fear of being ostracized from the group exerted a

compelling pressure to conform to the group norms. Intragroup

harmony was sought not only for its own sake but for the purpose

of goal attainment. This later found expression in the national
goal of surpassing the West.

As early as the seventh century Confucianism had been
introduced from China where it served to legitimize the authority
of China's ruling elite. Although Buddhism later became the
dominent Japanese religion, remnants of Confucianism survived
and were revitalized by the Tokugawa family. It became the
official philosophy and the ideological framework for the rigid
class system. Conformity to group norms was prescribed
above all else. Confucian precepts recognized the unity of
economics and politics, and recognized the importance of economic
activities provided they contributed to social harmony. Confucianism
played a role similar to that of the Protestant ethic in the West
in helping to breed the entrepreneurial spirit. The difference
was that one placed faith in the individual and the other in the
nation. Even today "The Analects of Confucius" is the most
admired book among Japanese managers. (59)

These concepts laid the basis for inter-company cooperation,
and set the stage for government encouraged monopolies and
oligarchies. (60)

As commerce developed it was necessary for the dominant
warrior or samurai class to control its development. This
furthered the trend toward control of commerce by the state.
Shoganate-sponsored semi-monopolies sprang up in certain
commercial lines. Progressive feudal lords saw the military
potential of modern technology and began defense oriented
industries such as iron and shipbuilding.

Slowly, power in the feudal society shifted to the merchant class whose ranks were invaded by the progressive samurai.

The majority of tradition-bound samurai were unable to make the transition into the new economy and soon found themselves in desperate financial condition. Higher tax burdens on the farmer coupled with envy of the rising merchants led to general discontent which found expression in Shintoism. This quasi-religious, quasi-political philosophy emphasized the glorification of the Emperor and the uniqueness of Japan as a divine nation. An intense nationalism developed and the Meiji Restoration followed in 1868.

The Restoration meant the removal of the political power vested in the Shoganate and the return to direct rule by the Emperor. This movement was led by progressive samurai, some of whom later became members of the ruling oligarchy. Acting in the name of the Emperor they began to build a militarily strong nation with a newly found industrial base. (61)

In the beginning, therefore, industrialization was related to the attainment of dominant national goals one of which was to catch up with the West. A sense of urgency coupled with the weakness of private capital placed all of the initiative with the government. It became the major promoter, owner, and administrator of industry in the early Meiji years.

In the 1880's the government decided to withdraw from the operation of most industrial enterprises and sold them to prominent commercial families. Among the recipients was the Iwasaki family of samurai origin. They had been operating

a shipping service since 1870 and had established the Mitsubishi

Company in 1886. The government-managed Nagasaki

Dockyard was released to them and Mitsubishi began to place

prime emphasis on shipbuilding. This gave rise to various

activities in the machinery industry which laid the foundation

for the subsequent Mitsubishi Group.

During the same period the government also looked to the

wealthier samurai and merchants to develop commercial banks

for the financing of further industrial growth. Few of these

families had banking experience and hence they were expected

to follow government instructions and guidance. In most

instances they were not considered as individual profiteering

bankers, but as semi-government bureaucrats serving the needs

of the State.

Zaibatsu like Mitsubishi, Mitsui, and Sumitomo, which

had come into being with government endorsement, were persuaded

to open banks. Shortly, they controlled numerous banks and

financial institutions. This included sizable blocks of shares

in the central government Bank of Japan. The narrowly held

shareholdings of the zaibatsu soon made it necessary for them

to cooperate with banks for the financing of expansion. The banks,

in turn, through loans and ownership, became intimately connected
(62)
with industrial enterprises./ Since the central government Bank

of Japan had regulatory powers over all banks, the government

could exercise effective control over industry. This has
since been referred to as "window guidance. " (63)

The pattern of interwoven relations between government,
banks, and companies accounts for the present unity of goals
between legally separate entities. This bias, grafted upon
traditional community-centred values, provided the basis for
ensuring the growth of the nation. Emphasis on the group or
collectivity was further cemented by the Civil Code of 1898 in which
the family, rather than the individual, constituted the basic
legal entity. Modern industrial indications of this can be seen
in the "company" club. The Mitsui Club, the best known, has
members from all the companies within that group.

The accelerated growth of Mitsubishi began around 1917
when various business divisions were incorporated into independent
companies and Mitsubishi Goshi Kaisha became the holding company
and controller. Among other entities which came into being were
Mitsubishi Bank, Mitsubishi Iron Works, and Mitsubishi Shoji.
The latter played the role of salesmen for the Group.

To promote rapid growth, the government encouraged
cartels and other collusive actions. As the larger firms progressed
their wage rates rose substantially above those of the smaller
firms. Zaibatsu and other large enterprises took advantage of
this through a system of subcontracting often combined with
financial control. These arrangements facilitated the rising
economic power of Mitsubishi and the other zaibatsu so that
after the Second World War the four biggest zaibatsu held nearly

one-third of the paid-in capital in heavy industry. Their banks extended over 70% of total bank loans, and their trading companies handled one-third of Japan's foreign trade. (64)

American postwar occupation introduced the legal concepts of free competition in the form of the Anti-Monopoly Act. The zaibatsu were most heavily affected. Family ownership and control were removed, holding companies dissolved, and subsidiaries were released to become independent corporations with widely diffused ownership.

Mitsubishi Goshi Kaisha had changed its name to Mitsubishi Honsha Ltd. At the time of the breakups it controlled the Group. Forty-eight subsidiaries, eleven affiliates, and sixteen related companies were all under the command of President Iwasaki. In general, Mitsubishi met the same fate as the other zaibatsu. Partition and dissolution resulted in the disintegration of the empire. Typical of the fate of other segments, Mitsubishi Shoji was split into 140 companies.

Organization

After termination of the Allied Occupation it was this shattered Mitsubishi Shoji that became the focus of the regrouping of Mitsubishi. At first there was extensive mutual cooperation among the small firms into which Shoji had been divided. The . traditional Mitsubishi principle of doing business on the strength of organization led to its reorganization into one firm in 1954.

Nearly half of the newly issued Shoji shares were allocated

to companies in the Mitsubishi Group. This system replaced

and reversed the pre-war system under which Mitsubishi Honsha

held control by owning stocks of the Group companies. (65)

The new mutual stockholdings arrangement set the pattern

for the reintegration of the other pre-war Mitsubishi companies.

Intercorporate ties were strengthened by increasing cross-

holdings of stocks within the Group. Reciprocal dealings in

production, sales and technical development swelled, thus

continuing their earlier cooperative strategy. The post-war

difference was in their legal and ownership interconnections,

not in the way they functioned. (66)

Before the war, ownership and overall management control

rested with the Iwasaki family. Now each former subsidiary

is an independent company with its own stockholders and board

of directors. Reflecting this change, the word "group" has

replaced the term zaibatsu. Cross-holdings of stock among the

Group have still assumed some importance, amounting to 17%
(67)
in 1965./ Current Group coordination is provided by the Kinyo-

kai or Friday Conference. This weekly gathering is attended by

the chief executive officers of approximately 26 major Mitsubishi

companies. Leadership at the conference is in the hands of a

triumvirate consisting of the top executive from Mitsubishi

Shoji (renamed Mitsubishi Corporation in 1971), from Mitsubishi

Bank and from Mitsubishi Heavy Industries. Coordination and

cooperation among the Group depends upon the collective
guidance exercised at these meetings. The resulting extra-
legal organization can be represented as shown in the diagram
on the next page.

Mitsubishi Group

Unlike the centrally dominated pre-war pattern, the
present companies are a loose confederation of independent
enterprises sharing common former zaibatsu ties and a certain
community of interest. The council of 26 Kinyo-kai executives
also differs in its power and function from the pre-war holding
company. The present organization, with a few exceptions, is
a council of peers, each representing an independent firm.
The officers of these firms do, in fact, place the interest of
their own company over that of the Group. They are willing to
cooperate only insofar as such collaboration will be beneficial
to their own firm. But it usually is, and although the council
lacks the ultimate authority once vested in the holding company,
its policy decisions are seldom ignored by the management of
a member firm.

There are more than 40 companies that are clearly
Mitsubishi aligned. As suppliers, customers, and traders of
equipment and technology they engage in a wide variety of
exchanges. It is estimated that as much as half of the Group's
total business may be done within the Group itself. (68). Of all

MITSUBISHI GROUP

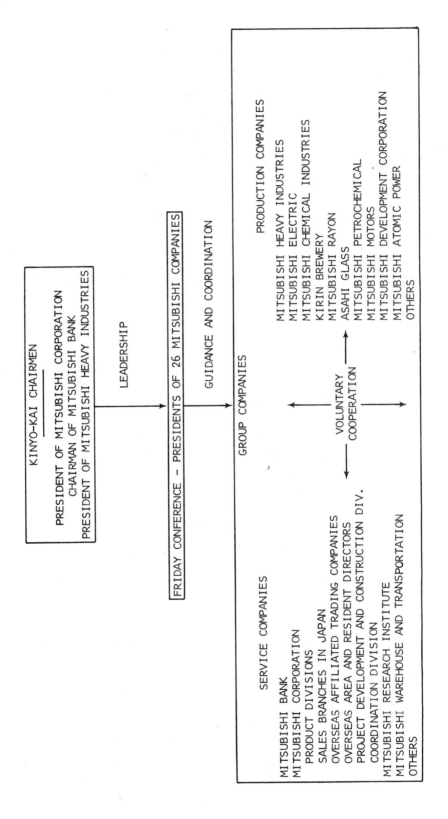

KINYO-KAI CHAIRMEN

PRESIDENT OF MITSUBISHI CORPORATION
CHAIRMAN OF MITSUBISHI BANK
PRESIDENT OF MITSUBISHI HEAVY INDUSTRIES

LEADERSHIP

FRIDAY CONFERENCE — PRESIDENTS OF 26 MITSUBISHI COMPANIES

GUIDANCE AND COORDINATION

GROUP COMPANIES

SERVICE COMPANIES

MITSUBISHI BANK
MITSUBISHI CORPORATION
PRODUCT DIVISIONS
SALES BRANCHES IN JAPAN
OVERSEAS AFFILIATED TRADING COMPANIES
OVERSEAS AREA AND RESIDENT DIRECTORS
PROJECT DEVELOPMENT AND CONSTRUCTION DIV.
COORDINATION DIVISION
MITSUBISHI RESEARCH INSTITUTE
MITSUBISHI WAREHOUSE AND TRANSPORTATION
OTHERS

VOLUNTARY
COOPERATION

PRODUCTION COMPANIES

MITSUBISHI HEAVY INDUSTRIES
MITSUBISHI ELECTRIC
MITSUBISHI CHEMICAL INDUSTRIES
KIRIN BREWERY
MITSUBISHI RAYON
ASAHI GLASS
MITSUBISHI PETROCHEMICAL
MITSUBISHI MOTORS
MITSUBISHI DEVELOPMENT CORPORATION
MITSUBISHI ATOMIC POWER
OTHERS

Group companies there are five which play key roles in the
Group's solidarity. They are Mitsubishi Corporation,
Mitsubishi Bank, Mitsubishi Heavy Industries, Mitsubishi
Research Institute, and Mitsubishi Development Corporation.

The importance of Mitsubishi Corporation (MC) is reflected
in its representation in the Kinyo-kai triumvirate. Its president,
Chujiro Fujino, is one of the three chairmen who hold the reins
of supreme leadership in the Group. MC is the overall marketing
and new project manager for the Group.

To appreciate the marketing or trading function of MC
one should envision placing the sales and purchasing departments
of forty of America's largest and diverse companies into a single
corporation. Not only is this difficult to imagine from an
organisation viewpoint, but by U.S. law it is highly questionable.
However, Japanese industry is centered around this international
trading company concept.

Not all sales of Group companies are handled by Mitsubishi
Corporation, nor are Group products the only ones sold by
the corporation. It is estimated that more than half of the
Group's exports and imports are funneled through the trading
company./ (69) This is consistent with the fact that over 40% of MC's
shares are still held by Group companies.

Although Group companies do carve out new and independent
paths for their firms, MC plays a significant role as Group
project manager. Much of this is administered by its Project
Development and Construction Division and its Coordination

Division. A recently proposed project typifies this function and also demonstrates the continuing closeness of government ties. A 56-company Japanese consortium headed by Mitsubishi Corporation was preparing competitive bid estimates on a multi-million dollar mass transit project in Hong Kong. The project was considered so gigantic that it would require a low interest government loan. Mitsubishi officials stated that they had conferred with Japanese Prime Minister Tanaka regarding the loan. (70)

MC's global sales network consists of overseas branch offices, or wholly owned foreign corporations. The latter are referred to as affiliated trading companies and are found in countries where local incorporation is necessary or advantageous. The heads of the other offices, not locally incorporated are designated as resident directors or area directors depending upon the scope of their responsibility. In all, MC has sales offices in approximately 100 cities spread over every continent.

Major product divisions within MC are fuels, metals, foods, machinery, textiles, chemicals and general merchandise. They buy and sell everything from cameras to beer, whale oil, logs, autos, flight simulation equipment and some of the world's largest ships.

The Group's financial backbone is Mitsubishi Bank (MB). It holds about 8 per cent of the shares of MC and varying portions of other Group companies. Together with Group members

Mitsubishi Trust, Tokyo Marine and Fire Insurance and Meiji Mutual Life Insurance it provides substantial amounts of financing for Group expansion. Total assets of these four exceed those of First National City Bank of New York, the second largest commercial bank in the world.

Mitsubishi Heavy Industires (MHI), the third member of the triumvirate, is the largest company in the Group. Independently, it ranks as the 19th largest industrial outside the U.S. The sheer magnitude of its shipbuilding, aircraft and other industrial systems makes it a focal point for Group subcontracting and coordination.

The web of Group solidarity was further strengthened in 1970 with the formation of Mitsubishi Development Corporation (MDC). Its initial capitalization was shared by 33 Group Companies. The president of the company is the president of MC and its staff is drawn from other Group members. The chairman is also the chairman of Mitsubishi Estate Company, the lessor of nearly a third of all rentals in Tokyo. MDC's primary mission is to undertake long term housing, city and regional development plans, as well as futuristic projects such as ocean development. Because it is launching programs that no single Group company could undertake, it works closely with the Project Development and Coordination Divisions of MC.

Mitsubishi Research Institute, also formed in 1970, is another example of Group integration. Its capitalization was shared by 27 Group companies and the president of Mitsubishi

Steel served as its first president. One of the Institut's three

nuclei is Mitsubishi Economic Research Institute which was

founded in 1932. Another is the Institute's computer complex,

the largest in Japan, and partly developed by Mitsubishi Atomic

Power Industries. The third element is the Advanced Techno-

Economic Information Center which at the time of its earlier

founding was meant to become Japan's center for gathering

technological information. All members of the Mitsubishi

Group have access to the Institute which is reported to be Japan's

best research environment.

The same pattern of cooperation can be seen in the chemical

and atomic power industries. In 1956 Mitsubishi Chemical

attempted to move into the petrochemical industry. But it

lacked the colossal sums necessary. Various Group companies

believed this new endeavor to be critical to the Group's future and

so the beginning capital for Mitsubishi Petro-chemical came

from Mitsubishi Chemical, MC, MB, Mitsubishi Metal Mining,

Asahi Glass, other Group companies, and one outsider, Shell

Oil.

In 1958 two dozen Mitsubishi-aligned companies gave birth

to Mitsubishi Atomic Power Industries and commenced the Group's

modern power generation goals. Subsequent activities displayed

the same teamwork. Design and engineering were initiated by

Mitsubishi Atomic Power. Major component manufacture and

equipment subcontracting was the role of MHI and Mitsubishi

Electric. MC handled sales arrangements. Import and sales
of uranium were the duty of Mitsubishi Oil and MC, while
nuclear fuel processing was done by Mitsubishi Atomic Power.
To insure uranium ore supplies MC made long term contracts
for Canadian ore, and Mitsubishi Metal Mining entered a joint
venture to mine uranium in Wyoming, U.S.A.

Group efforts, in association with Westinghouse, resulted
in Japan's first pressure water reactor for power generation.
An independent Group effort produced the Matsu, an atomic-
powered ship. While discussing these new Group activities and
goals, an officer of MC significantly stated: "To achieve
such purposes successfully, all the interested organizations
in our Group are taking actions. We aim at a 60 percent market
share in Japan in all areas of atomic energy industry." (71)

There are similarities between MG and large American
and European companies. The Western giants are composed of
subsidiaries, profit centers, or divisions which their parents
frequently profess to be independent. Their central services
are often available to the entire organization on a voluntary
basis. Divisions and subsidiaries are encouraged to purchase
parts and materials from within the company, although they are
generally   free to purchase anywhere because of their
separate profit accountability.

What the top officers are really managing is not simply
one major company but an industrial combine consisting of a

large number of firms, called divisions or subsidiaires, with

corporate headquarters as the nucleus for coordination. ITT's

directors, for example, attempt to establish policies for the

overall guidance of the company in the same way that overall

Mitsubishi policies are set by Kinyo-kai members.

The difference is mainly one of ownership. ITT owns

its divisions and the shares of its subsidiaries. There is no

single parent company that can make that claim for the Mitsubishi

companies. Mitsubishi cohesion is based on cross-holdings of

stocks, a community of interest, and a tradition of cooperation.

3. INTERNATIONAL MULTINATIONS (TRANSNATIONALS)

The Royal Dutch/Shell Group, Unilever, the Dunlop Pirelli Union and less than a dozen other enterprises have been classified as "international multinationals". These are organisations composed of two or more parent companies of different nationalities linked together by means of shareholdings, common directorial control, or contract; subject to a single managerial direction; and consisting of networks of connected companies of many nationalities.

These international multinationals are to be distinguished from "national multinationals, " like the Ford Motor Company. Ford's single parent company is incorporated in the U.S., and in spite of its many foreign subsidiaries, is clearly an American entity. The international multinationals, in contrast have two or more national parents, giving them dual, treble or additional nationality at the top.

3.1 ROYAL DUTCH/SHELL GROUP

Royal Dutch in the Netherlands, and Shell Transport in England, came into being near the end of the last century. Royal Dutch had discovered oil in the Dutch East Indies but did not have market outlets. Shell began by trading seashells as Victorian ornaments and then proceeded to sell Russian oil through its agents in the East.

To survive competition from Rockefeller's Standard Oil, the two agreed in 1907 to combine their complementary interests on a 60/40 basis. Both sides preferred a unified management for their combined assets, but neither wished to be merged into the other. Even if a merger had been acceptable, tax and fiscal factors presented formidable obstacles. The structure that satisfied both sides is, with minor alterations, the structure in use today. It can be seen on the next page.

At the top, each side has a parent company and a holding company. One set is incorporated in England and the other in the Netherlands. The Dutch parent has a 60% interest in both the Dutch and British holding companies, and the British parent has the remaining 40%. In turn, both holding companies own the stock of the operating companies located in over 100 countries. Whether an operating company is held by the British holding company or by the Dutch, is determined largely by tax considerations.

In effect, the Dutch parent exchanged a 100% interest in its assets for a 60% interest in the combined assets. The British parent exchanged all of its assets for 40% of the combined assets. From a public stockholder's viewpoint, an equal value of investment in either parent yields an equal value of dividend return. This is true except for inevitable differences in exchange controls, interest equalization, and varying standards of price/earnings ratios. These factors depend upon the nationality and location of the particular stockholder and have nothing to do with the basic investment equality built into and maintained by the structure of the Group.

ROYAL DUTCH/SHELL GROUP

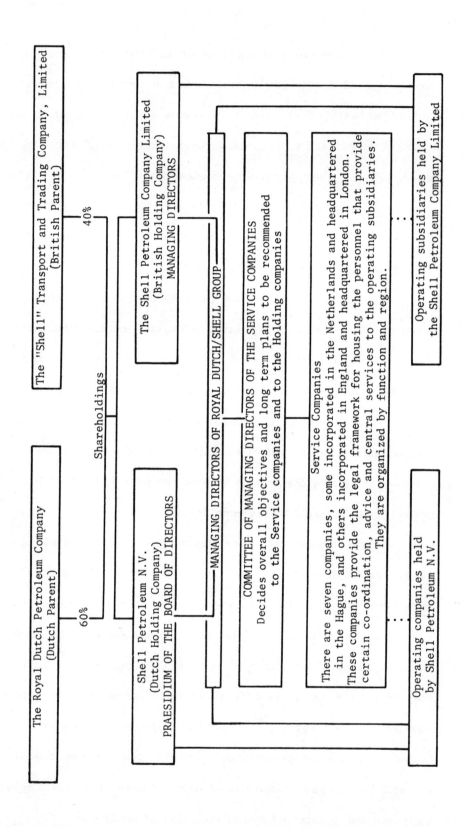

The Royal Dutch Petroleum Company
(Dutch Parent)

The "Shell" Transport and Trading Company, Limited
(British Parent)

60%

40%

Shareholdings

Shell Petroleum N.V.
(Dutch Holding Company)
PRAESIDIUM OF THE BOARD OF DIRECTORS

The Shell Petroleum Company Limited
(British Holding Company)
MANAGING DIRECTORS

MANAGING DIRECTORS OF ROYAL DUTCH/SHELL GROUP

COMMITTEE OF MANAGING DIRECTORS OF THE SERVICE COMPANIES
Decides overall objectives and long term plans to be recommended
to the Service companies and to the Holding companies

Service Companies
There are seven companies, some incorporated in the Netherlands and headquartered
in the Hague, and others incorporated in England and headquartered in London.
These companies provide the legal framework for housing the personnel that provide
certain co-ordination, advice and central services to the operating subsidiaries.
They are organized by function and region.

Operating companies held
by Shell Petroleum N.V.

Operating subsidiaries held by
the Shell Petroleum Company Limited

As parent companies, Royal Dutch and Shell Transport do
not themselves engage in operating activities. They are vehicles
for investment in the Group, and the means of channeling operating
company incomes to the stockholders.

The primary function of the holding companies is what the
name implies. They have the right, by law, to vote their shares in
the operating companies for the election of directors. They are also
responsible for long-range planning and appraisal of operating
results, though in practice this is delegated to the service companies
mentioned later.

Unified management of the combined enterprise is vested in
a group of persons called the Managing Directors of the Royal
Dutch/Shell Group. These persons play several distinct but related
roles. All are key board members in the holding companies and
directors of the service companies. They also form part of the
Committee of Managing Directors of the service companies. This
committee decides upon objectives and plans to be recommended
by the service companies to the operating companies and the holding
companies.

Approximately a half-dozen service companies, incorporated
either in England or the Netherlands, provide coordination, advice,
and central services to the operating companies on a contractual
basis. Service company management is organized by function and
by region.

Without overall guidance the operating companies could not

realize optimum success. Such guidance comes from the Committee of Managing Directors of the service companies. Each managing director has a portfolio of responsibility covering one or more regions and/or world-wide functions. Consequently, each part of the world receives attention from a managing director and, at the same time, each managing director maintains a global viewpoint through the eyes of one or more functions.

The structure of the Group's top management is similar to that of many American corporations. There is a resemblance between the Committee of Managing Directors and the executive committee of a U.S. corporation, and between the principal executives of the service companies and the functional and regional vice-presidents of a U.S. corporation.

Neither the Royal Dutch/Shell Group nor the other two international multinationals discussed below are separate legal entities. Each is a combination of parent entities tied together in unique ways. (1)

3.2   UNILEVER

Unilever Limited (British) and Unilever N.V. (Dutch)
together comprise what their identical annual reports label, simply,
Unilever. Its present structure is the outgrowth of the 1929 alliance
of the British soap company, Lever Brothers, and N.V. Margarine
Unie, a Dutch margarine producer. Combined on a 50/50 basis as
Unilever, they were able to produce a wide variety of household products.

Tax considerations prompted the structure of linked British
and Dutch parent companies. If both interests had been combined into
a single British parent, the profits of the Dutch operating companies
would have flowed to the British parent in the form of foreign Dutch
dividends taxable to the British parent. A similar extra tax burden would
have resulted if the combined interests flowed to a single Dutch parent.
This extra tax was avoided by devising the dual structure under which
the profits of the Dutch operating companies flow to Unilever N.V., and
those of the British to Unilever Limited. A diagram of the organisation
is shown on the next page.

The two parent companies are united by a legal arrangement
for common directors and by their Equalisation Agreement.

The directors of both parents are identical because N.V.'s
Articles of Association grant to the holders of ordinary shares
numbered 1 to 2,400 the right to draw up a binding nomination list
for the appointment of directors; and because Limited's Articles
provide that no person shall be eligible for director unless nominated
by the holders of the deferred shares.   N.V. Elmn,   a

UNILEVER

Equalization Agreement
Other Unifying Agreements

Unilever Limited
(British Parent)
Articles of Association provide that Directors
be nominated by holders of Deferred Shares

Unilever N.V.
(Dutch Parent)
Articles of Association provide that Directors
be appointed from a binding nomination list
drawn by holders of Ordinary Shares 1 to 2400

United Holdings Ltd.
Holds 50% of Deferred Shares of Unilever Limited and
50% of Ordinary Shares 1 to 2400 of Unilever N.V.

N.V. Elmn
Holds 50% of Ordinary Shares 1 to 2400 of Unilever N.V.
and 50% of the Deferred Shares of Unilever Limited

Directors of Unilever Limited —— Identical ——— Directors of Unilever N.V.

Make final decisions allocating resources
among Unilever Limited Subsidiaries

Make final decisions allocating resources
among Unilever N.V. Subsidiaries

Special Committee
Decides major questions of policy

**Product Co-ordinators, Regional Committees,
Heads of Central Services**
Manage the operations of Unilever as a single economic unit, regardless of
legal connections of the subsidiaries. They report to the Central Committee

Unilever Limited Subsidiaries

Unilever N.V. Subsidiaries

subsidiary of N. V. , and United Holdings, a subsidiary of Limited,
each hold 50% of those two blocks of securities. Therefore the two
subsidiaries draw up the nomination list for the appointment of
directors and since only the persons on the list can be appointed,
the directors of each parent are identical.

The Equalisation Agreement, embodied in the Articles of
both parents, assures continuation of the original 50/50 combination
by guaranteeing equal rights to the shareholders of each parent. It
intends to place the holders of the ordinary shares of both companies
in a similar position to that which would have existed if they held
shares in a single company. The result is that dividends paid to
both sets of shareholders must be the same. The same would be
true of any distribution in the event of liquidation.

To achieve the agreed dividend equality Unilver must
maintain a continuing balance of earning power between the parents.
Otherwise one parent's dividends would be held down by the inability
of the other to equal it, or inter-parent transfers might be
required in order to pay any dividend at all. Any such inter-parent
transfer would incur the extra tax which the dual structure intended
to avoid. The necessary balance is accomplished through capital
budgeting, reallocation of markets, assignment of new products
and, as a last resort, the transfer of physical assets.

Unilever has never had to reroute dividends from one
parent to another in order to pay stockholder dividends. However,
in 1937 it did make a substantial inter-parent transfer of assets.

At that time the earning power of the Dutch parent had declined considerably owing to economic and political developments on the continent of Europe. So the British parent transferred its interests outside the British Empire to the Dutch parent. From this transfer the Dutch acquired the Lever Brothers Company in the U.S.

The Royal Dutch/Shell Group does not have this balancing problem which stems from Unilever's Equalisation Agreement. The Group secures the 60/40 rights of the two stockholder groups by each parent's direct ownership of those percentages of both holding companies.

Today, Unilever operates approximately 200 principal subsidiary companies dispersed throughout more than 70 countries. By means of stockholdings about half of them are owned by each parent.

Decisions regarding the allocation of resources within each parent are made separately by each. However, major questions of policy are referred to the Special Committee consisting of the Chairman of each parent and the Vice Chairman of Limited. In actual practice both parents' boards delegate most of their powers to this committee.

As far as possible Unilever is operated as if it were one company. The common identity of the boards and the Special Committee makes this possible. In the Royal Dutch/Shell Group this unity was achieved by the 60/40 joint ownership of the holding companies, the Committee of Managing Directors and the service companies.

Below the Special Committee, Unilever is organized by
regional and product groups, with increasing emphasis on the latter.
Each product group has a Coordinator who is also a director.
Regional groups are called Committees for the particular areas.
Individual directors serve as members of those Committees.
Additionally, there are Heads of central services, such as finance
and research, who are also directors. This integrating web of
directors is similar to that found in the service companies of the
Royal Dutch/Shell Group. (2)

3.3 DUNLOP PIRELLI UNION

Prior to their 1971 union, the British Dunlop and Italian Pirelli each manufactured and sold on an international scale. Rubber products were their major lines. The 50/50 joinder was motivated by increasing economic integration in Europe and the threat of American competition. Also, the companies were complementary in geographical spread.

Although Union was to be operated as a single business, the separate legal entities of the parents were retained. This preserved each parent's well known name and trademark.

Oversimplified, the ownership integration was accomplished by Dunlop giving Pirelli a 49% interest in all its subsidiaries in eachange for a 49% interest in all Pirelli's subsidiaries. In this way the stockholders of each parent continue to hold the same capital, although it now represents half the former assets of each parent. The same method had been employed in reaching the 60/40 ownership exchange in the Royal Dutch/Shell Group.

The exact ownership arrangements were complicated by the fact that Pirelli consisted of two main holding companies, Pirelli S.p.A., incorporated in Italy, and Societe Internationale Pirelli S.A., incorporated in Switzerland. The majority of Pirelli's overseas companies were held by the Swiss parent with a significant number of outside stockholders. If Dunlop had been given a 49% interest in those holdings, it would have become the largest share-holder in the Pirelli overseas companies. That was not intended, so the exchange of overseas interests could only be 40% instead of 49%.

•

A more basic problem was how to effect the exchange of interests. Pooling of profits or dividends would have resulted in additional taxes on transmission to parents and public stockholders. Assets could not be exchanged for cash because of capital gains taxes in certain countries. Antitrust laws of the E. E. C., Germany, U. K. and the U. S. provided additional constraints.

A system of jointly owned companies or entities proved to be the optimum solution. After agreeing upon common accounting principles, seven companies or paper entities were established to own or reflect the combined operating assets. The two Pirelli parents and the Dunlop parent own varying percentages of these entities, but on the aggregate each side owns 50%. The Union organization is shown on the next page.

For political, fiscal and psychological reasons, the parents agreed that controlling interest in former Dunlop and Pirelli companies should remain with the original parent. This was to be reflected in the ownership distribution within the seven jointly own ed entities. Therefore the former Dunlop interests are found in those jointly owned entities in which the British parent has a majority interest. Pirelli, in turn, has the majority interest in those joint entities which now hold the former Pirelli assets. The only exception to this is the joint entity, Pirelli Limited, which contains the former Pirelli interests in England. Antitrust factors prohibited Pirelli from holding that majority interest.

The result is that the companies originally owned by each parent are still controlled and managed by them. Each parent has

DUNLOP PIRELLI UNION

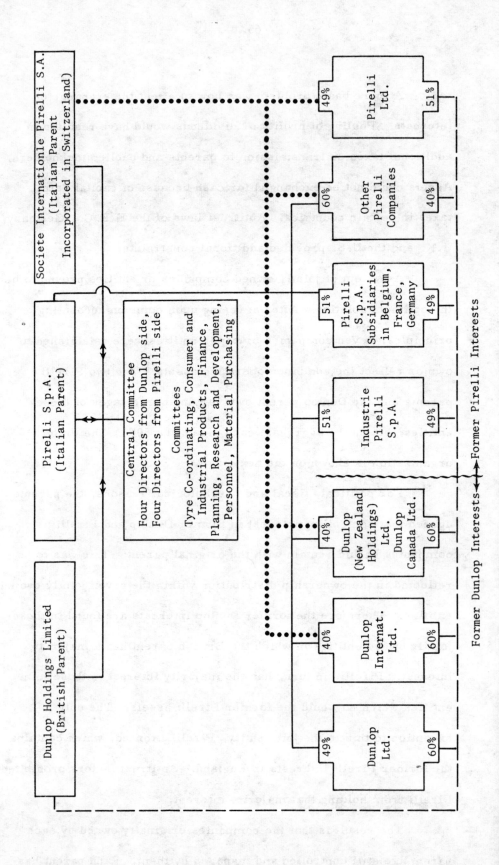

the right to be represented on the boards of the jointly owned

companies but management responsibility rests with the parent

having the majority interest.

In spite of the split management responsibility, the Union

is intended to function as a single business enterprise. Progress

has already been made in joint purchasing and research harmonization.

Various committees coordinate line management, product and country

strategies, and financial requirements. The responsibility for

all coordination is exercised by the Central Committee. The two

parents are equally represented on the Committee and its chairmanship

alternates between the two at three-year intervals. The function of

the Central Committee is similar to that of the Managing Directors

of the Royal Dutch/Shell Group and to Unilever's Special Committee.

In an inter-parent general agreement, Dunlop and Pirelli

agreed to insure that the flow of income from the jointly owned

entities would be sufficient for the parent companies to maintain

their existing dividends and to increase them with future growth.

This agreement was intended to secure the shareholders of each parent

against a dividend setback resulting from adverse income flow from

the assets formerly held by the other parent, or from some other

imbalance. This same shareholder's security is guaranteed in

Unilever through its Equalisation Agreement. In contrast, share-

holders on each side of the Royal Dutch/Shell Group simply accept

the risks and gains of the amalgamation.

Difficult and unforeseen business conditions in Italy during

1971 precipitated an adjustment under the Union agreement.   A former Pirelli Company, Industrie Pirelli S. p. A. , showed a loss

equivalent to 24 million dollars. This substantial loss threatened

the existing dividend level and the security of the Dunlop shareholders.

To offset it, the parents agreed to a change in the capitalization of

Industrie Pirelli S. p. A. , one of the jointly owned companies.

The British parent's 49% of ordinary shares in Industrie was

converted into preferred shares. Consequently, no part of the 1971

operating loss of Industrie was attributable to the British parent.

The agreement provides, however, that profits sufficient to offset

the 1971 loss will have to be made in subsequent years before the

British partner can participate in the profits of Industrie. To

rebalance the Union structure, reciprocal changes were made in

the capitalization of Dunlop Ltd. , a jointly owned company formerly

held by Dunlop. Pirelli's 49% interest in it was similarly converted

to preferred shares. Otherwise, the respective voting rights in

the two jointly owned companies remained the same. The balancing

of each parent's stockholder rights is a complication which is not

present when the form of amalgamation is an outright merger.

And such balancing is further complicated as the number of parents

increases.

In substance, the Union is a bi-national multinational because

the third Swiss Parent is controlled by the Italian parent. But

the presence of the Swiss parent in the Union structure does provide

an example of how a tri-national multinational might be organized. (3)

Analysis

As Endel J. Kolde has written: "Although influenced by it, the managerial organization (of the international business firm) seldom coincides with the juridic form". (4) / This statement is particularly true of the international multinationals.

As an enterprise grows, combines with others, and is challenged by new conditions, it modifies its organization accordingly. Ideally, the organizational structure should not be hampered by legal constraints. But it is. A major constraint is the notion of sovereignty. The basic organizational unit of the world is the nation state. Each of these political units presents varying impediments to the efficient organization of international enterprise.

"Regardless of the way their own industry may develop, the extent to which all international companies integrate their activities across national frontiers will increase". (5) / The key to successful integration across national frontiers lies in the degree of integration achieved at the managerial level. This integration cannot under present circumstances be achieved through merger. It must be accomplished in spite of the need to preserve separate national incorporation, separate capitalization and distinct sets of shareholders. Hopefully, if all goes well, the resultant enterprise will enjoy the advantages of rationalization, while at the same time retaining its former national allegiances, its original good will and trademarks, its historical stock market listings and other assets associated with its component nationalities.

The international multinationals do have the problem of balancing earnings capacities and the rights of shareholders of different parents. Some of these problems have been resolved by a variety of ingenious techniques over a period of several decades; but some distressingly painful problems remain. The Dunlop Pirelli Union remains in difficulty. Continuing losses seem to cast doubt on the wisdom of the "dual structure". Quite possibly the unhappy experience of the Union may dampen enthusiasm for the international multinational for a period of time. However, the transient writings of the popular business press miss the basic point. The fact that losses occur at a certain time in a particular segment of a large enterprise bears scant relationship to the worth of the overall organizational structure or to the viability of the enterprise. With no present outlook for the use of the merger as a means of accommodating to massive competitive pressures, the international multinational remains a potential if difficult alternative course of action.

4.   <u>LEGAL STRUCTURE OF MULTINATIONAL ENTERPRISE</u>

During the past century purely national enterprises have

been steadily growing in size and diversity.   This was a response

to changing economic and technological factors.   National legal

forces in the form of restrictive practices and monopoly legislation,

along with national market limitations, have pushed these enter-

prises across national frontiers.   Reduced tariffs and regional

groupings have accelerated the trend.

In order to exploit managerial and technological assets,

survive international competition, and to secure greater portions

of world markets, these national enterprises have been joining

forces and combining with other national enterprises.

Some of the amalgamating devices and forms they employ

are simply national techniques applied to the international scene.

In other instances the techniques are entirely novel. A primary

goal of the techniques is to provide a legal framework within

which managerial unity can function.   The statement which follows

is an indication of the significance of this aspect.   It is a comment

about international multinations but is applicable to all forms of

multinationals.

"One of the most important problems in international

multinationals is to secure unity of control of the

management. It depends on the effective arrangement

of that unity that the enterprise, composed as it is of

different national companies sometimes with centrifugal

tendencies, can be steered as an economic unit". (1)

The following is a list of these techniques and structures placed more or less in the order of their complexity.

4.1   Linkages Based Purely on Contract

        Prime Contractor/Sub Contractor Relations

        Long Term Supply or Distribution Relations

        Licensing and Cross Licensing

        Multinational Consortiums

4.2   Linkages Based on Cross Shareholdings and External

        Non-Legal Coordination Devices

        Mitsubishi Group

4.3   Jointly Owned Holding Company

        Fiat/Citroen

4.4   Jointly Owned Operating Company

        Panavia

4.5   National Multinationals

        Ford

4.6   International Multinations or Transnationals

4.61   Equalization Agreement and Common Directors

        Unilever   SAS

4.62   Jointly Owned Operating Companies and Coordinated

Management Committee

Dunlop Pirelli Union

4.63   Two Jointly Owned Holding Companies with Common

Directors

Agfa Gevaert

4.64   Two Jointly Oqned Holding Companies and Appointed

Group Managing Directors

Royal Dutch/Shell

4.65   Two Jointly Owned Holding Companies with Two

National Operating/Holding Companies

VFW Fokker

4.7   Public Transnationals

Air Afrique   Saarlor

4.1   LINKAGES BASED PURELY ON CONTRACT

Within the industrial countries there are companies,
especially in the construction industry, which expand their international
productive capacity through Prime Contractor/Sub Contractor
relationships. They bid on foreign country projects on the basis
that they will sub-contract portions of the project to miscellaneous
local companies. This permits them to function as if they were a
considerably larger enterprise. They can undertake projects
that would otherwise require larger capital and a greater range
of equipment. Work specialization among the sub-contracting
companies allows the project to be completed in a much shorter
time. And local licensing and labor relations are simplified.

Similar advantages of specialization can be gained from
Long Term Distribution Relationships. A national manufacturer
can accelerate its penetration into foreign markets by long term
contracts with foreign companies having extensive marketing and
distribution networks. This reduces the expense and time lapse
normally associated with new product introduction. Furthermore,
the foreign distribution company can tailor product packaging and
advertising to the needs of foreign customer and environment.
In some instances, especially with a smaller national company,
foreign laws and market peculiarities may be so complex that
direct selling would be highly impracticle if not impossible.

At the other extreme, long term contracts are often employed to secure the supply of raw materials only available from foreign nations. This technique is typically used by Japanese zaibatsu like Mitsubishi. Rather than undertake vertical integration backward, with all the complications, expense, and insecurity of large foreign investments, they contract for the output of a foreign producer. In many instances these contracts call for payment in the finished products of the Japanese company.

Foreign licensing and cross licensing is another method whereby national companies can exploit their existing technology and obtain the advantage of growing foreign research. A great deal has been written about this method as an early multinationalization strategy.

The Multinational Consortium is yet another contractual technique. It carries the contract device about as far as can be done without permanent integration of the participating foreign companies. These arrangements have become the usual tools of the extractive, aerospace, and electronics industry. The 1970 North Sea oil field discovery was the product of a four-company multinational consortium headed by Phillips Petroleum. The development of the Concorde aircraft was the joint development of France's Sud Aviation and British Aircraft Company. The construction of NATO's $U.S. 300 billion Nadge air defense system was done by a consortium composed of five European companies and the Hughes Aircraft Company of the U.S. (2)

The "consortium" is a recognised type of business

association, but it is not a separate legal entity. The word comes from the Latin "consors" and the Italian "consorzio", meaning partner or companion. I t is formed by private contract and in some countries it must be registered for the protection of third parties. Although contract terms vary, the parties are usually jointly and severally liable.

A simple definition of a multinational consortium is a contractual association of two or more business entities of different nationalities temporarily joined together for the performance of a limited task. Consortium formations are motivated more by necessity than for other practical reasons. They undertake huge projects involving substantial risks that any one company is reluctant or unable to undertake alone. Companies of different nationalities are involved either because the required technologies and skills involved are so diverse, or because of political considerations. The project may involve a foreign government or the key resources of a region. Combined national companies tend to blur the national images of the constituent companies. When the consortium's cash and profit flow takes several national routes there is less unsettling of national balance of payments accounts.

Coordination of consortium functions is performed by a non-legal central consortium management team consisting of representatives of the parties. For taxation or other legal purposes the consortium agreement may actually take the form of a partnership or some form of temporary company or corporation.

The relationship, however, remains basicly one of contract.

All of these contractual linkages have one common advantage. They expand the international horizons of a national company without the necessity of increased capitalization. They permit each national participant to do things that would otherwise be beyond its capacity. And there is near equal enrichment of the contracting parties without undue balance of payments impact on the nations involved. In some respect these techniques resemble the area complementation programs undertaken by national multinationals such as Ford. The use of these techniques can be expected to increase, especially by small and medium size national firms.

For larger national firms whose resources give them greater latitude of choice the advantages are not so clear. Long range planning necessary for continueing growth requires deployment, coordination and redeployment of all organization resources. This cannot be accomplished when the foreign management and facilities are merely temporarily linked by contract. There is no common profit linkage and views of successful long-term strategy may differ. The structures which follow intend to eliminate this deficiency.

In all the structures which follow the primary emphasis is upon the combining of two or more national entities to form a permanent unified managerial or economic entity, while at the same time preserving the national identity of the parties. In other words, the legal techniques of merger and consolidation are not the basic tools.

4.2   LINKAGES BASED ON CROSS-SHAREHOLDINGS AND

EXTERNAL NON-LEGAL COORDINATION DEVICES

Mitsubishi Group

Although the forty or so Mitsubishi companies are
presently Japanese companies, their overseas markets and
accelerating foreign investment dictates that the Group be
classified as multinational. A number of their manufacturing
operations are already jointly owned with foreign companies and
before long foreign parent companies will be members of the
Mitsubishi family. Its structure represents a proven style of
operation which may be emulated by other groups of companies.

MITSUBISHI GROUP

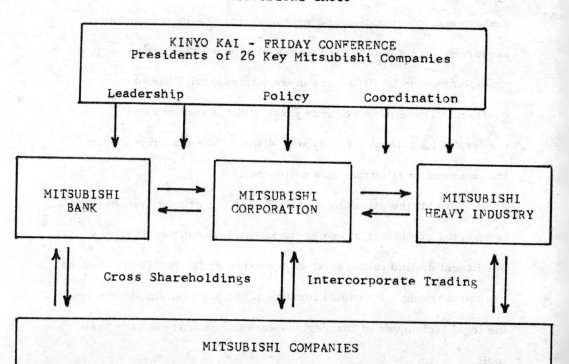

The three key Mitsubishi companies plus over forty others are all independent corporations. There is no parent corporation. In addition to national pride and a common cultural heritage for group cooperation, what links the companies together is an array of cross-shareholdings and intercorporate trading. Since the profits of one are partly linked to the profits of another, there is an inducement to give business to one another and to participate in continuing contractor/sub contractor, and other cooperative projects. These activities are coordinated by the Kinyo-kai or Friday Conference. It is led by the chief executive of the three key Mitsubishi companies, and attended by the presidents of 26 additional Mitsubishi companies.

In a broad sense, the Mitsubishi Group structure is not very different than American and European conglomerates which are groups of companies operating in multiple and diverse markets, coordinated to varying degrees by a central management group. The clear factual difference is that conglomerate companies are usually wholly owned by a single company. The resulting control power possessed by that single company is greater than the non-legal or non-ownership based powers of Kinyo-kai. However, the possession of power and its actual usage are two different things. Although the conglomerate parent has the power it generally sets general goals and policies., leaving individual companies to manage themselves with considerable independence. And the more diversified the conglomerate is, the truer this becomes.

This is another example of the continuing divergence between ownership and control.

One reason that groups like Mitsubishi do not exist in the U.S. or extensively in Western Europe is that monopolies and restrictive practices legislation prevents the Mitsubishi-like intercorporate behaviour. To some extent the U.S. viewpoint lacks logic. Such practices are forbidden among independent corporations but permitted if all the corporations are owned by a common parent. If the U.S. viewpoint was less restrictive some U.S. conglomerates would more closely resemble the Mitsubishi Group - cross-shareholdings instead of wholly-owned subsidiaires. (3)

If it were not for national and regional antitrust restrictions, more cross-border cooperating groups might come into being. Apprehensive of the uncertainties of legal and fiscal complications of complete merger, national companies forego crossborder mergers, and lesser cooperative arrangements that risk anticompetitive illegality. These factors, plus national governmental preferences for purely national combinations, have distorted the economic forces pressing for greater multinationalization.

4.3   JOINTLY OWNED HOLDING COMPANY

Fiat/Citroen

Fiat's drive for increased size and higher auto production volume could certainly be enhanced by cooperation with Citroen. In addition, Citroen could give Fiat a stronger position in France and greater innovation in auto design.   Citroen could gain from Fiat's scale and world wide distributor system.   A complete union could not be arranged as the French government did not wish to lose the Franch identity of Citroen or to have it controlled from outside.   A compromise was reached.

FIAT - CITROEN

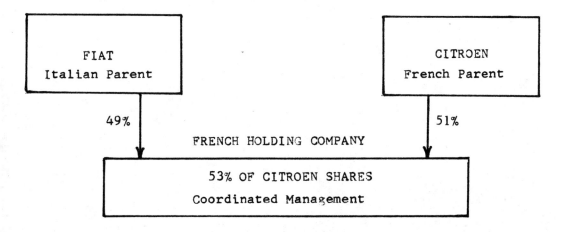

An acceptable combination required that Citroen, by far the smaller of the two, not be dominated by Fiat.   However, Fiat

desired a significant ownership interest in Citroen to make it
worthwhile to cooperate on a long term basis.   Under the agreed
arrangement Fiat holds an effective interest in approximately
26% of Citroen. This could have been accomplished by Fiat simply
taking a 26% interest in the Citroen shares.   However, this would
have diluted the French nationality ownership in this prized
company.   In addition, Fiat might obtain further control by
market purchase of the shares.   To avoid this, a French holding
company was established.   Fifty-three percent of the Citroen
shares were transferred to it.   Ownership of the French holding
company was then split on a 51/49 basis in favor of Citroen.

    This arrangement satisfied both parties   so that coordinated
management of both companies could commence.   (4)

4.4 JOINTLY OWNED OPERATING COMPANY

Panavia

As suggested earlier, the multinational consortium may be suitable for a one-time project, but for the long term production of competitive products, it is inferior to an enterprise unified under a common management and financial control. The jointly owned operating company has been the usual means of bringing together resources from two or more companies owned and controlled in different countries in order to attack a specific market. Many of these multinational industrial forms can be seen in the chemical and oil industries, aerospace, in banking, and in international hotel chains.

One of the most recent examples of this is Panavia established in 1970 to produce a series of aircraft.

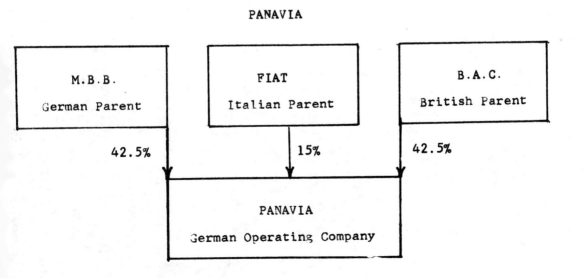

PANAVIA

M.B.B.	FIAT	B.A.C.
German Parent	Italian Parent	British Parent

42.5%   15%   42.5%

PANAVIA

German Operating Company

Even this structure has its limitations. The common interest that brought the parent companies together may disappear if one of them develops a competing product or some other conflict of interest develops.

Nevertheless, this structure provides a flexible framework within which the scope of the jointly attacked market could diminish or expand. If the parents wish to move slowly to complete managerial integration, they may progressively increase the assets of the jointly owned operating subsidiary until it takes over the entire activities of the parent companies and the parent companies become merely holding companies. (5)

4.5   NATIONAL MULTINATIONALS - FORD

Ford

At the present time the great majority of multinationals are national in origin, ownership, and control.   There is nothing unusual in this as corporate enterprise began within single national frameworks and it is natural that they first achieved size and diversity within the nation of their origin.

Their national strength then permitted them to expand overseas without the necessity of teaming up with a foreign partner of equal size.   Neither is it odd that more than half the world's multinationals are American.   Blessed with a huge national market, the commercial unification encouraged by the Commerce Clause of its Constitution, and its exemption from World War destruction, U.S. companies had a definite head start.

FORD

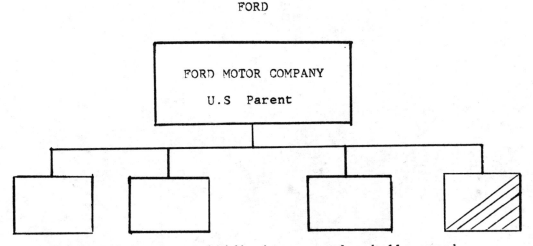

Domestic and Foreign Subsidiaries - mostly wholly owned

The Ford structure appears relatively simple - one parent
company plus an array of domestic and foreign subsidiaries.
This does not mean that the joint ownership or control of some of
the subsidiaries is not complex.

Some U.S. multinationals such as IBM have pursued a strict
policy of 100% ownership of all subsidiaries. This has been believed
to be necessary in order to maximize flexibility in planning and
deploying its resources on a global basis. If the optimum location
of a certain phase of production or operations is in country "X",
then there would be no objection from any joint partners in other
countries. In addition, the very nature of the product itself may
dictate greater or lesser control of coordination. There are
othere multinationals who encourage joint ownership of their
foreign subsidiaries. Ford's current policy favors 100%
ownership where possible. (6)

4.6   INTERNATIONAL MULTINATIONALS OR TRANSNATIONALS

This form of industrial structure is currently found only in Western Europe - the home of traditional international legal developments. Early industrial growth within the limited confines of those countries had some day to burst across national borders. This has happened partly in response to the needs of international competition. Now it is encouraged by the existence of the Common Market and the drive for economies of scale.

Some have referred to transnationals as cross border mergers. From a legal viewpoint this is not the best terminology as the word "merger" has definite legal meaning. In a true "merger" one company is merged into another and the former ceases to exist as a separate legal entity. In transnational structures true "mergers" are impossible or impractical because of various legal and fiscal barriers. Even if that were not the case, it is unlikely that "mergers" will be extensively used as national companies do not wish to be dissolved. Furthermore, there are definite advantages to the continued existence of the combined entities. Therefore, cross-border combinations or transnationals all presently preserve the combining foreign parent companies, but link them together with various unique devices.

4.61   EQUILIZATION AGREEMENT AND COMMON DIRECTORS

<u>Unilever</u>

Unilever stands in a class of its own. To date, no other enterprise employs the same type of structure.

UNILEVER

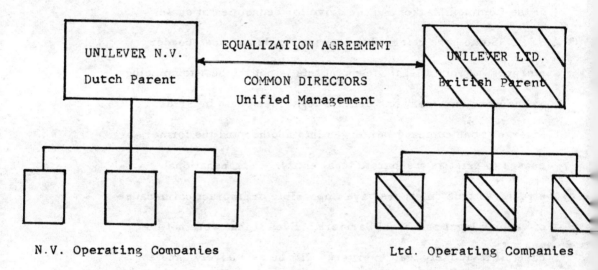

N.V. Operating Companies   Ltd. Operating Companies

Unification is achieved by contractual agreements between the parent companies. The agreed provisions are part of the Article of Association of each parent. The result of these agreements is that the stockholders of each parent are placed on an equal footing in every respect, just as if they held shares in one and the same company and the directors are the same for both parents. This control system has been referred to as the "identity of directorate of twin companies". (7)

Should one parent be prevented from paying a dividend because of the inability of the other to pay, then the former would have to make a sufficient transfer of funds to the latter so that it would be able to match the proposed dividend. This requires that the earning power of both sides to be kept in relative balance. Otherwise extra taxes would be incurred by any such inter-parent transfer of funds. To date this has never been necessary. These arrangements have sufficed to permit the Common Directors to maintain a totally unified managerial structure.(8)

SAS

SAS unification is based on the same contractual basis as Unilever except that the contract is for a limited period of time - 25 years, and that a board of directors common to both parents is not employed. The SAS Board of Directors are appointed by the directors of each parent, and from among their ranks.

SAS

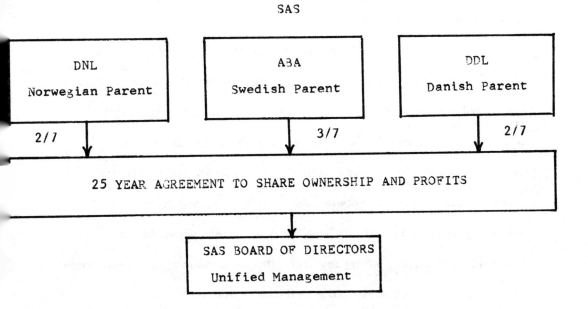

The parent companies of SAS are Sweden's Aktiebelaget Aerotransport (ABA), Norway's Det Norske Luflfartselskob A/S (DNL) and Denmark's Det Danske Luflfarlselskof A/S (DDL). Each parent is a public company half owned by private individuals and enterprises, and half owned by the respective governments. The 1950 agreement was approved by each government.

The parents provide the flight equipment and ground facilities for use in the jointly operated services and they divide the net proceeds in the following ratios:

ABA 3/7,   DNL 2/7,   DDL 2/7

Provisions of the Convention on International Civil Aviation prohibited the dual or multiple registration of aircraft. Consequently, ownership of the aircraft is retained by the parties and is registered in its country, but all aircraft are regarded as owned by them in the same proportions as mentioned above. The overall relationship is much like that of a partnership. The three parents are jointly and severally liable for any obligation or liability of SAS.

The SAS Board of Directors oversees the unified management of the enterprise. In appointing the various management personnel, the Board is obligated by the agreement to achieve an organisation which is as "rational and efficient as possible. Furthermore, appointments are to be made "with due consideration of achieving a reasonable proportion between Swedes, Danes, and Norwegians". Another provision securing a balance of interests provides that SAS shall make every effort towards allocating its business activities between the three countries in a reasonable manner.

91.

The SAS model provides a good illustration on the way several national companies might approach the Unilever structure for a limited time and then, if all went well, move ahead into the Unilever structure.[9]

4.62 JOINTLY OWNED OPERATING COMPANIES AND COORDINATED MANAGEMENT COMMITTEE

Dunlop Pirelli Union

The Dunlop Pirelli Union is a joinder of parents of approximately equal size. It involves more corporate restructuring than the previous enterprises. The ultimate goal of the parents is to achieve complete managerial unification as in Unilever. The beginning structure permits them to share ownership and profits on a 50/50 basis, to retain managerial control of their respective operating companies, and to commence a limited number of coordinated activities

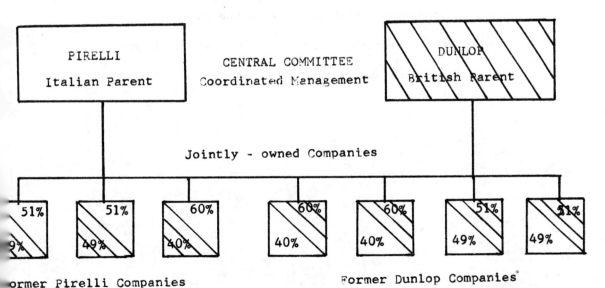

DUNLOP PIRELLI UNION

Ideally, each parent would have taken 50% of the shares of the operating companies of the other. However, because the Italian side actually consisted of two parent companies, one incorporated in Switzerland with substantial outside holdings, it was necessary to modify the proportions taken by each side. Otherwise control of certain subsidiaries may have gone into the hands of those outside shareholders. The resulting mixture of percentages does, nevertheless, bring about a 50/50 split of overall combined ownership.

It does so in a way that leaves the Italian side with a majority interest in those companies that were formerly Pirelli-owned, and likewise for the British companies. For this reason, and by agreement of the parties, management responsibility over the operating companies remains as it was prior to the combination. A Central Committee appointed by each side has commenced overall coordination and the beginning of joint research, purchasing and finance activities. This type of control system has been referred to as the "cabinet system". (10)

Agfa Gevaert

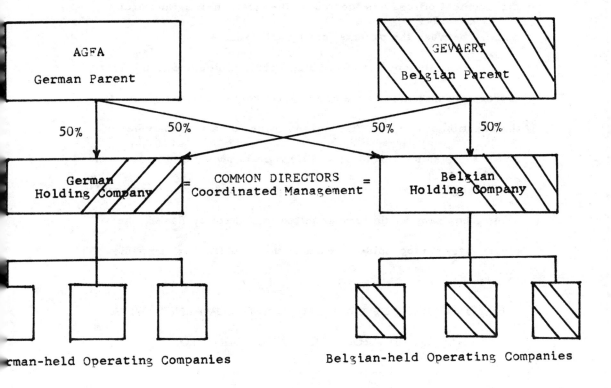

man-held Operating Companies   Belgian-held Operating Companies

Agfa Gevaert was formed in 1964.   It is a 50/50 arrangement and is much the same as the Dunlop Pirelli Union except
that the ownership split is accomplished through two jointly
owned holding companies.   The holding companies are Agfa-
Gevaert GmbH in Western Germany and Gevaert-Afga N.V. in
Belgium.   These companies have identical boards and are
responsible for the inegration of management.   To date, however,

the organisation is still in the stage of coordinated management

rather than a completely rationalized structure.   The integrated

management offices are located on the German-Belgian border

midway between the parents' headquarters.

As in the case of the Dunlop Pirelli Union and in the Fiat/

Citroen arrangement there are special considerations given to

the question of cont rol.   Gevaert is owned by a large number of

small Flemish shareholders, while Agfa is owned by the German

chemical giant, Bayer.   A pure merger or even a single national

holding company would have resulted in control by Bayer, the

single largest stockholder.   Hence, the twin holding companies. (11)

4.64   TWO JOINTLY OWNED HOLDING COMPANIES WITH APPOINTED GROUP MANAGING DIRECTORS

Royal Dutch/Shell Group

The Royal Dutch/Shell Group was formed in 1907 and

is the oldest and largest of the transnationals.   Like Unilever,

its management is completely unified even though the separate

parent companies continue to exist as separate legal entities.

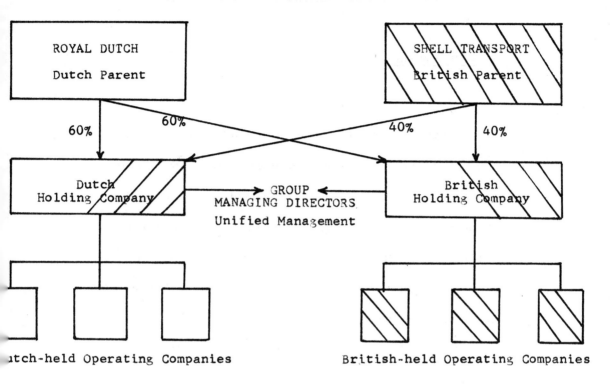

ROYAL DUTCH/SHELL GROUP

Its legal structure is identical to that of Agfa/Gevaert
except that the ownership split is 60/40 and the holding companies
do not have common directors. Key members of each holding
company board are appointed as Group Managing Directors and
they supervise the unified management. (12)

4. 65   JOINTLY OWNED HOLDING COMPANY WITH TWO
        NATIONAL OPERATING/HOLDING COMPANIES

VFW/Fokker

VFW/Fokker, Europe's first transnational aircraft enterprise, formed in 1969, is also based on the principle of equality. It is a somewhat advanced model of the Agfa/Geraert and Royal Dutch/Shell structures. A possible drawback of those structures is that unity of management is not formalized in a single legal entity. It was not felt sufficient to have common directors or appointed Managing Directors. So VFW/Fokker went a step further, employing the "central directing company" control system. It created a single holding company to act as a central management unit.   (diagram page 118)

The single holding company was created under German law, but as a concession to Dutch sensibilities its headquarters is located in Dusseldorf midway between the headquarters of the parent companies.

The single holding company was employed for another reason - to escape from the German laws requiring worker representation on boards of companies employing a certain number of employees. The single holding company keeps the number of employees below the minimum.   (13)

VFW-FOKKER

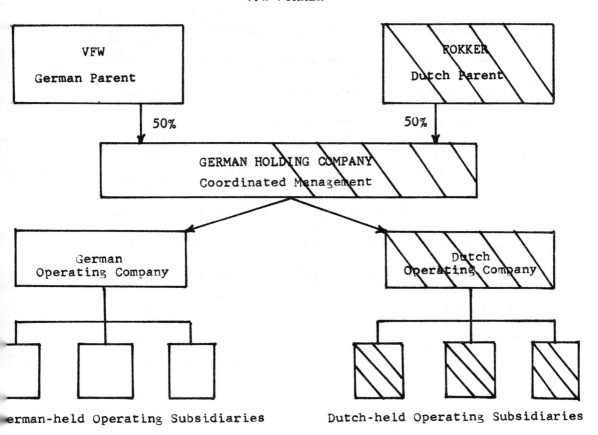

4.7   PUBLIC TRANSNATIONALS

There are a number of corporate entities which are commercial in nature, created by treaty, and owned or controlled by the treaty-making nations.   They can be placed into different classifications depending on the degree of their "international" character.   Some are given dual, treble or wider nationality according to the number of nations involved.   Others are truly international, taking on the status of international persons, not subject to any national system of law, but subject only to the treaty provisions and public international law.   Illustrations of these institutions are: the World Bank, the European Investment Bank, and the Asian Development Bank.

There are similar international institutions such as the Food and Agricultural Organization, UNESCO, and the United Nations itself.   These organizations and those previously mentioned banking institutions provide interesting models for future governmental institutions.   It is possible to envision their evolvement for use in truly international transportation enterprises or in world production of basic raw materials such as steel, food staples or fuels.   However, this is highly futuristic.   At the present time these institutions are confined to matters of international administration or social services, and banking and finance services.   In so far as categorizing these bodies they are more frequently thought of as simply international institutions or international public corporations.

Bodies such as Eurofina, Eurochemic, the Communications
Satellite System, Air Afrique and Saarlor are of more direct
interest here.(14)They can be referred to as "public transnationals".

Eurofina was established in 1955 by a convention between
14 participating governments for the purpose of unifying and improving
the construction and performance of railway rolling stock.
Because of the nonexistence of international company law proper,
and in order to avoid doubts as to its legal status, this enterprise
was established as a Swiss company, and is, therefore, governed
by Swiss law in its organizational and operational aspects.

Like the others, Eurofina is an example of the projection
of the public economic corporation to the transnational level.
Because they lack true international personality they cannot be
classified as international public corporations. (15)

Established two years later, in 1957, Eurochemic had as
its purpose the construction of a plant for the chemical processing
of irradiated fuel and related research and training. The
shareholders consist of the governments of the participating
European countries, their atomic energy authorities, public,
quasi-public, and private energy corporations. Its Convention
states that the Company shall be governed by the present
Convention, by its Statute and, residually, by the law of the State
in which its headquarters are situated, in so far as the Convention
or Statute do not derogate therefrom. The law of Belgium,
where the headquarters is situated, only applies in a subsidiary

capacity, as Swiss law does in the case of Eurofina. Eurochemic moves closer in the direction of a genuinely international company. (16)

These types of structures are also employed by the communist nations. With increasing East-West joint economic activity, their appearance will be more frequent. One of the first of these was Wismut AG, an East German corporation, formed between the Soviet and East German governments. Another is Scalda-Volga, S. A. a joint venture incorporated in Brussels in 1964 between a number of Soviet agricultural machine and tractor enterprises, and a Belgian auto transport company. (17)

Recently Yugoslavia, in pursuit of its new policy of free enterprise and competition, has authorized joint ventures between Yugoslavia and foreign enterprises. Among such joint ventures many make provisions for joint control and management, but not in the form of equity participation by the foreign enterprise. Usually the foreign enterprise shares in the final products in some agreed proportion. (18)

The Communications Satellite System, established in 1964, is an entirely unique transnational with both public and private participants. Its Agreement states that the participating national governments shall cooperate, in accordance with certain principles, to design, construct and maintain the space segment of a global communications satellite system.

The participating governments are represented by designated

communication entities which may be public or private. Most
are the state postal or telecommunications administrations.
Only in the case of the United States is the designated entity a
private corporation. It is the Communications Satellite Corporation
(CSC) of which the American Telephone and Telegraph Corporation
is the majority shareholder.

According to the Agreement, CSC acts as the overall
manager, following policy instructions from the . Committee.
The Committee is composed of representatives of the signatories,
roughly in proportion to their quotas. Voting is generally by
majority, except for certain veto powers held by the larger shareholders. In its present form this transnational enterprise appears
to be without international legal personality. (19)

Air Afrique

Air Afrique, formed in 1961, is not unlike SAS described
earlier. However, this regional air transport enterprise had
to be constructed without the benefit of existing air transport
companies as was the case with SAS.

This public transnational enterprise is the product of the
Treaty of Yaounde signed in 1961 by the governments of 11 West
African nations. The agreement established a single multinational
airline corporation known as Air Afrique with ownership divided
among the parties. It has a unitary structure but with a registered
head office and full legal personality and powers within each of

the member states. It enjoys the status of a national airline of each state.

The arrangement seemed preferable to creating individual companies in the several states and joining them together. The formation of separate national entities would have emphasised the diversity of national interests.

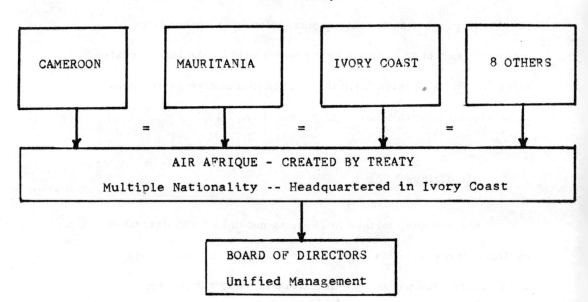

AIR AFRIQUE

Air Afrique is the direct owner of the aircraft equipment and facilities, the direct employer of all personnel, and is responsible for the operations and obligations of the enterprise. Its policies are established by a committee of the various

Ministers of Transport. Although the Treaty envisioned the

multiple registration of Air Afrique aircraft, they were first

registered in a single member country pending a ruling of the

Council of the International Civil Aviation Organization.

Air Afrique initially required the advice and assistance of

an experienced airline and consequently Air France and the Union

de Transports Aeriens hold minority equity interests through a

holding company called SODETRAF.

The enterprise enjoys exemptions from certain taxes,

customs duties and other charges within member states. This

stems from the mutual obligation of the states to harmonize

their respective laws on matters relating to Air Afrique activities.

The General Assembly of the shareholders appoints a

Board of Directors which is the managerial and decision-making

authority. The Board and its administration center are located

in the Ivory Coast. (20)

Saarlor

Saarlor is the product of a 1956 treaty between France and

Germany   to coordinate sales of coal produced in the Saar

and in Looraine.

SAARLOR

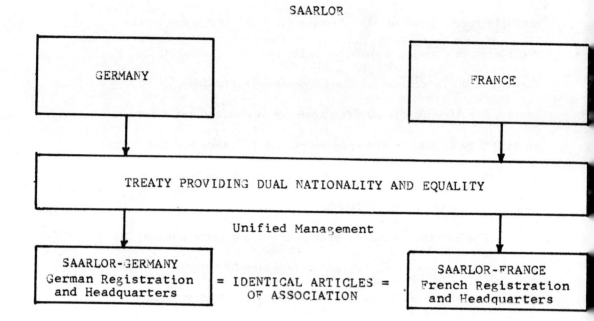

It is registered with identical Articles of Association both in France and Germany. Although it is meant to be one legal personality, it has headquarters in both countries and could be seen from a nationality viewpoint as two companies - one French and one German. A better interpretation is that it is one enterprise with dual nationality. In terms of ownership, control, liabilities, dividends, and all other respects, the nations are treated as equal shareholders. (21)

The foundation of the Saarlor dual nationality is different from that of Unilever, Royal Dutch/Shell, and the other international multinationals. They all have two or more companies formed under their respective national laws and are thereafter linked together in unique ways. Saarlor's dual nationality does not stem from pre-existing companies, but comes from the treaty - making powers of the contracting states.

The public transnationals do, however, resemble Unilever in that they are based on contract. The contract being between states, takes the form of a treaty. In both cases the unifying linkage is an agreement.

Virtually all existing multinational enterprises could be placed in one of the above classifications. In some instances the enterprise in the classification is the only model presently operating. In the future new multinational enterprises will bear the characteristics of combinations of the above categories, as well as new characteristics. In addition, nations and international institutions will no doubt fashion new legal structures beyond the existing contractual and corporate concepts. (22)

5.   LEGAL STRUCTURE OF FUTURE ENTERPRISES -

HARMONIZATION OF EUROPEAN COMPANY LAW,

EUROPEAN COMPANY, WORLD COMPANY

The success and dominance of existing multinational enterprise

has impelled governments, industrial leaders, and others, to explore new

means of encouraging the creation of similar enterprise. Certain facets

of the present structures are unsatisfactory, and there are numerous

obstacles in their creation and operation. Efforts in the direction are

most advanced within the European Economic Community. Although little

has yet been done elsewhere, the same efforts will undoubtedly follow

in regional groupings in Latin America, Asia and Africa.

It is clearly possible to form multinational enterprises under the

existing state of affairs as is evidenced by the structures described in

the previous chapter. National multinationals, the most prevalent type,

can be created by ownership of the shares of a group of foreign companies or

even by the ownership of unincorporated foreign branches. Except for

certain commercial activities such as banking, the latter variation is

generally not possible or practical.

The objection to this form is that such enterprises are owned and

controlled by a parent company from a single country, and its basic

structure, powers, and responsibilities are governed by the laws and

influences of that country. Although its foreign subsidiaries are governed

by local laws, its ownership and control by the parent make it a foreign

corporation for all practical purposes.

Transnationals answer this objection in part since additional parents from different countries present multiple nationality and national control at the top. However, their formation and operation present numerous complications. Since all of them to date are merely dual structures with dozens of subsidiaries in foreign countries, the nationality aspect is negligibly reduced.

Public Multinationals serve to reduce the nationality objection to its lowest ebb. Air Afrique, with the nationality and national control of a dozen different countries, illustrates this. The exact legal status of these entities is yet to be established. This, plus the fact that they are pbulic governmental entities, leaves the problem unresolved.

In those instances in which corporate national identity and national control are not objectionable, the national multinational structure can be employed, or the entities to be grouped can be legally merged into one national company. The latter solution is not generally possible because of the great variation among national merger laws. It is further complicated by the national diversity in the law of taxation, accounting and fiscal matters, labor relations, and other areas related to companies.

The fundamental problem is that the corporate legal structure of any company is governed by the laws of a single nation. According to the law in common law countries this is the place where the company was initially incorporated. In civil law countries it is generally the place where the company has its headquarters or seat. (1)

If industrialists from different countries desire to contribute equal capitalization to a proposed company for international operations, the company structure and its powers and duties must be governed by the law of one country. By that criteria, the company can be French, English, or Japanese, but it cannot be all three. This may not satisfy the sensibilities of the different nationals.

Should a group of foreign companies decide to join forces and form a single company, the same problem presents itself. The single company must be formed and governed in accordance with the laws of a single country.

There are ways around this as were seen in the previous chapter. But those means all have their complications and shortcomings. The proposed European Company is intended to reduce the nationality dilemna, at least as among parties within the E.E.C. A World Company would carry the solution out further.

Such structures might eliminate the single nationality problem but they would not eliminate the lack of uniformity in various national laws relating to companies. The E.E.C. has been dealing with this aspect in various directives aimed at harmonisation of European company law and related matters.

The steps being taken within the E.E.C. to integrate European business entities will provide a basis of experience for other world regional groups. Prospects for the future growth and political acceptability of multinationals will be heavily influenced by the success of these steps. Before discussing the European developments it is instructive to review the situation in the United States where the majority of existing multinationals are now headquartered.

In the United States

The United States, like other federal republics, provides a useful analogy when examining many international problems. The relationship among the states in the U.S. and between those states and the U.S. federal government can be compared to the relationships among nations and between nations and evolving supranational authorities such as the E.E.C.

There are no federal company laws in the U.S. Each state has its own peculiar company laws, taxation laws, and other company-related regulations. In the field of taxation and labor relations there are uniform federal laws, but side by side with these are additional regulations in each state.

A corporation can be a New York corporation or a Delaware or California corporation, but it can only be one of them. Its structure, powers, and duties are primarily governed by the laws of that single state.

When corporations began to expand their operations outside of the state of their incorporation, their activities were referred to as 'interstate commerce.' This can be compared to early multinational activities in the international arena. In early United States history there was acute rivalry among states and between regions. Corporations from other states were viewed as foreign. (2) Attempts were made to prevent the entrance of their operations or to discriminate aginst products manufactured by them. These efforts met with no success because the U.S. Constitution prohibited such state actions. Furthermore, the Commerce clause of the Constitution empowered the federal government to regulate interstate commerce. Regulations such as those relating to railroads were unified so that the industry might not be stifled by a myriad of state regulations. Interstate commerce flourished and has expanded to be international or multinational in nature.

In time, little was thought of the fact that a corporation was from another state or "foreign". In other words, identification with the state of incorporation ceased to become a significant issue. No doubt the same trend will evolve in other unified regional groupings and, ultimately, throughout the entire globe.

It is true that as corporations expanded from one state to others they encountered a certain number of laws that were unique to each state. This will no doubt remain the case in the U.S. and throughout the world. Local governments will always have some laws peculiar to their particular needs and desires. Complete uniformity is not desired nor sought. The lack of complete uniformity in the states of the U.S. was not a severe problem as there existed a common tradition inherited from the English comman law system. This is not the case in the E.E.C. where there is a wide diversity of legal systems.

The result in the U.S. is that a corporation from one state can expand operations into all the other states through a series of branch operations all confined under the corporate shell of the original state.

If the corporation in the original state desired to join forces with another coproration from the same state, this could be accomplished by the merger laws which existed in every state; or it could be achieved by the larger corporation purchasing the shares of the smaller and converting it into a subsidiary corporation.

As the merger and other corporate laws were approximately the
same in all states, these linking operations could be consumated between
corporations from different states. State identity, comparable to
nationality, was not an issue since all corporations were American, as all
EEC companies will, in time, be European rather than Italian or French.

The existence of national stock exchanges in the U.S. also
facilitated the grouping of corporations into larger economic units. Uniform
legislation such as the Uniform Commercial Code encourages continuing
uniformity of state laws. Uniform sets of laws relating to many matters,
including company laws, are continuously produced by law professors,
practitioners and judges. These serve as models for further movements
towards uniformity. To carry the process a step further it has been
suggested that the U.S. federal government should enact federal company laws
to permit federal incorporation. (3)

Should the U.S. adopt federal corporate chartering procedures
it will not be because it is sought by corporate leaders but because it
might provide a more efficient basis for government control or regulation
of corporations, especially the largest ones operating on an interstate
and multinational basis.

The dispersal, among states, of the responsibility to make
corporate chartering rules, has discouraged initiative for reform. Rather
than progressive reform, a sticter change of one state's laws will cause
corporate managers to reincorporate in a more accommodating state.
Delaware's reputation for this is widely known. Such liberal incorporation
laws have failed to control corporate power. For better or worse,

governmental control has been forfeited to other bodies of law and institutions, such as the antitrust laws administered by the federal Justice Department and the Federal Trade Commision. There are those who believe that the "control" function should be   partly administered in the chartering and re-chartering process. (4)

State incorporation law has clearly failed to control corporate power. Because of the state competition for corporate business, this failure can only be corrected at the federal level. While federal antitrust laws have failed to significantly deter the extraordinary concentration of American business, a strict chartering scheme might. One that has been proposed suggests such a procedure for only the largest corporations, those with assets in excess of one million dollars. Although there does not appear to be any prospect of this coming about in the near future, accelerating pressure of public opinion on issues like polution and consumers rights could precipitate earlier reform. What is interesting about the prospect is that the motivation for its realization is entirely opposite to that which inspires the forthcoming European Company. The latter hopes to encourage concentration and is not directed towards control of enterprises.

5.1   HARMONIZATION OF EUROPEAN COMPANY LAW

The goal of the E. E. C. is economic integration. This cannot be achieved without a certain degree of uniformity in the legal framework within which it is to occur. Since companies are the most important instruments of international trade, the treatment accorded to them when their activities cross national boundaries has a direct impact on the ultimate success of European economic integration. If transnational operations are unduly restricted, trade will not realise its full potential. Another way of putting it is that the intended attainment of the freedom of movement of persons and/or companies, goods, services, and capital will be impossible as long as great discrepancies remain in the legislation of the different member states.   (5)

The E. E. C. has already gone a long way toward removing trade barriers between member states. Companies now look to the whole of the E. E. C. as their market. However, there has been little crossborder concentration to create EEC-wide enterprises which could most effectively service this unified market. This dearth of European crossborder concentration has been due in part to a lack of harmonization of the national tax and corporate law systems with respect to the merger transaction, holding company techniques, and other transnational forms.   (6)

In recognition of these considerations the Rome Treaty contains both specific and general provisions designed to reduce those differences in the various national laws pertaining to the creation, operation, rights, duties and liabilities of companies which would hinder the realization of economic integration. Complete identy of laws is not intended or sought.

The U.S. experience and that of other federal countries has demonstrated that economic integration does not require complete uniformity.

The EEC intends to achieve harmonisation primarily by the use of Directives. These Directives are drafted by the EEC Commission and are submitted to the Council of Ministers for its acceptance or rejection.

Once a Directive is accepted, each member state must change its national law to be consistent with the directive. The aims of the directive are binding on the member states but the appropriate legislation or administrative means of realising the aims is left to the individual states acting separately.

At the present time there are about six directives in existance, all in various stages of realizing their purposes. Those which have a direct bearing on the formation and operation of crossborder enterprises will be discussed. (7)

Mergers

Purely domestic mergers are recongized in nearly every member country. However, there are wide variations among the rules pertaining to fusion, as the process is generally labelled. One of the chief problems involves the divergencies in the tax consequences of mergers. Another is a split in the fundamental commercial law of fusion. In some countries the merged company retains a legal existence within the framework of the acquiring company and remains liable for its debts until the final liquidation which occurs only upon fulfillment of all of its obligations. The other countries regard a merger as a complete fusion of legal personalities,

resulting in the liability of the acquiring company for all debts of the
acquired company.

Another obstacle is the theory, recognized by the continental
members, that a company must be created by the State in which it has its
seat. This makes it a theoretical legal impossibility to merge companies
formed in different countries without dissolution of both and re-creation of
the combined units in one country.

A need exists for harmonized legislation for the maintenance of a
company's legal personality when moving its seat to another country.
Preparatory work for negotiations among the member states for
harmonisation in this area has occured. In the meantime two countries
have enacted domestic legislation designed to help solve the problem.

Apart from legal difficulties encountered, numerous political
obstacles impede progress. EEC companies which wish to improve their
competitiveness frequently choose to associate themselves with American
or other non-EEC partners rather than to merge with their European
competitors. In some respects this is detrimental to the internal strength
of the Community.

The question which this raises is whether the advantages afforded
crossborder mergers should be reserved to companies which are authentically
European. As none of the member states wishes to express an overtly
discriminatory attitude, this problem remains suspended.

There are those who believe that crossborder mergers are not
crucial to EEC goals. They argue that complete legal integration between
foreign companies is not necessary for their economic integration. This
is demonstrated by the transnationals that now exist. In addition there

are numerous advantages to combinations which preserve the separate

foreign corporate shells through parent-subsidiary relationships and

contractual relationships. Nevertheless, there are many circumstances

when legal merger or fusion is more advantageous, especially in

combinations between very large and very small companies.

In the case of combinations between giant national companies,

reasons of nationalistic pride and independence will militate against legal

mergers. However, within the parents of transnational linkages, such

as Royal Dutch/Shell and the Dunlop Pirelli Union, there will be need for

operating subsidiaries to acquire smaller sub-subsidiaries by complete

merger.

The EEC Commission's Draft Third Directive (as amended) is

the first major attempt to harmonise the municipal law of mergers and

to introduce such an institution where it does not exist. It defines a

merger as the transfer of all assets and obligations in their totality,

without liquidation, from the disappearing company to the surviving

company, by issuing shares of the latter to the shareholders of the

former. Totality of transfer assures the continuation of the business

activity. It is not necessary to transfer ownership of assets to the

surviving company nor to transfer the individual liabilities.

Mergers may take place either by absorption of one company by

another or by formation of a new company. Special, simplified, provision

is made for the merger of subsidiary and parent companies.

To accommodate the wide divergance in the mechanics of executing

mergers, the draft offers a broad "merger plan". It requires a two-thirds

approval of each proposed merger plan at the general meeting of all companies involved. Each specific plan is to follow the national requirements of the companies involved. To protect shareholder interests the draft provides for a report containing the results of an audit regarding the exchange ratio of shares.

Among the other draft provisions, the most controversial one requires discussion of the report with workers' representatives before the voting at the general meeting. The workers representatives may produce a written statement which must be brought to the attention of the general meeting

The crossborder merger problem is also being attacked from another angle. Article 220 of the Rome Treaty provides that member states shall adopt a Convention for the "merger between companies or firms governed by the laws of different countries". Such a Convention has been drafted and may provide a solution if member states can agree on a final version.   (8)

Taxation in the Formation of Mergers and Combinations

Excessive tax burdens probably constitute the most significant obstacle to the formation and operation of multinational combinations, whether by merger, holding company system, transnationals, or otherwise.

The EEC Commission has stated that taxes within the Community should be harmonized so that tax hindrances should not influence the choice of forms that concentration take. In other words tax law should be neutral.

Under the present national tax systems the merger event is subject to effective taxation with certain relief provisions. The tax is on the seller's side and is measured by the gain on various forms of previously unrealized profit and the book profit itself. In addition to this tax there are registration and transfer taxes.

With respect to purely domestic mergers, all of the member states currently provide for some tax relief with respect ot the capital gains. Taxation is either reduced, extended over a period of time, or deferred until a later recognition of gain. The discrimination against crossborder mergers is intended. This is not the case in Belgium if the absorbing or newly-created company has its seat or principal establishment in Belgium, plus other conditions. In France the crossborder merger receives no discrimination even if the absorbing company is foreign. However, this assumes approval of the transaction by the interested government ministries, and the non-removal of the French assets. Italy now extends tax relief to all registration taxes and income taxes with respect to domestic and crossborder mergers. However, domestic mergers receive unconditional relief whereas a foreign absorbing company must meet certain criteria related to Italian competition policy. These are a few examples of the nature of the discrimination, other than outright and unqualified discrimination.

There is some justification for this unequal treatment. When the absorbing company is foreign, the domestic taxing authority may lose taxing jurisdiction over future gains with respect to local assets. Furthermore, various previously unrealized gains not yet reflected on the absorbed company's books may never be subject to domestic taxation.

This presents a different state of affairs from the purely domestic merger in which the domestic taxing authority maintains continuing jurisdiction over the profit generating assets.

Even if the various national relief provisions were extended to crossborder mergers, a major problem would still remain. The variation among relief provisions would bring about overall differing tax results depending upon the nationality or location of the merging companies. This could result in mergers always occuring in the same direction - away from states with stricter laws. This is similar to the kind of distortion that takes place in the U.S. regarding the preponderance of the of the Delaware formed corporation, only the implications are greater.

An EEC-wide agreement extending national relief provisions to all crossborder mergers would only be complete if the national systems were first harmonized so that the tax results would be identical no matter which direction mergers were consumated.

The Commission's 1969 Draft Directive on Merger Taxation proposes a uniform system of taxation covering part of the problem. The directive recognizes the need to protect the state of the absorbed company from losing its tax base, and to eliminate the discriminatory treatment of crossbroder mergers.

The proposed scheme is that there be a deferment of all capital gains resulting from the merger transaction. The member states would be obligated to permit this deferment only insofar as the assets of the absolved company are transferred to the books of a permanent establishment (branch) of the absorbing company, located in the state of the absorbed company. This places crossborder mergers on the same basis as domestic

mergers so long as the absorbed domestic company is maintained as an

operating establishment (branch) in its original home state. The absorbing

foreign corporation would be able to transfer some assets as long as it

paid the capital gains tax attributable to those particular assets. (9)

Income Taxation of Multinational Combinations

Assuming the elimination of all legal obstacles and inequities

relating to the formation of crossborder combinations, there are still

income tax inequities with respect to their operation. Income tax

treatment is not the same as between purely domestic companies, local

permanent establishments or branches of foreign companies, and domestic

subsidiary companies of foreign parents. The latter two are seldom

treated the same as the first category. This stems from non-recognition

of the economic unity which exists in the latter two categories.

Profits of subsidiary companies are taxed, then taxed again when

dividends are distributed to the parent company. And some states tax

the parent company differently depending on whether it distributes holding

company profits to its shareholders. States with provisions mitigating

taxation of intercorporate dividends generally do not allow such mitigation

to apply to foreign holdings in domestic companies. This is sometimes

offset by the tax laws in the country where the holding company is established.

Those laws provide relief in the form of the exclusion of previously

taxed or foreign income, or by tax credit for taxes paid in another country.

Tax treaties also affect this. But any ultimate adjustment is complicated by the dividend withholding tax levied when the dividends are paid to the foreign parent.

In addition to the intercorporate dividend problem, no provision now exists to allow parent or holding companies to file EEC-wide consolidated tax returns so that losses of one subsidiary may be set off against gains from another. Some member states have consolidation privileges but they are generally applicable only for the benefit of domestic companies with foreign subsidiaries, and for purely domestic holding company systems. Hope for harmonisation is further complicated, though perhaps advanced, by the unique situation in Germany. It does not specifically provide for the filing of consolidated tax returns, but that result is realized by recognition of "related groups of companies" as a single entity. However, this is only applicable when all members of the group are domestic companies.

The Commission has attempted to deal with the tax inequities respecting companies with permanent foreign establishments (branches) in another part of its Draft Directive on Merger Taxation.

The directive reiterates the right of each member state to tax permanent establishments within its borders. However, it proposes that the company with permanent establishments abroad be allowed to opt in favor of being taxed on its worldwide profits. This will allow such companies to deduct from profits in its home country the losses incurred by its permanent establishments abroad. The proposal also calls for a scheme of avoiding any double taxation of previously taxed profits of the foreign branches.

The matter of intercorporate dividend taxation is dealt with separately in the Draft Directive on Parent-Subsidiary Taxation. The basic proposals are to exempt profits which a parent corporation receives from its subsidiary; to eliminate withholding taxes on dividends paid by a subsidiary to a foreign parent; and to provide for a system of consolidated profits parallel to that proposed with respect to mergers. (10)

It is recognized that harmonization of national laws on mergers, related taxation laws, and worker participation is a long term prospect. In addition to attempting to harmonize the laws with respect to all companies, the Commission is considering the creation of a separate EEC company law to permit the formation of large crossborder enterprises in the form of European Companies.

5.2   THE EUROPEAN COMPANY

If the structure for a European Company (Societas Europaea, SE)
becomes a reality during the 1970's it will be the most progressive form
of corporate business enterprise yet devised.   Even the present examples
of imaginative multinational and international companies cannot compare
with it.   They are ingenious devices employing combinations of national
corporate forms and international treaties.   The SE will, in contrast,
provide the first supranational corporate structure, recognizing that
economic enterprise ignores national boundaries.   (11)

The EEC Commission submitted a Draft Statute for the European
Company to the Council of Ministers in 1970.   It was largely the product
of proposals suggested a decade prior to that.   Its purpose is to provide
an additional type of company to encourage integration and cooperation
within the Common Market, Since the larger European companies have
demonstrated their ability to accomplish this under present laws, the SE
will aid medium and smaller size firms to accomplish the same result
in simpler fashion.

The proposed European Company law will not replace, but supplement
the national company laws existing in the member states of the EEC.   The
SE would exist side by side with the already available national company
forms.   Business leaders will then have an additional option in choosing the
legal structure which their enterprise will take.

Those choosing the SE form will be governed by its nearly 300
articles which will constitute part of the company law of the EEC Community.

Matters governed by these statutes shall not be subject to the national laws of the member states. The European Court is responsible for statute interpretation and administration.

When litigation in national courts is governed by the Statute, those courts must follow the intention of the Statute as expressly stated or as interpreted by the European Court. When no such guidance is available then the interpretation shall be resolved in accordance with the general principles upon which the Statute is based, or in the alternative, upon the general principles common to the laws of the member states. National law is only involved when questions fall outside the scope of the Statute.

The structure of the SE is based upon progressive aspects of corporate forms in operation in the member states. SE powers are divided between the general meeting, the supervisory board, and the executive board. This system is similar to that in Germany, France, and the Netherlands.

The supervisory board is conceived as the controlling organ of the management of the company by the executive board. Two-thirds of its members are appointed by the general meeting for terms not exceeding five years. The other one-third are workers' representatives and are elected by the members of the works councils in the national establishments of the SE pursuant to national laws. The workers may not be represented if two-thirds of the employees of the SE so decide.

Provision is made for an annual audit of the accounts completely independent of the SE. Independent auditors are appointed by the general meeting.

The executive board is the motivating managerial force of the company. Its members are not elected by the general meeting, but are appointed by the supervisory board. It is felt that the supervisory board is in a better position than the general meeting of shareholders to select suitable directors. The national corporate laws of several states already reflect this. The international dispersion of SE shareholders make this even more compelling. The draft requires that executive board directors be nationals of member states where the board comprises only one or two members. In other instances those nationals must be in the majority.

A fourth organ of the SE is the European Works Council (EWC). It also possesses considerable power. Works councils are generally provided for under the laws of the member states though their exact constitution and authorities differ. They will remain in existence in the national establishments of the SE. The EWC will be superior to them when the SE has establishments in more than one country. In those cases the EWC represents the employees in matters which concern the SE as a whole or several of its establishments.

The EWC, which is elected directly by the employees of the establishments, has rights to be informed, to be heard, and, in some instances, to approve. These rights relate to company matters which affect the employee. The incorporation of the EWC into the SE structure attempts to make the relation of management and labor more of a cooperative one, rather than one of conflict. Because of this, it has been said that the Draft Statute contains "enterprise law" rather than company law in the classic sense, where labor does not play a role at all.   (12)

Since the purpose of the SE Statute is to facilitate Common Market inegration, its application is restricted to those instances in which that result is likely to follow. Hence, the founders of an SE must be public companies of which at least two are incorporated under a different national law. The neutral form of the SE will only be available when there is an international factor as the basis of the creation of the SE. And only public companies formed under the laws of one of the EEC member states can act as founders. In theory this would exclude all American, Japanese and other non-EEC companies. But since these excluded companies can form subsidiaries within the EEC, those subsidiaries could qualify as founders.

Use of the SE form is envisioned when founders from different countries wish to merge, form a holding company, or a joint subsidiary. When a complete merger is intended, 500,000 units of account (about U.S. $500,000) is the minimum required capital. In the other two instances it is 250,000 units.

Assuming that some form of the SE Statute becomes Community law, what impact will it have? Its proponents believe that it will significantly reduce the psychological nationalistic barriers to crossborder mergers and that it will provide a vehicle for crossborder integration among smaller EEC companies; and that such SE forms will provide a symbol and working example for further EEC integration.

Its critics, however, believe that the real impediment to crossborder company integration is taxation, and that the SE form does not affect the taxation barriers at all. / Furthermore, there are some who
(13)
believe that having a group of connected foreign subsidiaries gives greater flexibility.

No doubt there are situations in which the SE form would be advantageous for the merger of two or more small companies, or instances in which a subsidiary of a giant multinational could make good use of the SE form. However, it does not seem likely that there will be a stampede into this new form. As more literature is published about the operations of multinational enterprises, it appears that "flexibility" is their chief asset. If this is so, then any question of loss of flexibility in the SE form will rule out its adoption. In the area of labor relations it is clear that the various workers' representation schemes of the SE could limit management flexibility. The day when labor's multinational strength will equal that of management's is coming. When it does, management will not be immune from it, whatever form the enterprise takes.

On the other hand, it should not be overlooked that the SE form does provide management, labor, shareholders, and creditors with a framework that gives its multinational operations a single form, integrated financial standing, and unified corporate regulations. Another significant advantage is that the SE would have easier access to all European stock exchanges and forms of capital. It is also contemplated that SE taxation will be simplified. The exchange of shares involved in the formation of an SE holding company does not give rise to any tax so long as the new shares are shown on the books at the same value of the old shares. The proposed tax scheme requires that the profits of an SE establishment be taxed exclusively in the state where the establishment is located. And SE's would be allowed to elect the option of being taxed on worldwide profit - permitting an SE to deduct in the country of tax domicile the losses suffered by establishments abroad. Even the losses of 50%-owned subsidiaries could be deducted. This makes it possible to set-off profits and losses of companies which are legally distrinct, yet part of a larger economic unit.

The SE would also eliminate problems concerning the transfer of the corporate seat.

Recognition of Groups of Companies

Another main feature of the Draft Statute is that segment which concerns "groups of companies". Those rules go to the heart of the present multinational structures insofar as they are connected to SE's. (14)

The principle underlying the rules is that the individual interests of the respective companies which constitute a group are generally subordinated to the interests of the group as a whole. Consequently, related enterprises are considered under the Statute as an integrated group or unit which should be subject to certain uniform rules. These rules will effect all related companies which act as an economic unit, but which are legally separate entities. This is a subject which requires attention in all parts of the world but which, to date, has only been treated systematically under German law. (15)

The provisions of the Draft Statute are extended to any such group in which an SE is either directly or indirectly the controlled or controlling enterprise in the group. These provisions are applicable to non-EEC enterprises as well as EEC ones. They seek to establish a legal framework in which the interests of groups of affiliated and related companies can be reconciled with those of minority shareholders and creditors. To protect the rights of those minority shareholders of a controlled company whose seat is in one of the member states, provision is made for these shareholders to exchange their shares for shares of the controlling company if it is an SE or EEC member company, or to settle for a cash payment as soon as the company becomes a member of a group.

To help safeguard the rights of creditors, the Draft Statute provides that the controlling company is jointly and severally liable for all the obligations of the dependent undertakings. Provision is made for the publication of certain notices with regard to whether an SE forms part of a group.

What these "groups of companies" rules represent is the beginning of what may evolve into a fully coordinated EEC policy toward all multinational enterprises.

In many respects company law can be viewed as a key basis of a nation's economic structure. The importance of the SE Draft Statute is that it is the first major move towards enterprise law which narrows the gap between economic realities and legal structures.

5.3   WORLD COMPANY

When the prospect for a World Company is discussed, it is necessary to clarify what is meant. There are two possibilities. One is the extension of the idea of the Draft Statute for a European Company to the global level. This can be viewed as the "de jure" world company.

The other possibility can be called the "de facto" world company. It refers to the factual existence of an enterprise which is thoroughly integrated and involved in all nations of the world. It is a world company or enterprise, even though its existence, regulation or control is not governed by any supranational company law or institution.

Both of these prospects require some attention in order to set the stage for the various interrelationships to be discussed in the forthcoming chapters.

First the "de jure" world company. As early as 1944 Professor Schmitthoff suggested the registration of international companies at the International Court of Justice at The Hague.(15a) This order of thinking is now reflected in the proposed European Company (SE). Let us assume that the SE becomes a reality and goes on to fulfill at least some of its intended goals. It is certainly possible to envision that the same kind of economic and political forces that brought about the SE could bring about a similar structure on a global level, especially if it were on an optional basis.   The concept of a "Cosmocorp", a stateless corporation, has already been introduced. (16) In the field of global communications - radio, sea and air transport, and postal services - we already have global regulatory bodies. (17) The orderly exploitation of the oceans have raised the suggestion for a supranational institution to issue corporate charters to enterprises entering that field.(18) History has demonstrated that the restructuring of institutions is more often the rule than the exception.

It is becoming more obvious that "most of the rules of behaviour for international business are set in fragmented ways by nation - states, reflecting not concern for the over-all international system or a world system, but for the narrow interests of (national) subsystems".(19) This realization has already become a matter of urgency, and not choice, in matters relating to pollution and aerial hijacking.

Although sometimes exaggerated, the present decade has already seen many publications suggesting that the multinationals are on a collision course with nationa states. The subject is now under examination by a United Nations panel of experts selected by the Economic and Social Council. Although this panel began with the idea of suggesting a "code of good conduct" for giant multinations, they have tentatively concluded that such a code would be inadequate and that some form of coordinated government control is necessary. It is not yet clear where this will lead, however, it certainly points in the direction of a possible body of world company law for the largest multinational enterprises. Several general chartering and regulatory schemes were even discussed prior to the convening of the U. N. panel. (20)

The "de facto" idea of a world company is one that is rapidly coming into existence irrespective of whether the ideal legal framework is available or not. In fact, the truth of the matter is that the prospect for giant world companies has impelled nation states to consider machinery and structures for their control and regulation, not to accelerate their existence or growth.

Multinational enterprises can be equated with large

enterprises. Though not all large enterprises are multinational, most multinationals are large. There is a limit to the size an enterprise may reach when it confines itself to one nation. The trend in mergers, take-overs, and other forms of amalgamation is clear. In the United States, Europe and Japan smaller firms are forged into larger ones, and the size and concentration of enterprises is accelerating. As the size of any national enterprise increases, the likelihood of its going multination also increases. And many acquisitions and takeovers are crossing national borders. The American corporate invasion of Europe has been proceeding for several decades and is now being followed by a Japanese invasion. European and Japanese enterprises are now entering the U.S. in larger numbers. All this, plus the diverse multinational investment in the less developed areas makes the course of events unmistakable. (21)

In addition to these facts there are those who believe that "to avoid a Darwinian debacle on a global scale we will have to use our resources with maximum efficiency and a minimum of waste" and that the multinational enterprise is the vehicle to accomplish this. (22) In other words, not only is the prospect of genuine world companies a fact, but there are those who believe this realization should be accelerated. Indeed, the intention to increase size and concentration is an express policy goal within the Common Market and in Japan. It is already recognized that adoption of many modern technologies is feasible only with economies of scale attainable at the regional level. Enterprises such as INTELSAT are testimony to the fact that this concept has been accepted at the global level. As the magnitude of problems facing mankind become increasingly global in scale, they call for solution by enterprises global in scale.

Reduction in trade barriers has not resulted in a more equitable distribution of wealth among nations. It has opened the doors to the prospect. Many believe that the multinational enterprise can be the vehicle for redistribution of the benefits of increased world production. (23)

The probability for a genuine multinational or world company is yet in the distance. The primary obstacle to such a realization is the fact that the world's wealth is not equally distributed among nations. This reality impedes the true multinationality of ownership.

In spite of this, a nearly genuine world company or enterprise could presently come into existence. Although various national and regional antitrust and monopolies laws are functioning, there has been little objection to the conglomerate merger or amalgamation – the combination of companies in different industries. This is especially true when the entities are from different nations and regions.

However presently improbable, it is possible to imagine combinations such as UNIMITFORD, a combination of Unilever, Mitsubishi, and Ford, all in different industries, and headquartered and owned in different countries. The improbability of this stems mainly from the psychology of nationality. But these barriers are falling. It has already happened in banking. Witness the international merchant bank, Orion, controlled by Chase Manhattan, Mitsubishi Bank, National Westminster Bank, Westdeutsche Landesbank Girozentrade, the Royal Bank of Canada, and Credito Italiano.,

6   <u>OWNERSHIP AND CONTROL</u>

The separation of ownership and control in large corporate
enterprise has been recognised for some time. The legal device
of the holding company system played its role in this development.
Part of this process has resulted in the distinct separation of the
legal structure and the managerial structure. As both structures
of an enterprise encompass the entire globe, the separation becomes
greater. All the implications of the separation of ownership and
control are compounded.

At the root of the function between multinational enterprises
and nation states are the concepts of ownership and control. It is
important to know what impact the multinational enterprise (MNE)
has had, and what policy choices are open to it, what the reaction
of the nation state (NS) has been and what options are available to
it. This can be best accomplished by taking the broadest possible
view of the subject and by incorporating the views of a wide variety
of commentators. Because public opinion plays such a significant
role in this area, the chapter relies almost exclusively on an
organised series of verbatim quotations of leading experts.
"To a remarkable extent the ownership and control of both
production and distribution, outside of the Communist countries,
has passed into the hands of gigantic corporate organisations. " (1)
Although significant notice of this has only recently been taken, the

process has been taking place over a long period of time and the
NS has yet to retard it. "The multinational corporate enterprise
represents the contemporary stage of development of the national
corporate enterprise, which in turn developed from the local
corporate enterprise, which in its turn evolved from the non-
corporate local (though sometimes national or international)
enterprise. At each stage of this evolution, there has been protest
and attempts to arrest or control the emergent next stage." (2).
In short, the MNE has emerged because its superior economic
efficiency has surpassed various political processes.

Given an expanding world economy and the rise of the
multinational corporation, national boundaries may follow the history
of state boundaries in the United States, which failed to confine the
American corporation or prevent the growth of a national economy.
(3) The trend is undeniable. It represents a move beyond international trade into an internationalisation of production. (4).

Ownership and control once confined to the boundaries of
a single nation are now not only separated from one another but
splintered among many nations. Now we find that the physical
assets of production and distribution may be located in one country
but owned and controlled in another. Absentee ownership is nothing
new, but it has never before been seen on the scale that is emerging.
The dilemma of the NS is that it cannot easily live with it and cannot
live without it. The response of the Canadian Government has been

that the economic benefit of the MNE exceeds the cost of having no
direct foreign investment at all. (5). Not all nations see it that
way.

"The ultimate debate between corporations and nation-states may
boil down to the pursuit of international interests by the former
and of narrowly national interests by the latter. " (6)   If a clash
is coming, there are those who see the MNE gaining momentum.
"The difference between countries and corporations - in size,
influence, capabilities, even in the number of people whose lives
they directly affect - are no longer as great as they once were.
If General Motors were a nation, it would rank 14 among the
countries of the world in gross national product. " (7)

What has made the ownership/control problems especially
complex is that the really significant economic resources are now
technology and management. (8) These assets enjoy the quality of
mobility as well as scarcity.   Manufacturing operations formerly
found in a few nations are now widely dispersing throughout the
world. (9)

A number of developments, including GATT, have moved
the world closer to free trade. But those developments have not
brought the expected benefits to the poorer nations. Developing
nations are increasingly unwilling to accept as 'equitable' the
distribution of economic benefits produced by free trade. (10)

The free trade institutions have assumed that removal of

trade barriers would produce maximum benefits for all countries.
What has happened, according to some observers, is that, in
practice, free trade has served to maintain and even magnify the
existing comparative advantages of the developed nations. (11)
"What we see is not a world of individual traders with large flows
of both short and long term capital, as prevailed in the first half
of the century. Instead, we see a world of nations increasingly
dependent for their economic development on infusions of foreign
technology, management, capital, and marketing skills. This
infusion . . . . . enters principally through private channels, not
under government sponsorship. Rather than trade effecting the
integration of the world economy, production owned and controlled
by foreign-based corporations is altering the pattern and composition
of international trade by tying enterprises together, primarily
through the spread of direct investment and foreign licensing. " (12)

This excellent description of what is happening in the
world economic arena suggests that the fate of the developing nations
really depends upon the operations, ownership and control of MNE.
It also makes plain that the associated problems can always be
viewed from two extremes - investing nation and host nation.
Control or regulation of MNE whether by national, regional or
international devices is also complicated.
"In the economic area, regulation is endangered by the growing
gap between the rich and the poor countries, by Western growth

patterns, and stagnation elsewhere, by a growing mismatch between and separation of production, distribution and consumption activities, by technological gaps and by the distortion of the reward system. " (13)

It is clear that there is an inherent conflict of interest between managements that operate in the world economy and govern-ments confined to a national scene. (14) Nations which are the home country of MNE are gaining dominance over the others. Jean-Jacques Servan Schreiber, in the American Challenge showed that the economically strong countries always make direct investments thereby gaining control while weak countries only make portfolio investments abroad and do not get control. This is not a new phenomenon. Nearly 70 years ago a book called The American Invaders was published in England and described the threat to British enterprise posed by Singer, Heinz and other American corporations. (15)

Host governments increasingly see the MNE as a new form of imperialism. (16) In extreme cases they see themselves becoming 'branch plant countries'. (17) The irony of the NS predicament is that the more it enforces its own set of priorities, the more costly will its environment appear to MNE. (18) And it generally needs the foreign capital, technology, and management of the MNE. The gut issue has been said to be whether the national short-term goals are permitted to prevail over long-term global benefits. (19) Those who put it in extreme terms have asked the question about which institution is more likely to be around a century from now - France or General Motors. Two keen observers place their money on France. (20)

Of course there is another view of all this. Some have described the MNE as "the hope of the world because of their potentials in disseminating technological know-how erasing national boundaries." (21) A more balanced viewpoint is: "The coming age of multinational corporations should represent a great step forward in the efficiency with which the world uses its economic resources, but it will create grave social and political problems and will be very uneven in exploiting and distributing the benefits of modern science and technology. In a word, the multinational corporation reveals the power of size and the danger of leaving it uncontrolled." (22)

The pursuit of economic efficiency has resulted in the ever increasing size of the firm and the widening integration of operations. The MNE provide one device by which interdependent activities in different countries can be co-ordinated in a flexible and adaptable institution. "Not only are they a projection to the international scene of a well-known and well-tried national phenomenon, the group of companies, but they offer the advantage of making possible the seemingly impossible, to sit on both sides of the fence. In the host countries their national subsidiaries are regarded and treated as national companies, and yet in the home country the whole cluster of connected companies is regarded as a national unit." (23)

The present trend is clear. The multinationals have for some time been increasing their production and sales faster than most countries have expanded their gross national product. (24) An American professor sums up the situation: "... 100 years hence our descendants will look back at the second half of the 20th Century as a significant turning point in world history when we accomplished the transition from a basically nation-oriented society to one in which global institutions were ascendant, and that one of the foremost instigators of this transition was the multinational firm." (25)

6. 1   OWNERSHIP

Probably the most significant aspect of share ownership is the associated power or right to control the enterprise. This aspect or function of share ownership is dealt with in detail in the section on 'control'. The remaining aspect of share ownership is the right to receive the dividends or profits.

Let us assume that the parent corporation and the bulk of its shareholders are in the United States and that its wholly owned subsidiary corporations are located in numerous countries around the globe. This means that the flow of dividends or profits is all in one direction - toward the United States. Or if it is directed elsewhere for reinvestment, the redirection is determined by the US parent. The national balance of payments implications are obvious; so too, are capital accumulations.

Labor groups in the United States had criticized the American multinationals of adversely affecting the US balance of payments. In the Congressional hearings which followed the facts demonstrated that the opposite was generally true. And as a generalization it is fair to say that the long-term flow back of dividends far exceeds the initial outflow of investment, if any. It cannot be ignored that foreign investment can be wholly or partly financed from foreign local sources.

The flow of profits has other implications stemming from

the fact that profit can be reduced by various national taxes. This
influences the location of production, intercorporate pricing and
other decisions of the enterprise. "Profits can be recorded in other
units of a global system, including holding companies located in
tax havens, through control of transfer prices for goods and services
supplied by the parent company or exports to other affiliates." (26)
Prices charged for intercorporate imports have been shown in some
instances to be far above prevailing world prices and conversely
those for exports have been below world prices. (27)

When ownership, management (control), and location of
production were all combined together in a single nation, these
new cash flow complexities did not exist. However, "new industrial
technology requires economies of scale which cannot always be
contained within existing national frameworks." (28)
"There are further gains to be made through economies of large-
scale production. These economies are of greater significance to
those countries too small in area and population to permit the
erection of industries of optimum size, but they can be obtained
through enterprises big enough to serve a number of such nations
through their operations." (29)

For this and other reasons the internationalization of
production is rising and is likely to continue rising. One of the
explanations for foreign direct investment is that once one com-
petitior does it, the others must follow. (30)

The consequences of this are far reaching for both developed and developing nations. "For example, in the United States we used to have a very large megnetic tape industry for home entertainment. One hundred percent of that industry moved to the Far East. (31) In that instance location of production facilities changed completely and ownership changed only partly, because of American reinvestment in the Far East. The ownership change that did take place in this industry occurred largely because of wage differentials. Though that factor accounts for numerous other international industrial relocations, in time wage differentials will narrow. In the future those who own capital, management know-how, and technology will determine the global location of industries. "Land is totally immobile; the mobility of labor is difficult at best, and everywhere is restricted by positive law; therefore the mobility of capital and management becomes even more important than in a theoretically free market. " (32) The significance of technology has been illustrated in the Canadian setting. General Motors of Canada is technologically dependent on its US parent and this would not change even if it became 100% Canadian-owned. "This underlines the fact that technical assistance is a continuing affair, and the real controlling influence in multinational enterprises rather than stock ownership. " (33)

Ownership Policies

Multinational corporations generally exercise control over

their foreign affiliates through complete or majority ownership. In certain unique circumstances effective control can be exercised from a minority position. At least 80% of Unites States affiliates and 75% of United Kingdom affiliates are either wholly-owned or majority controlled. In terms of total investment these two countries have about 90% in affiliates which are at least majority-owned. Majority ownership and control appears to be a general characteristic of multinational corporations from other home countries, except in the case of Japanese multinational corporations, where a higher proportion of affiliates and investment are minority-owned joint ventures. This difference in ownership pattern is apparently influenced by differences in methods of control as well as in the industrial and geographical distribution of foreign activities. (34)

Cash flow and investment are interconnected with ownership policies. When investment cash is short two joint venture affiliates may complement the MNE system better than one wholly-owned. (35) Theoretically, when a MNE parent decides which subsidiary should supply a certain export market it should choose a wholly-owned subsidiary over a jointly-owned subsidiary, all else being equal. (36)

"The common cure recommended for strained relations between host nations and inter - and multi-national corporations is the joint venture". (37) However, the large MNE has sometimes responded to host country pressures for local subsidiary partici-

pation by urging the purchase of the parent's stock. This permits

the parent to maintain complete control over the subsidiary. (38)

Where local subsidiary profits are higher than parent profits this

policy may not satisfy local investors.

Recent studies have revealed some interesting facts about

joint venture operations. "Nearly one-third of the international

corporate marriages of large US firms have ended in divorce or

in significant increase in the US firm's apparent power over its

partner." (39) This has posed the question why many large US

multinationals have converted one-time joint ventures into wholly-

owned subsidiaries, increased their shareholdings from minority

or 50-50 positions to majority holdings, or sold out to their once

joint venture partners." The desire of product-concentrating

firms eventually to implement marketing and production rational-

ization policies was found to be associated with joint-venture

instability." (40) The overall conclusion was that joint-venture

survival varies with the particular multinational strategy.

Another study confirms that profit management is closely

related to ownership policies and that it is the strategy of expansion

which generates the policy. (41) "We found that a close tie between

strategy and structure exists regardless of what industry the firm

is in; managers in enterprises following similar strategies in

quite different industries have developed similar organizational structures and ownership policies. " (42)

Multinational enterprises are not, however, reluctant to share their ownership of foreign subsidiaries if there are other means of retaining control. In this regard it is significant to note that host countries are sometimes more concerned with who appears to have control rather than who actually exercises effective control. "There is a difference, however, between the attitude of US foreign investors (whether they have reached the stage of being multinational enterprises or not) toward proposals to alter their control pattern and their attitude toward proposals to change the ownership pattern. Many US enterprises are willing to sell shares of the affiliates to the public up to 30 per cent or so, or even to take some joint-venture (minority or fifty-fifty) partners, if internal company arrangements make certain that full control is held by the majority partner. In the developing countries, which are much more against foreign ownership than the advanced countries, a number of techniques are permitted (or are at least employed) through which the majority (or even minority) foreign partner achieves substantially full management control. They include management contracts and provisions in licensing agreements which cover product introduction, quality control, production schedules, marketing and prices. Some multinational enterprises which publicly proclaim their adherence to host-government wishes in forming joint ventures have carefully restructed the management responsibilities and authorities of the local partner. The tacit acceptance by host governments of such

provisions indicates that, at least for some countries, the

problem is not so much the <u>exercise</u> of control as it is the <u>evidence</u>

of control, ie, ownership. " (43)

In the future novel forms of corporate ownership should be

devised to meet the needs of the MNE and the host country. MNE

may be allowed complete control as long as they continue to make

a critical contribution that cannot be made by others. As that

contribution diminishes, so local control will increase. Various

'fade-out' arrangements have already been implemented and more

are appearing in the legislation of developing countries. The use

of management contracts is also likely to become more frequent. (44)

"One suggestion is that the equity shareholding in the capital of MPE's

should be shared between the different countries in which they

operate according to the proportion of the total sales or assets

accounted for by them. " (45) MPE stands for multinational producing

enterprise and is another variant of terminology.

Some Canadian observers have made a significant

observation about 'ownership'.

"Concentration on ownership of enterprises through ownership of

shares in corporations obscures at least two things of fundamental

importance. One involves the relation of ownership of shares to

actual control and management of an enterprise. The other involves

the relationship of corporate ownership, and the management which is assumed to go with ownership, to general public interest. " (46)

What is becoming obvious is the need to recognize the separation of ownership and control in the MNE, and to devise new techniques or concepts for non-control ownership participation. Complementing this is the necessity of understanding the difference between internal and external control of MNE and the inter-relationship between the two. This is discussed in the section under 'control'.

Genuine Multinational Ownership

The term 'MNE' as generally used today refers to enterprises that have operations and activities in many different nations. It does not mean that the enterprise is owned by nationals of many different countries. Quite the contrary, the major MNE's are most often owned nearly exclusively by the nationals of its home country. The majority of existing multinationals are headquartered in the US and are American-owned, with minor exceptions. The few European transnationals with dual parent companies are mainly owned by the nationals of the two parent companies. For the present, therefore, there is no genuine multinational ownership of MNE. Subsidiary companies are mostly wholly owned by the parent company and the parent company is owned by the nationals of the parent country.

International Business Machines, an American MNE, is a case in point. Its foreign subsidiaries are almost always wholly-owned. Its executive officer explained it this way: "... to really get going internationally you need to plough back a lot into them (foreign subsidiaries), and local partners who are interested in dividends don't always want to do this." (47) The relationship between ownership and control over strategy is another explanation. Put in broader terms: "it is clear to me that national ownership in local subsidiaries impedes the fulfillment of the world corporation's full potential as the best means yet devised for utilizing world resources according to the criterion of profit; an objective standard of efficiency." (48)

The disadvantage of local ownership interests is that they think in national and not in global terms. Matters of prices, dividends, plant utilization and location are viewed with a narrow perspective.

The solution most often suggested is that interests share ownership in the parent company rather than in the local subsidiary. "This leads me to suggest that we might do well to approach the problem at a different level, not by nationalizing local subsidiaries but by interrationalizing or perhaps more accurately denationalizing the parent." (49) "This means among other things that share ownership in the parent must be spread through the world so that the company cannot be regarded as the exclusive instrument of a particular nation. .... Of course, in view of the underdeveloped state of most national capital markets, even in the economically

advanced countries, this is not likely to occur very soon. .... But
eventually, as savings are effectively mobilized for investment in
more and more countries, companies will assume an increasingly
international character. At the same time, we can expect a gradual
internationalizing of boards of directors and parent company
managements. " (50)

The basic conflict between local national interests and
global efficiency is somewhat solved by local ownership interest in
the parent if that can be accomplished. In the extreme case where
overall efficiency requires closing the local plant and producing in
another country, local interests will still have their interest in the
parent dividends. However, the local national interest in full
employment and other obvious considerations is ignored. 'Ownership'
interests may be satisfied, but 'control' or self-determination is
not. Admittedly, the example is extreme and seldon occurs over-
night, but it does suggest the need for a more complete resolution
of the conflict. Production location exclusively by considerations
of world efficiency ignore other traditional governmental interests.

Another advocate of internationalizing the ownership of
parent company company stock is the President of the American
Pepsi-Cola Company. (51) He outlines a number of the problems and
some solutions. Shares in the local subsidiary are often more
desirable since the subsidiary is well known locally and may be
more easily traded than the stock of the parent company. Dividends

and earnings retention policies tend to match local desires and interests, including local tax laws. In many countries there is no other alternative as local laws prohibit citizens from acquiring or holding foreign assets, including stocks. Or if it is permitted it is not on an equal basis with the holding of local stock. The interest equalization tax in the US is an example of this. Differences in national taxing systems and the absence of tax treaties add to the complications. Another problem is the need for multilingual stock certificates.

"Perhaps the major barrier to multinational ownership of multi-national companies, however, is that the investment habit has not yet taken hold in other countries as it has in the United States. " (52)

Kendall's proposal is for the parent company to create a special class of 'blocked stock' that could be traded only in a limited geographical area and not be allowed to return to the parent country. According to this proposal, for instance, a US company could go abroad, acquire a local company and use parent company stock for the acquisition. This stock would be the same as that traded in the US, except that the certificate would be stamped with a restriction making it negotiable only in the country for which it was issued or in a limited surrounding region.

The shares of a number of well-known worldwide companies are already listed in numerous stock exchanges outside of their home countries. This is true of American, English, European, as well as Japanese companies.

Restraints on direct foreign investment from the US have already compelled some American companies to finance foreign investments from foreign sources. One technique is to use debentures fully convertible into parent company stock, to achieve this purpose. A similar trend could develop with respect to executive stock options. In 1965 General Motors gave parent company stock awards to its foreign executives outside the US and Canada.

Another theory explains why there may be a trend toward multi-national ownership of parent shares rather than those of the subsidiaries. Shares in a foreign subsidiary are inherently worth more to the parent firm than they are to an autonomous shareholder. The control of the resources of the subsidiary are worth more to the MNE system than to an autonomous local firm or investor. "A theory of the international firm can be developed by pursuing this line of reasoning to identify the conditions under which productive activities in different countries will earn a higher total income if their control is internationally centralized." (53)   The point here is that the whole is often greater than the sum of its parts.

Kendall says that : "There will be no truly multinational companies until there is multinational ownership. And there will be no multinational ownership in any real sense until there is some worldwide sharing of ownership in the parent company. It would not then be too long or difficult a step to move toward worldwide corporate management. A truly multinational company would be one in which there would be no national bias in filling these roles. " (54)

What Kendall advocates seems more likely to materialize first in Europe. "European companies interviewed, especially in countries such as Sweden and Switzerland, have devised ways of spreading, to a certain extent, the ownership of the parent company among foreigners without diluting national control in any way. " (55) This is often accomplished by forms of non-voting shares.

6. 11   DOES IT MATTER WHO OWNS MNE?

Generally, foreign investment does advance economic systems of a nation, indeed some cannot advance without it. The Scandinavian countries and Japan have done quite well without foreign investment. Japan, however, did import extensive foreign technology. "The Communist countries, rigidly excluding foreign venture capital, have made relatively more progress towards industrialization in recent years than have most of the less developed capitalist countries that have welcomed foreign investment. Even in the non-Communist world, the most remarkable progress in the past half-century has been made by Japan, which has followed a policy of excluding foreign capital only slightly less rigid than Soviet Russia's. " (56)

It may be that those countries have unique conditions or assets which have enabled them to advance economically from within. However, a large number of countries, developed and developing, have found it advantages to welcome production facilities owned

by enterprises from other nations. As time has elapsed a certain
amount of friction or conflict has arisen between these enterprises
and host countries. The complaint of the host countries generally
suggests that the foreign-owned enterprise is in some way taking
advantage of the host country or that the enterprise is taking more
out of the country than it is putting into it. The apparent contra-
diction in this is that while those same host countries are levelling
that complaint they admit additional foreign-owned enterprises.

This may be a situation as with human individuals who
complain about the bad aspect of a person or situation but find that
the good aspect is sufficiently good so as not to warrant a change.
There is no doubt that many nations do not welcome foreign investment but they cannot move ahead without it. But this only raises the
question why is the foreign-owned technology, know-how, management skill, or whatever, so loaded with nagative aspects simply
because it is foreign-owned. Simple nationalistic pride is no
doubt part of it but let us look beyond that.

One interesting aspect is that some studies have demonstrated
that foreign-owned enterprises pay better, are more efficient and
contribute more to the local economy than locally-owned competition.
"The assertion that the international firm exists because of its
technical or administrative superiority finds apparent empirical
support from studies that have compared foreign subsidiaries with
their domestic competitors in the same industry. All of these

studies have found that foreign subsidiaries are typically the
dominant firms in their industries in the host country. They are
consistently larger and more productive, and they pay higher wage
rates than domestic firms producing in the same industry." (57)
Another study shows that United States controlled subsidiaries in
many cases have been more responsive to local needs than have
the host country's own firms and agencies. (58)

These studies are not surprising as MNE's would not
enter a country unless they were fairly certain of being able to
compete against local or regional competitors.

Canada probably has the highest proportion of its industries
made up of foreign-owned MNE subsidiaries, and the associated
functions. The question has been repeatedly raised whether those
subsidiaries would behave differently if they were Canadian-owned.
Or to looking at it another way: "Are Canadian capitalists different
from American capitalists?" (59) The word 'capitalists' may
perhaps be too narrow. 'Enterprise administrators' would include
a wider array of nationalities. A similar question has been asked
about the president of the American MNE, Xerox: "Does he view
Xerox as Canadian, American, English or French? Or does he
view Xerox in terms of productivity wherever it does business?" (60)

"The owners of the mature corporation, the shareholders,
exercise little control over the technostructure; the autonomy of
the technostructure is nearly complete. Can it be said that if

General Motors sold all their shares in the Canadian operation to
the Canadian public, the technostructure would not find it necessary
to engage in the same kind of planning as it has done so far? Or
that its motivation would be any different? Is the motivation of the
technostructure of General Motors of Canada any different from
that of the technostructure of Massey-Ferguson or Stelco? Ownership is not the proper focus of attention; it is the power of the
technostructure. " (61)

In response to this, studies suggest that enterprises,
regardless of their nationality of ownership, generally operate in
response to a given institutional and economic sitting in order to
improve their economic position. (62) And, going a step further
that the enterprise is free of the bounds of ownership and functions
as an independent institution.

"The claims to ownership are sub-divided in such fashion and are
so mobile, that the enterprise assumes an independent life, as if
it belonged to no-one; it takes an objective existence, such as in
earlier days, was embodied only in state and church, in a
municipal corporation, in the life of a guild or a religious order....
The depersonalization of ownership; the objectification of
enterprise, the detachment of property from the possessor, leads
to a point where the enterprise becomes transformed into an
institution which resembles the state in character. " (63) and:

".... one cannot help wondering whether conflicts of loyalty are not unavoidable conflicts between corporate and government policies, rather than problems created by differences of nationality. The root cause of most conflicts may well be in absentee ownership rather than divergent national objectives. " (64)

Government Enterprise and Ownership

One solution to both absentee ownership and conflict between corporate and government policies is the transfer of ownership to the public sector as is done in systems of state capitalism or decentralized socialism. (65) Whether that is a satisfactory resolution of the problem or not, the current trend in nearly all countries is toward increased state enterprise in one form or another. (66) Increasing government expenditure on social services and government procurement, including defence, is narrowing the 'free market' sector and increasing the 'public' sector of the world economy. (67)

Galbraith's answer regarding large mature corporations in the United States is to convert them into fully public corporations by the government purchase of their shares with fixed interest - bearing securities. (68) His view is founded on the belief that the 'market economy' no longer functions and that the large enterprise or technostructure plans the economy and is in fact now a quasi-public or public institution. His claim is equivalent to saying that these large enterprises perform the economic planning function that is performed by the state in the Soviet system.

In contrast to this there is a somewhat opposite trend
regarding 'ownership' problems in Eastern European countries.
There, state owned enterprises are making certain compromises
so as to accommodate participation with western capitalist-
type enterprises. "Yugoslavia was the first Eastern European
country to break with Communist tradition by inviting foreign
firms to invest capital in local enterprises on a share basis.
Since its initiation in 1967, Yugoslavia joint venture legislation
has provided for a 'pooling of resources', not strictly speaking
equity in the traditional western sense, but equity in terms of
sharing control income and proceeds from liquidation. " (69)
The new Yugoslav joint venture laws provide a legal framework within which the partners can work out the details of each
relationship by contract agreements, subject to the ultimate
perogative of the workers council. Some of these contracts
have protective clauses which do limit the workers council
perogative in certain specific matters. More than a hundred
joint ventures with foreign enterprises have been concluded
in Yugoslavia since 1967. Romania and Hungary have passed
joint venture legislation, and Poland is moving in the same
direction.

The significant aspect of these new co-operative ventures
is that they clearly separate the ownership aspect from the control
or management aspect, or at least, in form, they appear to do so.
Underlying philosophical considerations may prevent them from

openly conceding that, western partners are actual 'part-owners' of the enterprise. So that the foreign partners rights do not stem from ownership but from the various specific contractual rights conferred. Decision-making rights are defined in the contract as well as the percentage of profits or surplus over costs. Sometimes, instead of a percentage of the profits the foreign partner is paid in a proportion of the total product output. In other instances substantial management fees are paid to foreign partners, taking the place of dividends. These new methods of sharing ownership and control are typical of new approaches that are gradually evolving in all countries of the world.

What appears to be happening everywhere is a merger of government and enterprise. This has been taken to its extreme in the Soviet Union. And in that respect the Soviet Union could be viewed as the worlds largest enterprise.

Returning to the more immediate problems of ownership, it is becoming clear that absolute and indivisible ownership concepts connected with capitalism are unsatisfactory for international economic harmony. "Everyone agrees with the principle of the free flow of international capital, particularly to developing nations, but the insistence of the cosmocorps on attaching absolute ownership and property rights to their capital invites growing hostility and the certain destruction of the system in which they have prospered." (70)

Another way of stating the situation is: "The problem
of the technostructure, as we shall presently observe, is whether
it can be accommodated to social goals or whether society will
have to be accommodated instead to its needs. The nature of the
legal ownership has an undoubted bearing on the amenability of
the technostructure to social goals. " (71)

Control, Not Ownership, is the Real Issue

Ownership of MNE has its significant aspects whether the
owner is foreign and private, local and private, or the host state.
However, when one analyzes the ownership debates in each of these
contexts it is apparent that the conflicts are not so much much over
who enjoys the ownership but rather who controls the enterprise and
towards what end. "Merely changing ownership will not result in
an equitable and socially salubrious distribution of corporate
resources. The problem is not ownership, but accountability.
Soviet lakes are polluted too. " (72) Or to put it another way even
state enterprise has problems of control. And; "It cannot be
assumed that indigenous ownership without regulation of business
behaviour will produce desired results. " (73)

Even in those nations which have switched completely to
state enterprise there has been a tendency to move backward to
the employment of traditional capitalistic management techniques.
And the state enterprise system is sometimes praised not for its

unique merit but for its resemblance to the 'free economy' system. "Goals seem to be reached more often in planned economics when they have been set by industrial managers, based on the narrow interests of their enterprise, a system only slightly different from our present one." (74)

The following is an excellent summation of the ownership (property)/control problem in large corporate enterprise from the public policy point of view, and serves to set the stage for the next section specifically devoted to the subject of 'control'.

"The review of corporate powers over participations that has preceded, sufficiently indicates the use of a power which is virtually new in the common law. This is in substance the power of confiscation of a part of the profit stream and even of the underlying corporate assets by means of purely private processes, without any test of public welfare or necessity. As they stand these powers are nominally uncontrolled.

It requires little analysis to make plain the fact that private property, as understood in the capitalistic system, is rapidly losing its original characteristics. Unless the law stops the wide open gap which the corporate mechanism has introduced, the entire system has to be revalued.

It is entirely possible and some students of the situation are beginning to contend, that the corporation profit stream in reality no longer is private property, and that claims on it must be adjusted by some test other than that of property right. ......

It is the purpose of this chapter to state this theory, with

full realization of the possibility that private property may one day

cease to be the basic concept in terms of which the courts handle

problems of large scale enterprises and that the corporate

mechanism may prove the very means through which such mod-

ification is brought about. " (75)

6.2   CONTROL

As multinational enterprises increase in power and
independence, control over their operations and goals is becoming
the paramount issue. Nearly all of the present MNE's are
privately-owned by large numbers of small shareholders who do
not exercise control over the enterprise. Control is already in
the hands of the management structure or technostructure. Even
if ownership were to shift so that MNE's became state enterprises
of the home country, the control situation would not have changed
dramatically. Managerial technocrats will simply be relabelled
'bureau-technocrats'. As between nations, the 'control' problems
may or may not be simplified.

The subject is first discussed from the viewpoint of the
multinational enterprise itself. 'Internal' control problems of
managing and organizing the enterprise should be understood before
tackling the ultimate problem of 'external' control.

Following that is a review of the position of the nation
state, its need to control multinational enterprise, and the regulatory
steps that have been taken. That leads to the regional and international regulatory efforts and their future prospects. The final
section takes a broad view of corporate control and the function of
legal systems.

6.21   INTERNAL CONTROL PROBLEMS OF MANAGING AND

ORGANIZING MNE

"The qualitative evidence on the structure of business enterprise and
its evolution through time suggests that both size and internationality
have important positive effects on a firms strength and ability. " (76)
It is these two factors - size and internationality - that complicate
the internal control problems of MNE. The enormous dimensions of
this are suggested by those who view the multinationals as, in effect,
centrally planned economies like Russia. They see MNE as
enlarging the domain of centrally planned world production and
decreasing the sphere of decentralized free markets. (77)

At present, it appears that these challenges are being
responded to more effectively by MNE than by national government.
However, as state and private enterprise join forces it will be more
difficult to make such assessments.

In studying the 'control' of the MN enterprise itself, it is
difficult even to determine exactly who possesses and wields the
control powers. A recent example illustrates this. A large American
company announced plans to form a Luxemberg-based holding company
to issue loans to five European companies which were to be integrated
through a common board of directors set up in France. The American
company would own 80 per cent of the holding company, but will only
have half of the directors, with the remaining half divided among the

the five. The companies were from France, Belgium, Italy and Spain. Questions were posed regarding the proposed scheme. "Where was control centered in the new structure? Did it reside in the board of directors, in middle management? Does the board's composition of half Europeans with a European Chairman provide any necessary indication that the corporation will respond any less to corporate as contrasted to national interests. " (78) In addition to this type of situation, there are those wherein control of critical patents, technology or markets by one minority owner may give that partner overall effective control.

The Question of Centralized versus Decentralized Control

"One of the critical tasks of managing multi-national operations is to design an effective managerial control system to allow top management to co-ordinate and guide activities of a large number of far-flung foreign affiliates into a unified whole." (79) Meeting this challenge is partly a matter of striking the correct balance between centralized and decentralized control. The tendency and present trend seems to be to accentuate centralized control. "Strategic planning on a global basis is likely to become more efficient and more effective. The accumulation of experience and the development of more sophisticated computerised data processing and control systems will both assist this process. One implication of such trends is the greater centralisation of resource allocation and control at corporate headquarters. This is already becoming noticeable in several large international firms. " (80) "Despite the idealogy of decentralization, the trend is toward closer control by the head office. " (81).

There are a number of unmistakable illustrations of this. "From what was once described as a kind of holding company in which, at one point, managers were literally told to ignore New York directives and 'just send earnings back home', ITT became a tightly centralized organization" (82) Regarding British Ford: "You control a company if you control its capital expenditure, its products and in great detail its operating budgets, " said one ex-finance man. "All these are controlled by Americans over here and ultimately by Detroit. The amount of paper flowing to Detroit and back is unbelievable. " (83)

From another viewpoint there is a limit to the extent of centralized decision making that is effective. "The parent corporation is only in the position to set broad policy, to rationalize operations; it cannot substitute its judgment for the plant manager as to events in the field. " (84) "At the same time, the philosophy of decentralising to give foreign profit centres a large measure of autonomy remains strong. It could well be sustained by the greater interest of national governments and the authorities of regional groupings in the activities of multinational corporations. Their efforts to ensure beneficial effects for their respective territories from the operations of international firms are almost certain to result in some shift in the internal balance of power of the latter from central headquarters to national operating units. " (85)

In any event, the last quotation makes it plain that there is a correlation between internal and external control, each one influencing the other.

An analysis of the organizational development of American MNE suggests that the firms moved from an early period of uncontrolled experimentation, which gave considerable autonomy to the subsidiaries, to the subsequent establishment of international divisions which curtailed this autonomy, and then away from the international division to worldwide product or area divisions embracing the entire enterprise. Some have since adopted mixed structures of product and area divisions. In all instances, the particular structure was found to relate to the firms strategy. (86) Studies of non-American multinations have demonstrated that they tend to rely more on informal modification of structure and procedures in their internationalization.

The international division concept is generally the result of an attempt to make a distinction between its domestic and international activities. Separated, the international division becomes a single centralized, semi-autonomous unit with its own profit responsibilities. Both the international and domestic divisions can then be organized along functional, product or regional lines. However, the international division is itself organized, its basic job is to co-ordinate the operations of the various foreign subsidiaries. Its goal is to raise the overall foreign subsidiary performance above the level that would be possible if each subsidiary behaved autonomously. Where there are transfers of goods and services among the foreign subsidiaries, the international division may reduce the overall taxes by coordinating the adjustment of prices. The alternative to the international division is the global approach which ignores national boundaries. Whether that is accomplished along product or functional lines, informal coordinating committees play an important role in the structure. These committees take varied forms and some like Sperry Rands 'umbrella companies' are even legal entities. (87)

Perhaps one of the most advanced forms of MNE structure is that of the transnationals such as Unilever and Royal Dutch/Shell. All of them originated in Europe and differ from the American multinationals in that both their ownership and control are clearly from two different nations. It has been said that they function as "an international coalition rather than as a command hierarchy." (88) Projecting their dual national control structures into enterprises controlled by a larger number of national entities suggests one possible resolution of the international control dilemma.

Internal Control and External Aspirations

Corporate leadership continues its search for more suitable organizational structures to suit their needs and goals. The scope of their pursuit should not be underestimated. As one commentator put it: ".... it is not a surprise that some executives see themselves as engaged in worldwide institution-building, with the multinational firm potentially a new kind of social architecture, particulary suitable for the last decades of the twentieth century. " (89)

Most of the rules regulating MNE are presently established in fragmented ways by nation-states, reflecting not concern for the overall international system or a world system, but for the narrow interests of national subsystems. MNE adapts and responds in ways which are typically classified as ethnocentric, polycentric or geocentric management. "Only in the geocentric category does the idea of a 'world corporation' become vaguely visible. It offers the possibility of designing policies which take the whole world into account - a possibility which is not realistically available to existing political structures, including the United Nations and its agencies. They are geared to the classical process of political bargaining rather than to searching and forming viable policies for the world. International business has been the most successful institution to date in traversing the boundaries of nation - states and even of power blocs. It is now to its interest to be a leader in the develop- ment of world institutions, which will eventually include effective political institutions. The role of business will be crucial in the forthcoming period. " (90)

What Jantsch advocates is that MNE broaden its functions to include a political role; or, putting it another way, that MNE is itself a regulating mechanism which should mold itself to the needs and demands of world society. He suggests that MNE is more likely to find opportunities to participate in regulation of the world than it will find opportunities to develop such a role within a nation - state.

It is questionable whether business, multinational or otherwise, has the capacity for playing such a role. "The mechanism of business, like all authoritarian institutions, is not well suited for coping with basic change outside its product matkets. Business has no strong internal mechanism for criticism of its performance in the community. Unlike an institution like Congress, it has no constituency that votes it in or out on the basis of its success in community life." (91) Business leaders operate in an internal environment which is essentially authoritarian and carefully structured in hierarchial fashion. This is generally perceived as the most efficient way to govern, in spite of some modern managerial trends to the contrary. Cassell goes a step further regarding the enterprise in the domestic environment. "The reluctance of the businessmen to share authority with others in the community represents a deep desire for order, the need to control his situation (as he has been taught in business schools), and the need to assure the continuity of the firm." (92) And he is not alone: "No institution is more undemocratic and more vulnerable to the charge of authoritarianism," says Professor Melville Watkins of the University of Toronto. (93)

The question, both in the domestic and international scene, is whether business enterprise is to adjust to society, or the other way around. The issue on a world scale precedes that on a national scale because on the world scale, the nation-state is itself threatened. Cassell asks old questions about business enter-prise, but they are the correct ones. How can it be justified solely on the basis of profits? What about the welfare of the people and

the good of society? Does not business exist at the pleasure of

the people? And regarding business education, he rightly points

out that we say little about how authoritarian organizations such

as business clash with the underlying notions of democracy. (94)

Whether business enterprise internal control

mechanisms are compatible with a broader role is open to

speculation. Historically, corporations have had broad social

and quasi-governmental aspects. Some see this recurring.

"Indeed, the corporation may be the institution of the future in

much the same way as the city was the institution of the future

at the close of the medieval epoch." (95) "The multinational

corporation is perhaps the best example of an institution operating

within the constraints of the present while, at the same time,

developing the institutional framework of the emerging global

society." (96)

A broader future role may fall to MNE by the simple

default of the nation - state. "As with the reaction of the trade-

union movement, there is little or no sign that national

governments are, in practice, prepared to make the leap to

internationalism that industrial managements have been regarding

as commonplace for one and two decades. It seems for the moment,

as if industrial management is the only organism which has found

the capacity to emerge from the restrictive and increasingly

irrelevant chrysalis of the nation-state." (97)

A better approach is to enquire whether it would be
desirable for MNE to assume some of the powers and responsibilities
of the sovereign state. (98) The 'company town', like those in remote
mining areas, has seldom been a favorable example of business
playing the broader community role. This does not mean that it is
not possible, however. Japanese business enterprises have been
successful in embracing a wider spectrum of their employees' lives.
Enterprises in various parts of the world now provide educational
and medical services for employees and their families. Recreation
facilities and retirement and stock investment plans are similar
illustrations. Contrasting this with the nation-states' movement
in the direction of state enterprise suggests that the roles of
business enterprise and the nation-state may be converging.

For the present, it is clear that business enterprise will
seek every opportunity to optimize the use of men, money, markets
and machines on a world scale with the nation-state generally
acting, on the whole, as a barrier to this optimization process. (99)
Corporations have made some modest attempts at self regulation
or internal control regarding their relationship with nations. One
example is the adoption of vague and broadly worded policy statements of 'Rights and Responsibilities of the International
Corporation.' (100)   However, it remains likely that the enterprise
independent of national or other control will continue to pursue the

maximum worldwide use of its overall resources, exercising
its internal control powers towards that end, to the virtual
exclusion of others. Plainly, the enterprise without external
control has a greater latitude for profiteering.

6.22 NEED FOR EXTERNAL CONTROL BY THE NATION-STATE

"The total program of the firm is managed on the principle
of maximization of investment, productive resources and profits
of the international firm as a whole, a process in which the
subsidiaries in various countries merely play their part in
the total scheme. The role of the particular subsidiary may
have little to do with the long-run fortunes of the subsidiary and the economy in which it is operating; it may be
required to forego opportunities which it would seize if it
were independent of control, and be required to maintain
production and other activities that cease to be in its best
interest as an individual company." (101) Although this is
a one-sided view of MNE, it does evidence that the MNE, as
an independent institutional force, considers its own goals
as primary. Numerous nation-states constitute the environment
in which it operates. Since World War II, the surge of international business pursuits has colored this environment in a
fashion not unlike that of an 'international gold rush'. The
rush has yet to be effectively controlled by the nation-states
and this suits MNE. "Executives of most big companies said
they would rather take their chances in individual countries
than be bound by a multinational code." (102)

Dilemmas for the Nation-State

MNE is taking advantage of this situation as is the nature
of their institution and they are encouraged by some business
scholars to go even farther towards maximization of profits through
various financial manipulations between national MNE units.
"Indeed, from the point of view of maximizing its profit potential,
the distinctive aspect of the multinational enterprise is that it is a
system operating in a multiplicity of economic environments with
varying Tax rates, costs of money and currency values. Yet few
enterprises try to integrate the financial links available to them into
a grand design that embraces all elements of the system. " (103)

Intercorporate pricing 'adjustments' among MNE units is
one method of shifting Income Tax burdens from one nation to
another. An extreme illustration follows: "... when the entire
output of the foreign-owned subsidiary is absorbed by a parent in
the investing country, the price of this output may be set at an
arbitrary figure which prevents the subsidiary operating at a profit.
This practice not only artificially depresses the earnings of the
workers in the subsidiary firm, but it also deprives the host
governments of the normal revenue from corporation Income Taxes.
By way of illustration, a large manufacturer of high-alpha wood-
pulp in British Columbia is a wholly-owned subsidiary of a large
artificial fibre producer in the United States, which purchases the
entire output of its Canadian subsidiary. For years, the price of the

pulp was set at a figure which permitted the Canadian firm to earn no profits, so that no corporate Income Tax was paid to Canada. All corporate Taxes earned by the joint enterprises were paid in the United States. The recurrent losses of the Canadian firm were met by 'transfer by way of gift' from the parent firm to its subsidiary. " (104) Another method has been to use overpricing for wholly-owned affiliates as an alternative to royalty payments. However, there is some evidence that this tactic has been reduced both by governmental pressure and by internal control. (105)

A broader concern faces those nations who are attempting to plan their national economy. They see the MNE as a foreign instrumentality that may frustrate their designs. This is especially true where the foreign enterprise is one of the largest employers and consumers of local labor and materials. "The problem is something like this: how can a national government make an economic plan with any confidence if a board of directors meeting 5,000 miles away can by altering its patterns of purchasing and production affect in a major way the country's economic life. " (106)

There is also the problem of MNE affect upon national enterprises. A French commentator states: "It creates new competition which may weaken French firms or lead to their destruction. Furthermore, the foreign parent company will make decisions in its own interest which will affect French interests .....

it may even decide to dissolve a French subsidiary to continue business through a more profitable subsidiary in a neighboring country. " (107)

The size and internal organizational flexibility of MNE has also premitted it to reduce 'sales' type taxes. This has changed somewhat with the advent of the value added tax. Nevertheless, it illustrates the nation-states' control dilemma when viewed in the context of inter-national transfers. "Another tax advantage of bigness which formerly flourished in Europe was the general turnover tax, which was imposed on every resale of a product from raw material producer to consumer. When the successive stages of manufacture and distribution were performed by separate enterprises, the tax was imposed many times, and became known as a 'cascade tax'. But if the enterprise were integrated from one end to the other, the tax might be paid only once. " (108)

National balance of payments problems is another area where there is a need for greater control over MNE. This is becoming more acute as financial control within MNE becomes more centralized, permitting the inter-subsidiary flow of sums of money that are large in relation to the size of the central reserves of the host country.

The laws of one nation sometimes come into conflict with the laws of another through the linkages of MNE units. This has occurred in the attempts at overseas enforcement of antitrust

laws and trading restrictions. An example which received
considerable publicity follows: "In December, 1961, six Viscount
airlines were sold by a British firm for delivery in China. Part
of the navigational equipment of these machines was manufactured
by Standard Telephones and Cables, a British firm owned and
controlled by International Telephone and Telegraph Company of
New York. Although the equipment had been designed and produced
in a British factory, and not under any United States patent or
license, the United States holding company, under pressure from
the State Department, forbade its British subsidiary to provide any
equipment for any aircraft destined for China." (109) The same
observer made an overall rather uncomplimentary summary:
"The tendency for foreign investment to be followed by political
and military interference in the domestic affairs of the host country
by the government of the investing country, has behind it a long and
dishonorable history." (110)

The Overall Dilemma

"Few countries have been strong enough to use foreign capital freely
without sacrificing both their economic independence and a large
measure of their political independence as well. This is not because
of the 'uncontrolability' of foreign capital. The state has ample
legal power to compel business operations within its borders to
serve the public interest or to cease operating. However, it rarely
has the courage to use this power to regulate foreign-owned

business when that business can call on the military and diplomatic support of a much more powerful government. " (111)

More to the point today is that nations are dependent upon the MNE for new investment, modern technology and marketing channels for their products. "The firm or unit of enterprise is the primary instrument for realizing a country's industrial strategy. " (112) Europeans have expressed dissatisfaction with the dominance of American multinationals, but: "There is ambivalence, however, because on the whole American firms are performing well in Europe, helping to speed modernization and to improve its productivity. Ford of England is the country's largest single exporter and Chrysler-owned Simca of France exports more cars to the rest of Europe than Renault, Peugeot and Citroen combined. " (113)

"Now the stakes seem to have gone up. In order to reap the gains from international exchange, a country has to become integrated into a corporate international structure of centralized planning and control, in which it plays a dependent role. " (114)

Essentially, individual states are competing for the resources and capabilities of multinational firms. (115) and MN firms have the commercial flexibility to trade one nation off against another. (116) The consequence of this is a ... "reduction in the ability of the government to control the economy. Multinational corporations, because of their size and international connections, have a certain flexibility in escaping regulations imposed in one country. The nature and effectiveness of traditional policy instruments - monetary policy, fiscal policy, antitrust policy, taxation policy, wage and income policy - change when important segments of the economy are foreign-owned. " (117)   Those nations that try going it alone are forced to shield domestic enterprise from foreign competition. Much evidence suggests that such strategies have resulted in increasingly archaic technologies and managerial methods. (118) There are exceptions, Japan is the most striking.

The main thrust of the nationalistic movement today is to protect the national environment for soccoeconomic reasons - to maintain employment social well-being. (119) It is widely accepted within the national framework that this is being done in close association and co-operation with large-scale enterprises. (120) What is happening, but not yet completely accepted, is the widening of this co-operative process to include foreign enterprises.

A genuinely co-operative process cannot evolve unless the parties have equal bargaining power. "Analyses of the role of foreign investment in underdeveloped countries often focus on the great disparity between the bargaining power of the government. The corporations are large and modern and have international horizons. The governments are, typically, administratively weak and have very limitied information outside their narrow confines.

In any particular negotiation between one country and one
company, power in the form of flexibility, knowledge and
liquidity is usually greater on the private rather than on the
public side of the table. " (121) Adding to this is the typical
host country shortage of competent government administrators
capable of bargaining effectively. (122)

The overwhelming power of the modern corporation has
been compared to the concentration of religous power in the
medieval church and even to the political power of nation-states.
(123) The prediction has even been made that: "... it is not at all
unlikely that a large portion of the world's economic activity will
be systematically organized by a relatively few huge economic
units able to mobilize people, technology, capital and management
far more efficiently than has ever been done before. " (124) Its
tremendous capacity to increase trade and economic growth means
that a nation   will exclude MNE at its own peril. (125)
"The growth of the multinational business and of attendant
multinational finance is unquestionably one of the most significant
structural changes in modern economic history. Before its
concentrated power, the ability of the nation state to control-its
own economic system is being put into question. Already the
nation-state, while it continues to reign, seems to have been
deprived of its power to govern. It is steadily being sapped of its
power over its economy, for example, in its helplessness to

contain inflation. The odds against its not succumbing in a slow
but steady retreat are very long indeed. In terms of either their
accumulated assets or annual production, the multinational
companies are shaping up as formidable rivals to nation-states, ...
On the basis of output, among the top one hundred countries and
enterprises with a volume exceeding $2 billion annually, fifty-four
are business enterprises and only forty-six are countries....
Given that multinational investment is moving at a faster rate than
economic growth (about two to three times) the relative weight of
enterprises to states will expand in favor of the enterprise. " (126)

    If MNE gains the upper hand in this matter, then it will
be up to them to assume some of the 'welfare' responsibilities
formerly deemed to be the province of the nation-state. This is
not presently viewed as satisfactory. "The multinational
corporation cannot, of their nature, set themselves up as
guardians of social welfare, security, or environment, for their
whole justification rests on profitability and change, which
depends on rejecting those areas and businesses which cannot be
profitable. If uncontrolled, they can undermine the basis of
welfare and security, through evading taxes, stimulating inflation,
or speculating in currency. " (127)

The Need for Control

Recent interviews with some five hundred French and British leaders
indicates that the toughest problem in the interaction of nationalism

and the multinational firm is in the area of control over global business
and national affairs. (128) As put by another report, the problem is
one of control - the capacity of a nation-state to shape its own means
and ends. (129) The resolution seems to be to give nations themselves
sufficient regulatory capabilities, so that they can control their
economic development. As opposed to the alternative of supranational
institutions, most nations would prefer to exert direct controls or
coordinated intergovernmental controls. (130)

6.23 REGULATORY CONTROL BY NATION-STATES

The interesting aspect of this is that nations seem to be more
concerned with 'controlling' the limited number of 'foreign' enterprises
within their borders than with controlling domestic enterprise.
Nations that are clammering loudest about the 'multinational' threat
have often done the least about controlling pre-existing enterprises.
In this sense, MNE has served a good purpose - the awakening of the
nation-states to their historic responsibility to ensure a proper
environment, economic and otherwise, for their societies. Before
plunging into the MNE issue, it is important to ask whether nation-
states have ever really 'controlled' domestic industry. It is the
nation-states liberal policy towards private capital movements and
mergers that resulted in the MNE. (131)

When industrial practices and institutions arise which are
clearly against the national interest, whatever nationality of
institution is involved, the governments should take corrective

action. In doing this, however, it must be recognized that influencing the behavior of foreign-owned firms or segments of MNE requires policies that differ from those required for purely national firms. (132)

The underlying difficulty for the nation-state is that excessive regulation may discourage needed foreign investment. That is the cost of 'control' "The gain would be whatever advantage the country saw from imposing the control over the investments that did remain there, or did come and the business activities which remained there. They will now be in the country on better terms, in terms of the country's objective function. The country has gained something and on the other hand it has lost something. As these countries are rational, ... they will raise their controls to the point where the gains from the controls are no longer any greater than the cost." (133)

Canada and the United States

Canada is probably the nation with the highest percentage of foreign-owned enterprises within its industries. Its national government has extensive experience with the process of weighing the benefits of control or exclusion against the loss of foreign investment and technology. The Canadian response has favored the reception of MNE, perhaps in the extreme. According to the Watkins Report, Canada has opted for the economic advantages, against expressions of sovereign independence; for rationalization and against nationalization. Although it has been accused of becoming an American satellite (United States investment is the heaviest), there are many indications to the contrary. Vigorous Canadian dissent over Viet Nam, troop withdrawal from NATO and Red China trade are some examples. In overall effect, however, the Canadian Government has contented itself with a natural evolution of the global enterprise. (134)

Many Canadians are not satisfied with this approach. "The main thrust of Canadian policy in my view should center on regulation of the multinational corporation. The objectives of such a regulatory policy, ... extend beyond the traditional and limited aim of regulatory agencies, namely to control the financial abuse of monopoly powers when an industry is not subject to the discipline of competition. The aim should be instead to restore national control over a much wider range of functions, from research and development policy through to assuring the presence of Canadian personnel at the operating and management levels. The objective of this regulation should be to restore the Canadian priorities on a broad front. The primary emphasis, then, is not on titles to property, but on putting an increasing number of functions of ownership under national control." (135)

More to the point is the comment of an American observer: "The Canadian 'presence' in the management of subsidiaries of foreign corporations in Canada, whether through management or directors, is not likely in the long run to prevail in favor of Canadian national objectives over the requirements of efficiency. If Canada wants such objectives, it must achieve them through positive direction of corporations by government. " (136) What Kindleberger is re-emphasizing is the inherent tendency of the enterprise to pursue its own objectives and the necessity of the nation to set and pursue overriding goals.

Nevertheless, beginning in 1964, Canadian federally incorporated insurance and trust companies were required to limit the portion of total shares which might be held by all non-residents to 25%. At the same time, the proportion held by any one non-resident owner was limited to 10%. A year later, the same regulations were brought to the banking industry. It was felt that financial institutions, because of their potential as bases for influence and control, held a critical position in the direction of the economy. Canadian ownership and control was believed to facilitate the implementation of Canadian economic policies.

The guidelines approach has also been attempted to induce desired behavior on the part of MNE subsidiaries. The Guidelines of Good Corporate Citizenship, issued by the Minister of Trade and Commerce in 1966, represented a blend of ownership and control regulation with regulation of behavior. (137)

Perhaps the most progressive approach yet is the Canadian-American Automobile Agreement of 1965. Although limited to one industry and two nations, its basic approach could be adopted on a wider scale. This agreement was a negotiated compromise among the nations and the private automobile manufacturers. It dealt with problems of production expansion, trade and monetary issues, employment, tariffs and overall integration and rationalization of the North American automobile industry. (138).

Since the United States is the dominant country in the nation-state system, as well as the home of most of the multinationals, attention is focused on it. However, to date, nearly all foreign investment within the United States has taken the form of portfolio investment. With respect to MNE, it functions as an 'investing' country and has not had to face the problems of host countries. As an 'investing' nation, it has employed regulations on United States direct foreign investment as part of its balance of payments policy. The irony of those regulations is that in the long term overseas investment by United States multinationals has proved to have a favorable impact on the United States balance of payments. Recent United States Congressional hearings have also thrown light on the overall impact of American multinations on the United States domestic economy. Whereas labor interests contended that those enterprises had an adverse affect upon employment, factual evidence demonstrated the contrary. The hearings clearly demonstrated the importance of the need to accumulate facts and to analyse them before embarking on regulatory programs.

There has not been an overall policy towards the American multinational, but rather a series of separate regulations dealing with specific problems, most of them pertaining to the overseas activities of the enterprises. (139) The United States Government has devised a number of specific policies to deal with particular multinational firm problems as they arise, but there has been no comprehensive approach to the subject. 'Ad hockey' has been the rule. There have been, for example, guarantees of their investments, measures to discourage foreign government from expropriating them, application of United States antitrust laws to their activities abroad, prohibition on trading with selected foreign countries, revised tax laws applicable to their earnings, and orders that they deploy their financial resources to accord with the United States balance of payments objectives. (140)

One major significance of such regulations is that they often come into conflict with host country regulations. Overlapping and conflicting regulations among host and investing countries constitutes one of the chief obstacles to effective national regulatory schemes.

There is another broad area of United States regulatory process that may be instructive. Since United States multinationals have enjoyed some success in world competition, the regulatory environment in which they first thrived may be some clue to the approach other nations might take in accelerating the growth of their own multinationals. The same is true for the British, German, Dutch, Japanese and other environments which are the homes of numerous multinationals. And, insofar as control of the MN enterprise itself is concerned, it is instructive to review the control devices employed in connection with giant state enterprises. (141)

Europe and Elsewhere

Regulation of foreign-owned investment has generally taken the simple form of complete exclusion, exclusion of select industries, screening of individual proposals, or exclusion unless jointly owned with local nationals.

A complimentary approach has been the requirement for a minimum number of local nationals in the governing or managerial structure. (142) Professor Schmitthoff, who is against such regulations, gives a concise summary of that. "Provisions requiring that some or all directors or shareholders shall be British residents or nationals are unknown in British law, ... The liberal attitude of British company law is shared by the company laws of the Republic of Ireland, France, Belgium, the Netherlands, West Germany, Austria and Israel. Other company laws have attempted to meet the danger of foreign domination by discriminatory provisions. Thus in Spain, apart from exceptional cases, three-fourths of the capital and in Mexico and the Arab Republic as a rule fifty-one per cent at least of the share capital, must be owned by nationals. In Sweden and Finland the articles must require that at least four-fifths of the capital are owned by nationals and cannot be transferred to aliens; .... In some countries, the directors and managers must be local nationals or residents. Thus in Sweden, Norway Denmark, Finland and Switzerland, all or the majority of the directors must satisfy this requirement, but in some cases the Government may dispense with it. These protective provisions have not always achieved the intended result, as they can be evaded by hommes de paille,

unless the legislation contains stringent provisions against such

evasion. Regrettably, the proposed statute of the European company

contains a discriminatory provision relating to the board of

management. " (143)

The Inevitable Retreat to Supranational Institutions

One of the reasons MNE has been the target of nationalistic

attack is the criticism that they have taken more out of the local

economies than they put in. (144) This criticism itself suggests that

the nation-state is a helpless observer. On the other hand, however:

"There is no doubt that governments have an ability to opt out of a

situation resulting from the existence of affiliates of multinational

enterprises; they can destroy, alter or control any affiliate within

their borders. During World War II, both the Allies and the Axis

powers took over foreign-owned entities for their own use. There

was no conceivable challenge to the sovereignty of these governments

from affiliates of foreign-owned companies. Ultimate powers resided

in the governments. This power continues to reside there today. "

(145)

This apparent anomaly is explainable. Any nation-state

can absolutely exclude foreign enterprise and nationalize existing ones.

But few nations can afford to exercise their sovereign powers in such a

manner. Enterprises which are nationalized are then separated from

the remainder of their parent enterprise system and hence are without the focal point of their capacity. And all future foreign investment will cease or decelerate.

It is true that some proposed MNE subsidiary operations might not be advantageous to a particular national economy and may be excluded under a nations investment screening process. But this only points up the obvious - no nation now controls MNE at all. The national controls that exist merely regulate incoming investment. No nation can alone control MNE because the bulk of its operations are always located elsewhere. This is why, speaking generally, nation-states appear to be helpless observers. They cannot do without MNE altogether and those they have are difficult to control because of the local subsidiaries myriad connections with the remainder of its MNE system.

One solution suggests that ".... big business and big government are going to have to work much more closely together in a spirit of partnership - rather than, as generally in the past, with 'adversary' points of view - if we are indeed to get the economic growth and stability we are looking for."(146) This sounds good and may be working on the national level, but the international scene is altogether different. It is possible, however, that certain combinations of nations and their multinationals may ultimately form coalitions competing against similar groups. Likely or not, it does not pose an ideal solution.

The challenge to the nation-state is not that of asserting sovereignty for its own sake, but rather, like business enterprise, to delineate and pursue its goals. (147) When its control problems exceed its national capacity, then it must associate its power with that of

other nations. The bilateral cooperation between home and host

countries such as in the Canadian-American Automobile Agreement

is one example. The multilateral approach is ideally suited for

problems of balance of payments, export controls, antitrust, taxation

avoidance and financial disclosure. If the multilateral strategy is not

successful, then additional supranational institutions like GATT and

IMF must be created. "The main problem, ... is as follows: if

national power is eroded, who is to perform the governments' functions?

For example, if nation-states, because of their openness of economy,

cannot control the level of aggregate economic activity through traditional

monetary and fiscal policy instruments, multinational agencies will need

to be developed to maintain full employment and price stability. " (148)

For the present, the difficulty is that internation business

integration, led by MNE, is proceeding at a much faster rate than

political cooperation and integration. (149)

The other dilemma is that: "The multinational firm is useful

to society precisely because of its capacity to make effective use of

economic resources and differentials on a globally managed basis. If

we distort the economics with assorted nation-oriented artificial conditions,

we weaken its contribution. " (150) The goal is to make MNE both

efficient and equitable.

If nations discriminate against enterprises on the basis of

nationality of ownership or control, this goal will not be met. If a

conflicting patchwork of national controls develop, the goal will likewise

be lost. If nations cannot do it on a rational, cooperative basis, it
will either not be done, or be accomplished by regional or
international institutions.

6.24 REGIONAL AND INTERNATIONAL CONTROL

By and large each nation has developed its own separate
nationalistic position regarding MNE, each attempting to maximize
its own growth and to establish a good bargaining position for the
future. Their efforts have been addressed to individual subsidiaries
and not to the MNE entity as a whole.

The internationalization of production and the splintered
reaction by nation-states has "... brought with it many new problems
along the national-corporate interface. The lack of a consistent set
of rules regulating the relationship between national governments and
corporations, particularly in areas such as antitrust regulations,
ownership rights, capital repatriation, labor relations, tax laws and
the issueance of securities has been costly, particularly for poor
countries, because of apprehension and mistrust. No two nations have
identical rules governing all aspects of a multinational corporation's
activities. This results in overlapping, conflicting and inconsistent
regulations in some instances and in others no regulation at all......
The net effect has been to inhibit the flow of capital and perhaps more
important, technology from rich to the poor countries." (151)

Disparity in economic regulation is not surprising, considering
the differences in basic cultural values and attitudes. Compare Asia and

the East to Western civilization: "For them, achievement is not a dominant theme for life on earth and work is not a value in itself. While Christian man, expelled from Paradise and condemned to work, has made work his new Paradise, Asian values have favored learning and contemplation as man's Paradise on earth." (152)

As individual nations attempt varying regulatory controls, multinational enterprises respond with a mixture of evasionary tactics. Individual national regulations become more extreme, thus discouraging further investment and MNE evasionary tactics further disrupt its activities and efficiency. It has been predicted that, at some point, managers of MNE would begin to find that their interests lie in cooperating with governments in the development of policies for uniform regulation. (153)

"Ideally a procedure should be agreed between each government and the international companies with which it is concerned whereby the two sides maintain contact with each other and the government can check on the individual company's activities. .... The procedure should take the form of an annual review of each company's activities. The company would explain to officials from the relevant ministry the outline of its plans and show how its local subsidiary would fit into them. There would be an emphasis on investment in new plant and machinery, the proposed sources of raw materials and components for the various factories, the allocation of export markets and the proposed financial movements into and out of the subsidiary. The procedure would be informal. The officials would respond to the company's presentation with an account of their government's hopes and plans and make counter-suggestions

to the company's proposals if they felt that their national interest

was not being sufficiently taken into account. .... Each side would

simply be keeping the other in touch with its plans for and views of

the future. ... The review would have to be conducted in complete

confidence to be of any value, ... " (154) Another who sees

cooperative, teamwork possibilities says: "A pattern of organized

development effort is emerging slowly and is likely to become clearer

over the next decade or two. It will result in the gradual

rationalization of government and private activities, with the slow

disappearance of distinct operating units, and the growth of a mixture

of the two .... (155) Hyman suggests the coming into being of a

World Market Research Service, a World Personnel Service and

similar organizations.

In spite of these predictions and suggestions, the atmosphere

both among nations and on the part of MNE is not especially cooperative

at present.

One of the approaches, therefore, has been to establish

institutional machinery to resolve nation-state/MNE conflicts. "The

need for established international arbitration procedures to solve

disputes between national governments and multinational corporations

is evidenced by the fact that two efforts have already been made. One

was an effort by the World Bank to establish an International Center

for the Settlement of Investment Disputes. The second was the Court

of Arbitration, organized by the International Chamber of Commerce. "

(156) If such tribunals are used they could provide the experience to

evolve a set of rules or guidelines similar to those that have evolved between labor and management out of labor arbitration. This is a slow process and is yet to show even a strong beginning.

Another tack is for nation-states to control the size and power of MNE through the traditional antitrust mechanism. The same theory that justified systems of national antitrust can be extended to justify international antitrust. (157) A number of commentators make a useful analogy when they compare the position of the multinations with that of the Catholic Church in medieval times. Kings and emperors of the period were threatened by the church's international organization and power and finally took steps to divide and conquer it.

Since the conflicts that arise from the operations of MNE are international in character, control devices limited to one nation are simply not effective. Consequently nations are undertaking more cooperative actions in the direction of harmonizing MNE policies. To understand how such actions might evolve, one can look to the international cooperative developments in the field of communication, transportation and pastal services. The MNE is not an entirely unique problem and nation-states can profit by their experience in these other fields.

One suggestion is that there be one master cooperative agreement that might be called a General Agreement on the International Corporation, analagous to the General Agreement on Tariffs and Trade. (158)

Regional Schemes

At the regional level, the most progressive measures are
those that have been adopted by the Andean Group in South America.
Those countries have adopted a set of procedures and guidelines
with respect to foreign investment and the transfer of technology.
Existing investors are required to sell majority holdings to local
investors and new investors from outside the region must take
minority positions, within fifteen to twenty years, in order to be
eligible for Andean Pact trade concessions. The nations have agreed
upon those sectors which are closed to foreign investment and have
devised a disinvestment schedule to reduce existing foreign ownership
in those sectors to 20%. (159) By increasing the size of the bargaining
unit from national to regional, the six member countries can now
impose rules upon, and command concessions from, Multinational
enterprises that could not have been realized by any one of the member
countries acting alone. Further, by expanding the size of the market
to which a foreign investor can gain access, thereby increasing the
profit potential, the member countries have provided an added
inducement for potential investors to conform to the rules of the
region.

Professor Behrman's outlook which he calls the 'sectoral
approach' is worth reviewing. (160) He says that what is needed, as
between nations, is greater sharing in the process of production as
well as in the consumption of goods produced and, that this interweaving
of the demand and production capabilities of nations be accomplished by
focusing sector by sector on the needs and objectives of nations in both
industry and agriculture.

Part of the problem, he claims, is that many countries have
not formulated sophisticated, national industrial policies. We need
more 'buying' countries insisting that foreign 'selling' companies sub-
contract certain production aspects to companies within the buying
country. For example, if Boeing wished to sell 747's to Belgium, a
condition of purchase might be that it sub-contract the manufacturer
of aelerons to the Belgian company, SABCA; or a sale to KLM might
be facilitated if the Dutch company, Fokker, were to build the tail
assembly. Behrmann concedes that this approach violates the
principles of free trade and reduces overall productivity, but,
within bounds, he asserts that it produces greater equity. All out
efficiency should not be the sole criteria in these matters.
Utilization of existing labor supply and social welfare should share
priority with efficiency. He suggests the formation of an Organization
for International Industrial Integration and predicts that government
decisions on industrial policies, rather than the trade and investment
decisions of private companies, will increasingly determine the use
of industrial resources.

A recent significant development is the attempt by host
countries to gain participation in or control of multinationals in their
territories. Where such countries get together to form unified groups
as in the case of the Organization of Petroleum Exporting Countries
they have negotiated a scheduled increase in participation towards the
end of a complete fadeout of foreign control and ownership. In some
instances, participation in the ownership of the parent oil companies
has also been negotiated.

Obsolescence of the Nation-State and the Rise of MNE

To get some idea of what regulatory or control devices and
institutions are likely to arise, it is useful to review the perceptions
that are held regarding the future evolution of these institutions.

The fundamental development is that growing participation
in a worldwide web of business interests and other activities is
raising a doubt about the usefulness of continued national loyalties.
Barbara Ward has stated it better than anyone else: ".... we have
become a 'single human community', yet the structure of our world
political system erects barriers which are not only disfunctional in
a systematic sense, but also preclude the encouragement of new forms
of behavior which are to be an inherent quality of the global society."
(161)

"The nation-state has a necessarily narrower, often more provincial
mission than a world institution like the multinational firm." (162)
The insular requirement of particular citizenship to hold a job is
imposed by governments, not business. (163) In a few years, many
multinationals will have true multi-national management at the top
such as Shell, Texaco, Olivetti, IBM and others do now. "National
identities, which seem to become accentuated in such forms as the
United Nations, tend to disappear in the multinational company. In
that sense, multinational business has already started to build an
effective community." (164)

Trudeau's overview is that the history of civilization is the

chronicle of the subordination of tribal nationalism to wider interests.
(165) The role of MNE in this evolution is nicely put by Matthews:
"It is perhaps not too fanciful to imagine a future world in which the
nation-state system will be transcended, for many purposes, by a
totally new organization of affairs where countervailing powers are
exercised by great international corporations and international labor
unions with the public interest being assured through controls
maintained by some sort of international regulatory agency." (166)
"As countries become more integrated economically and more
interdependent ecologically and socially, the list of problems which
cannot be solved at the national level lengthens. ... In a competitive
international economy it may be almost impossible to control some
forms of pollution without establishing standards or, at least, guidelines at the global level. Those firms adopting costly pollution -
control measures in one country may find themselves unable to
compete in world markets with firms domiciled in countries with less
stringent requirements." (167)

Professor Eells concurs: "... the public international
organizations - notably in the common markets - have moved appreciably
toward supranational status with consequent undermining of claims to
absolute sovereignty on the part of member states. All of these
developments may foreshadow the dominance of functionalism over
traditional legalism in the structure of the world arena. ... This trend,
heightened during the past half-century, is a response to many regional

and worldwide needs that the conventional international system of sovereign states could not meet effectively."(168)

Events in the field of global communication tell the same story. "Where the concept of sovereignty was initially applied with complete and exclusive validity resulting in a bilateral regime of services (airspace) it gradually tended to yield to the inherent nature of these services which could not be organized on a global scale through bilateral channels only. Bartering in relation to services is as futile as it is in respect of world trade, and even the most sovereign-minded governments are ultimately driven into multinationalism if they wish to respond to the social reality of world interdependence." (169)

George W. Ball recognizes it is a typical historical pattern - commerce moving in advance of politics and recommends: "One obvious solution is to modernize our political structures - to evolve units larger than nation-states and better suited to the present day." (170)

"According to Max Mark, 'the central fact of contemporary international politics is the obsolescence of the nation-state'. Most of the societies that we label today as nation-states cannot meet the most fundamental obligation of the nation-state - namely, providing a defence shield for its citizens." (171)

"The political institutions and government structures of our countries, whether they be communist and totalitarian, authoritarian or democratic, stem from the era of the steam engine. It is as clear as daylight that in such circumstances they are not fitted to cope with the problems of the atomic age." (172)

Another statement against national control: "The free play of economic forces will, apart from a few exceptional cases, make the economic welfare of the whole world greater in the long run than any alternate arrangement of resources. " (173)

In connecting with the forthcoming ocean society: "It is evident that an extension of the nation-state system to the realm of the ocean seas would lead to a division of marine resources that would be less than equitable ... " (174)

International or Supranational Control

It has been proposed that a MNE information centre be established at the United Nations to gather, analyze and disseminate information on such things as inter-affiliate flows of goods and services and their pricing, national regulatory measures, ownership a nd other methods of effective control, etc. (175) Such an organization would eliminate the duplication of national efforts, make data available to nations who could not otherwise afford to collect it, and create a repository of data which would result in more uniform practices and minimum standards.

A further suggestion is that a limited number of multi-nationals, presumably the largest, be registered with a United Nations agency to be called the Centre for Multinational Corporations and that they be accountable to that body. (176) Recent proposals for the creation of an international authority for the regulation or exploration of resources of the sea-bed beyond the limits of national jurisdiction indicate further possibilities for the creation of supranational machinery.

Professor Vernon's thinking is similar. "The basic
asymmetry between multinational enterprises and national governments
may be tolerable up to a point, but beyond that point there is a need to
re-establish a balance. When this occurs, the response is bound to
have some of the elements of the world corporation concept:
accountability to some body, charged with weighing the activities of
the multinational enterprise against a set of social yardsticks that are
multinational in scope. If this does not happen, some of the apocalyptic
projections of the future of multinational enterprises will grow more
plausible." (177)

The broad criteria for MNE controls have said to include the
key points "that we should restructure, in a global control system, the
control goals of the national leadership groups- and that the control
system should be directed at the center of the control system of the
multinational firm, rather than trying to dismember or maim that
system by hacking at its arms on the local level." (178)

Professor Burchill is the author of one of the most elaborate
proposals "(a) All corporations incorporated under a national
government should be required to keep at least ninety per cent of their
assets, both tangible and intangible, within the boundaries of the
incorporating nation. (b) Corporations not qualifying for national
incorporation under this rule would become multi-national corporations,
and would hold less than ninety per cent of their assets in any one
country. They would have no national status and would forfeit any claim

on any national government for protection of property and personnel

located outside the jurisdiction of that government. They would be

subject in any country to the same taxes and regulations imposed by

the national government on national corporations and to no additional

obligations. (c) Multinational corporations would be incorporated under

the United Nations and would have the legal status of world citizens.

They would be entitled to raise capital in any country permitting the

export of capital and to invest in any country whose laws permitted the

import of capital. In each country, they would be required to conduct

their business in accordance with the laws of that country, and in

international transactions would be required as well to conform to a

code of conduct established by mutual agreement, under the authority

and the jurisdiction of the United Nations. They would also be required

to pay to the United Nations certain taxes on their international trans-

actions, in addition to the taxes paid to national governments on

business done within national boundaries. (d) International carriers -

shipping companies and airlines, as well as telegraph, telephone and

satelite communication systems - would necessarily become multi-

national corporations. But communications and transportation within a

nation, as well as its coasting trade, would continue to be under national

jurisdiction. Ideally, also, inter-oceanic canals and the management

and use of international rivers, should similarly be placed under

international control .... If the valuable flow of capital from areas

where it is plentiful to areas where it is scarce is to continue, a new vehicle must be developed. The world corporation, operating under world law, and for the advantage of the world's peoples rather than for the advantage of a small class in a few states, may be the vehicle that is needed. " (179)

Arnold Toynbee and Orville Freeman also recommend the establishment of an international corporate chartering system. "There remains the problem that few multinational corporations are truly multinational; most identify with the nation-state in which they are domiciled. ... The exclusive authority to grant charters to all corporations wishing to operate across national borders should be granted to a neutral authority, perhaps one situated on a small island. This would have the effect of divorcing or, at least, greatly weakening ties between nation-states and corporations, reducing the extent to which one could use the other to help further its basic political or economic objectives. " (180) Professor Eells also suggests that such an authority be established on an island, such as Malta, or on a technological island in mid-ocean created expressly for the purpose. (181)

George Ball's idea is that: ".... world corporations should become quite literally citizens of the world. What this implies is the establishment by treaty of an international companies law, administered by a supranational body, including representatives drawn from various countries, who would not only exercise normal domiciliary supervision but would also enforce antimonopoly laws and administrative guarantees with regard to uncompensated expropriation. An international companies law could place limitations, for example, on the restrictions nation-

states might be permitted to impose on companies established under

its sanction. The operative standard defining these limitations might

be the quantity of freedom needed to preserve the central principle of

assuring the most economical and efficient use of world resources.

.... The international company's operations in its home country would

be subject to local laws, to the extent that they do not infringe the over-

riding regulations of the organic treaty. .... Yet the international

companies act, as I see it, has intrinsic merits. It offers the best

means I can think of to preserve the great potential of the world

corporation for all society. ...... Nor is this suggestion far beyond

present contemplation. It is merely an adaption in a larger arena

of what is likely to be created within the next few years in Europe:

a common companies law for the European Economic Community

together with a body of regulations to be administered by the EEC. "(182)

The Pesimistic Side

Professor Vagts has reviewed these ideas but is pesimistic

about the prospect for their realization. "The concept of international

incorporation has been put forth, but in such terms as to make it rather

purely facilitative, that is, a convenience for the MNE that would assure

it entry into countries without corresponding submission on its part to

more effective regulation. ...... A regulatory model has been suggested

in several variations implying different intensities of control. The

likelihood of adoption of such a proposal seems remote. The EEC has found it hard to unite six rather similar countries with many interests

in common upon a single policy vis a vis investments from outside.

The Andean countries have gone so far as to agree upon a common

code for testing foreign investment, but they have left implementation

to the individual governments. To bring both less-developed and

developed countries - some capital exporters, some capital importers

and some both - into one functioning agency would be an enormous

political feat. The result might be a rather horrifying, over-developed

bureaucracy. .....

At a less ambitious stage writers have conceived of a GATT-

type arrangement, one in which countries acknowledged certain basic

principles and agreed to consult and bargain as to any departure there-

from. GATT in dealing with trade as it has done with fair success -

handles a set of topics as to which there is a fair amount of reciprocity -

all countries both export and import goods. In the capital area the

interests of nations tend to be more sharply divided. Nor has the

tradition in favor of a general freedom of trade flows been paralleled

by as general a consensus on liberality as to capital flows. Paralleling

GATT's non-tariff provisions would require the evolution of a

moderately specific code of behavior towards foreign investors and,

capital-importing countries would insist, a matching code of behavior

on the part of those investors. Surveying the scene, one simply does

not see a consensus of those dimensions. " (183)

Vagts is not alone in his lack of optimism. "For governments

to create an institutional structure capable of making decisions concerning

.the location, ownership and control of international production, so as

to solve the central problem of equitable participation would require

an uncharacteristic farsightedness and unusual co-operation. " (184)

Louis Turner thinks the same. "The more visionary commen-

tators have sometimes gone one step further, suggesting that as

multinationals spread round the world, their ownership and control

should pass to the United Nations, itself. .... For a body made up

of so many different idealogies suddenly to accept control of the

multinationals would involve a completely new thinking from many

delegations. If anything like this does happen, the moves toward it

will be gradual. It could happen like this. A UN-sponsored conference

on multinationals should be possible by the end of the 1970's. Precedents

suggest that it takes between 10 and 20 years for an issue to move from

the stage when national governments perceive a problem, to the stage

where global action is necessary. " (185)

"Essentially, this search for a supranational companies law is an

attempt to place the cosmocorp, whether it be the multi-flag, multi-

branch, multinational or international variety, beyond the reach of

politics - to make it apolitical. This is an impossible dream. Corporate

planners may know how to do things better. There is no doubt that they

can apply greater resources - capital, technology and management

skills - to given operations. But they cannot decide for a people how

their nation's resources should be allocated. " (186)

"A supranational status that would protect the cosmocorp from perfectly

normal political pressures, resulting in a distorted allocation of resources away from a nation's own priorities, would not survive very

long, at least where politics and political expression exist. " (187)

6.25   CORPORATE CONTROL AND THE LAW

It has been recognized for some time that 'control' has been

separated from 'ownership'. First the separation was confined to

national boundaries. Now we have a situation where dependent foreign

subsidiaries, even if majority-owned locally, are controlled by parent

companies in other countries. The implications of this expanding

separation of 'control' from ownership, and international absentee

ownership and control, are yet to be recognized and acted upon by the

law.

The observations of Berle and Means went to the heart of the

matter. "The law holds the management to certain standards of

conduct. This is the legal link between ownership and management.

As separation of ownership from management becomes factually greater,

or is more thoroughly accomplished by legal devices, it becomes

increasingly the only reason why expectations that corporate securities

are worth having, can be enforced by the shareholders. ....

With this problem the law has only just begun to cope; it is

still incomplete; and it has to be considered rather as a framework

to be filled in than as a set of settled rules. .....

Economically, the problem is likely to change in form as

corporations gradually increase in size and as stock distribution

increases, to the point where the 'control' is virtually in the hands of

self-perpetuating Board of Directors like that of United States Steel
or American Telephone & Telegraph Company. But with this class
of control the public up to now has little quarrel; nor does it usually
thrash out such problems in the courts. It is conceivable, therefore,
that the problems of 'control' here discussed may become academic
within another generation. It is more likely that the law will deal,
blunderingly, with each situation as it comes up on its individual
merits; and most likely of all, the transactions by the 'control',
lying outside the technical sphere of corporation action, will remain
outside the normal cognizance of the law. " (188)

Berle and Means recognized the large corporation as the
dominant institution of the modern world. When the state emerged
victorious over the church, nationalistic politics superseded religion
as the basic world force. Economic power still remained diffused.
The situation has steadily changed. Multination enterprises have
created a concentration of economic power which can compete on
equal terms with the state. The role of the law has become more
critical.

Purely on the national level control is a complex matter,
especially as more enterprises become systems of linked companies.
"Even more dangerous is if subsidiaries acquire shares in the parent
company, and financial transactions take place between members of
a group. The whole structure may become so involved and complex
that no shareholders, if not on intimate terms with the directors, will
be able to form a clear view of the position. ......

Before general corporation laws were passed, corporations were generally held to be under the control of the government which granted them their charter. This supervision was exercised chiefly in order to ascertain whether the conditions laid down in the charter were complied with. ..... Generally, however, companies manage their affairs without governmental interference or supervision, and it was up to the shareholders to exercise their rights within the limits of the law. " (189) Although it is clear that shareholders cannot, for practical reasons, exercise effective control, the corporate law has not been modernized to correct the situation. The larger and more 'international' the enterprise the more helpless the existing legal machinery becomes.

Hadden's review of this state of affairs is one of the most progressive and comprehensive. ".... there can be no doubt that the large modern company has developed a separate institutional existence independent of its precise legal form. ..... The account of the growth of managerial power and the effective replacement of shareholder control through the general meeting by newer pressures from organized labour and the government raises important questions on the adequacy of the traditional legal framework for the large modern corporation. ......

This process of expansion may readily be contained within the original corporate structure of the business, and the needs for managerial and financial control of the various aspects of the business may be met by the creation of informal divisions or accounting units within it.   But it is often a good deal easier to create a new company

for each of the various activities undertaken, since this provides a

ready-made formal structure for accounting and control. . . . . . But

whatever the pattern of development, the fact that shares in a company

are as likely to be held by another company as by an individual raises

important issues in all areas of company law and practice. . . . . . .

Where one company is a major or controlling shareholder of

another or where the statutorily defined relationship of holding company

and subsidiary companies applies, wider problems of accounting and

responsibility arise, problems of which increase in complexity as the

relationship of simple holding and subsidiary companies expands into

more complex group inter-relationships between larger numbers of

companies. The precise financial position of any one company in the

group in terms of solvency and profitability can no longer be ascertained

from its individual accounts   a fact which in itself opens the way to the

entrenchment of control over the group, to the concealment of improper

transactions, and to the potential oppression of minority holdings in

individual subsidiaries. . . . . . The question for the company lawyer in such

cases   is   whether the interests of the consumer and the community

may safely be left to the management of the companies concerned or

whether some additional formal control or supervision is necessary.

Further problems are created by the development of multinational

companies whose operations are so extensive as to make any attempt

at control by a single national government largely ineffective, since

the company will often be in a position to switch its production and investment, and the employment and wealth which it creates, to other areas. " (190)

The perspective of Wolfgang Friedmann is much the same. "The fundamental issue is the relationship between the public interest and the economy when the scale of the economy dwarfs the representation of the public interest and the complexity of economic structure escapes the control of any government or legal system. This is an issue on the same order of importance for the future of international law as the control of force, the peaceful settlement of international disputes, ...

It poses in an acute form the international analog of the question of the place of the state in the complex modern community, a question the difficulty of which in political philosophy and constitutional law becomes still more difficult when transposed to the world scene and scale.....

The essence of the multinational corporation is that it has no coherent existence as a legal entity; it is a political and economic fact which expresses itself in a bewildering variety of legal forms and devices. It is the complexity of its legal structure, or rather of the interplay of legal entities and relationships constituting that structure, no less than the size of its resources or the scale of its operations, which makes its power so elusive and so formidable a challenge to the political order and rule of law. It is therefore inherent in the nature of the multinational corporation that there is no simple solution for the problem of its relationship to states, the world of states, or an organized world community; ....." (191)

The Legal Profession and Corporate Social Responsibility

The problems of controlling large corporate enterprises, especially the multinationals, cannot be met without the attentions of an imaginative and creative legal profession. Most lawyers, the world over, are employed by private or public persons to perform specific tasks directed at well defined specific and microscopic issues. Private employers and most governments have not directed massive efforts at a renovation of the fundamental corporate control structure. To the contrary, business interests impeded such efforts. The little attention it has received comes from the law professors, who often lack the practicle experience to produce effective and manageable solutions. In a few nations attention is beginning to focus on this. On a global scale the problem is easier to see. The irony is that the problem may be dealt with on a global scale before it is dealt with on a broad national scale. The opposite view can also be taken - that if the matter is not or cannot be effectively solved at the national level, then it certainly cannot be resolved at the global level.

The indication of a beginning is the new attitude toward enterprise systems. "The legal profession appears to have adopted an ostrichlike defence against the developing concept of enterprise in business. ...... It is good to learn from Mr Teleux and others that the legal profession is beginning to come to grips with the phenomenon of enterprise; and it may well be that our ideas will be further clarified when the lawyers have established a clearer legal basis for enterprise in general. " (192)

French and Belgian law does little about: ......

regulating the relationship between companies that are affiliated or

constitute portions of a whole. ...... , law and jurisprudence

are fragmentary and in essence, limit themselves to the functioning of

of each of the individual companies.   Moreover, the rules do not

distinguish whether the companies in question form part of a national

or multinational group, except, in the second case, in order to keep

unreasonable and arbitary demands in check.   This almost complete

refusal of the law to take cognisance of economic realities is

doubtless explained by the absence of a juridicial concept of the

'enterprise' as an economic entity, as distinct from the incorporated

company in the technical sense, and by the confusion which in

consequence prevails between these two notions. ......

German law, like the law of the Netherlands in its latest

form, has already started along the road towards a recognition of

the law of enterprise. " (193)

The general difficulty is that the internal managerial

control system which pursues efficiency is in conflict with the external

governmental control system which is directed at wider social and

political goals confined to narrow geographical boundaries.

In the international arena this finds expression in statements

such as: "On the one hand the shareholders of corporations have a

right to expect a reasonable rate of return on capital and a chance

to earn income in relation to entrepreneurial risks.   But, at the

same time, a foreign government is quite validly concerned with

the ability of corporate managements to influence the employment
and indeed the prosperity of the country. The dilemma arises
because neither the people nor the government of the country in
question plays a part in selecting the directors or management of
world corporations. ...... Since it is only through national legislation
that managements can be made in any way responsible to the local
people, there is bound to be frustration when the managements of
world firms are out of reach of such legislation. " (194)

If corporate entities can fit themselves into a more acceptable
role in the wider social community the overall situation could take
another direction altogether. "The developments outlined in the
preceding section show that large international companies are
gradually beginning to improve their position and to regain some of
the lost prestige attached to private enterprise as described in the
first part of this book, when private companies could be almost
sovereign powers ruling vast territories in their own right. It must
be remembered that one reason why the position was lost was the
unaccountability of companies except to their own shareholders, and
the incongruity of the almost life and death powers which some of them
possessed. " (195)

One of the obvious changes within the corporate community
itself is a growing emphasis on social responsibilities. (196)
Hopefully, events will take the direction that Friedmann suggested:
"The corporate organisation of business and labor have long ceased
to be a private phenomenon. That they have a direct and decisive

impact on the social, economic and political life of the nation is no longer a matter of argument. It is an undeniable fact of daily experience. The challenge to the contemporary lawyer is to translate the social transformation of these organizations from private associations to public organisins into legal terms. " (197)

Corporate Law as the Constitutional Law for the New Economic State

Implicit in the operations of MNE and its confrontation with the nation - state is a question of political philosophy - the legitimacy of power. (198) It has been suggested that the problem is one of the hierarchal, non-democratic nature of the corporate enterprise. But it is more than that. Eells points out that those criticisms can also be levelled against churches and universities and yet there has been no similar universal concern over those institutions. (199) They do not present the overwhelming power and threat of MNE.

Galbraith recognised that power resides more and more with what he calls the 'planning system' - the large corporations, and less and less with the 'market system'. (200) In effect governments have failed to preserve the conditions necessary for the preservation of the 'market system', or events have evolved this way for the better, depending on viewpoint. Either way, the result is the blurring of public and corporate interests. Friedmann's reaction to this is: "If the legal order representing the community as a whole has no response to this kind of unholy alliance, where public power is merely an aspect of private economic power, then we shall have to admit

that the 'public interest' is no more than an empty phrase .... "
(201)

The comments of Eells regarding MNE are similar.
"This conception of business corporations as a species of private
government, though resisted at first, is now widely accepted. ......
The corporation of the future will eventually be seen in an enlarged
constitutional framework that accounts for this organic relationship
of the firm to the several economies to which its destinies are tied. "
(202)   He suggests some scheme whereby managerial authority can
be shared by trade unions and governments citing another example
of the possible future evolution of this: "The jet age thus had an
impact not only on the organization of single airline companies but
also on a new form of private government - the IATA - which
transcends national frontiers and reaches into all parts of the globe
as a power - and authority - wielding entity. ......   This latter
instrument of government supercedes not only the authority of
individual airlines but the authority, in practice, of public
governments as well. " (203)

Berle and Means, however, were the first ones to hit the
heart of the matter.   "The future may see the economic organism,
now typified by the corporation, not only on an equal plane with the
state, but possibly even superseding it as the dominant form of social
organization.   The law of corporations, accordingly, might well be
considered as a potential constitutional law for the new economic
state, while business practice is increasingly assuming the
aspect of economic statesmanship. " (204)

Within the American national framework Buchanan's views
are interesting.   He observes that the U.S. Constitution is completely
silent on the subject of the corporation as such.   Since the U.S.
government is, in a sense, the parent of all U.S. corporations,
and hence most multinationals today, this is an engaging point.   He
also compares the large corporation to a sub-community trying to
meet all of our needs like a large family from which he says the
corporation originally grew.   He raises the question of which
regulates which when it comes to government and business.   "It
was a suspicion and an accompanying fear of civil war that Thomas
Hobbes in seventh century England made two prophetic observations
on the new style corporations that were then exploring and
organizing the new world.   He said they were 'worms in the body
politic', and that they were 'chips off the block of sovereignty'.
By the first he meant that they were private associations that were
taking on a kind of spontaneous autonomy in their parasitical way
of life; by the second he meant that they were no longer mercantile
arms of the state, but had taken some of the power of the
government into their own management. " (205)

Eells' American view which he calls 'corporate
constitutionalism' is intended to make corporate enterprises bear
the responsibility of the 'governmental' power they wield.   "The
courts would view the actions of corporate officialdom for violations
of the due process and equal protection clauses just as they now
review the acts of federal and state agencies for possible

encroachment on private rights by public officials". (206) He predicts

that: "Politically, the now relatively autonomous business corporation

could conceivably degenerate into a mere administrative arm of the

state or its ecological successor. " (207)

Recently in the United States, consideration has been given

to the creation of a federal corporate chartering control system

to take the place of the state chartering system which now exists.

There is a useful analogy here - comparing the individual states

and the federal government to the individual nations and a yet-to-be

supranational authority.

In the United States corporate chartering law has, in

practice, functioned as mere enabling legislation. Actual control of

corporate actions is accomplished, with varying degrees of success, by

individual regulations directed at specific acts. Henning contrasts this

attitude towards corporate control with constitutional government control

or limitation. "However, we have not attempted to control the super-

corporations in the same way that we have controlled the power of

government. Through anti-trust policy and regulatory agencies,

federal regulation proceeded by a series of attempts to prohibit

specific acts. A very different approach to the control of

governments' power was taken by the founding fathers in drafting

the U.S. Constitution. They chose to reorganize, regularize and

disburse government power rather than to prohibit specific acts. " (208)

"The notion of federal chartering is not new. At the

Constitutional Convention James Madison proposed unsuccessfully that Congress be empowered to charter corporations.   Presidents

Roosevelt, Taft and Wilson all advocated federal chartering or

licensing. ......

The (proposed) act may, for example, require that no

corporation be chartered to serve more than twelve percent of

any relevant market. ......   However, enterprises with profound

national and international impact would be required to conform to

structural and institutional standards developed to meet the special problems

that size and power generate. ......

(regarding the largest corporations)   The principle of

rigorous external examination and supervision, now firmly

embedded in the banking community, ought to be transferable to

the corporate community. ......   There is no reason why such an

audit must be confined to the historical indices of success and failure.

It could involve examination of a corporation's responsibilities to

hire and promote members of minority communities, to refrain from

polluting the environment and to manufacture socially useful products. "

(209)

Henning also raises the question of the difficulty of rescuing

politics from the dominance of business.   He cites those who see

corporate power gaining over the state and the suggestion that

corporate autocracies and oligopolies be transformed into democratic

political institutions.   "If the old social contract with government

has not been fulfilled, enter into a new one with the super-

corporations. " (210)

Managerial Structure and Legal Structure

There have been extensive efforts by management writers
and practitioners to modernize the managerial structure to meet the
'control' needs of large and diversified corporations.   These efforts
are now being devoted to the complex problem of the control of
multinational enterprises.   In contrast, it does not appear that
the same efforts have been devoted to the evolution of the corporate
legal structure.   Managerial structures have radically changed and
continue to do so, whereas fundamental changes in corporate legal
structure have just begun.   As is generally the case with legal
change, there is a considerable 'lag' element.

In addition to this there is a tendency for 'management'
people to view the legal structure as an incidental necessity.   The
result is that for purposes of 'internal' and 'external' control the
law has not fulfilled the role that it might or should.   An understanding
of the views and perspectives on this must precede its resolution.

"For a number of reasons (e. g. , local legal requirements,
tax advantages, or need for financial control), a company creating a world
enterprise often sets up a statutory corporate structure that differs
from the more fluid and informal (though very real) lines of
communication followed in the day-to-day operations of the business.
The statutory organization is designed to put the pieces of the company
together into a legal structure that optimizes cash flow, for the
overall corporation.   The manner in which the company is actually
co-ordinated and run involves a set of working relationships that are

constructed to fit the managerial requirements of the company. ......
Recognising the distinction between the formal statutory organization
and the manner in which the total business is co-ordinated and
managed dispels much of the fog that surrounds all foreign
operations. " (211)

Galbraith goes to the core of the matter when he discusses
the consequence of the changes in the relationship of control and
ownership.   "In consequence, nearly all study of the corporation has
been concerned with its deviation from its legal or formal image.
This image - that of an association of persons into 'an autonomous
legal unit with a distinct legal personality that enable it to carry
on business, own property and contract debts' - is highly normative.
It is what a corporation should be.   When the modern corporation
disenfranchises its stockholders, grows to gargantuan size, expands
into wholly unrelated activities   is a monopoly where it buys and a
monopoly where it sells, something is wrong. ......

Thus the corporation adapts itself well to the needs of the
small enterprise.   This adaption, it will be observed, conforms (as the
large corporation does not) to the design that is adumbrated in corporation
law and celebrated in the well-regarded textbooks. " (212)

Chandler's classic study of business strategy puts the matter
in wider perspective.   "And here the distinction between legal and
administrative developments must be kept clear.   The truly
consolidated enterprise operating on a national scale required both new
legal and new administrative forms.   Legally, it called for an instrument

that would permit it to operate in many different states.

Administratively, it demanded a structure to provide for

centralized co-ordination, appraisal, and planning for its extended

plant and personnel. " (213)

In 1889 in the United States, the state of New Jersey amended

her general incorporation laws to permit one corporation to own the

stock of another corporation.   All of the states soon followed.

Chandler saw this as a significant turning point after which

administrative innovations were much more important to the

development of American business than legal ones. (214)

Chandler also makes the observation that market forces have

had a far greater impact on corporate enterprise than the various

regulatory laws or controls.   This raises the question of whether or not

the law has played an effective role.   "The market, the nature of their

resources, and their entrepreneurial talents have, with relatively few

exceptions, had far more effect on the history of large industrial firms

in the United States than have antitrust laws, taxation, labor and welfare

legislation, and comparable evidence of public policy.   Possibly tax

regulations have had more of an impact on the strategy of expansion

since World War II, but their influence has not appreciably altered

broad trends in the structure and strategy of great enterprises. "

(215)   He excludes the impact of government spending, especially on

defense.

The recent study by Stopford and Wells makes a similar observation.

"This treatment of structure excludes any recognition of the legal or

statutory features of an enterprise. But the legal structure is designed,
in accordance with government regulations, for cash-flow and tax
purposes; it seldom reflects the way in which the enterprise is managed.
Because this book is concerned with managerial practice, the legal
structure can be ignored. " (216)

Perhaps the most astute insights into the managerial/legal
dichotomy have been made by Endel J. Kolde. ".... another source which
to date has escaped the scrutiny of organizational theorists - the legal,
or juridic form of organization as defined by the respective country's
law and imposed upon a company by its official charter. Although
influenced by it, the managerial organization seldom coincides with the
juridic form........

Although to some extent conditioned by official charters, the de
facto management of the foreign-based affiliates is often different from
the de jure administration and is invariably subordinated to the parent
company's international headquarters whatever its form. No clear cut
interrelationship between the de facto and de jure managements exists.
In some companies they are completely divorced. In others they are
quite closely interwoven, with most titular officers serving as operating
executives also. But in the great majority of cases the actual management
is in the hands of people other than the law-prescribed directors and
officers.......

The complete separation of de facto and de jure administrations
is illustrated by the organizational structure of a large West Coast
company which operates affiliates in a number of Latin American countries.

Each of these affiliates is incorporated under the laws of the respective country, but none of them functions as a separate administrative unit; instead, they 'buy' their management from a U.S. subsidiary of the parent company, organized for that purpose exclusively........

If there were no legal restrictions, the managerial hierarchy, primarily because of performance criteria, would also constitute the formal organization. However, this is seldom the case. The laws of each country provide not only for different business charters but also for different qualifications for company officers, different numbers of stockholders, and different ownership distributions.

Most of these provisions are based upon nonmanagerial criteria and, thus, have a general restraining effect upon business efficiency."(217)

Something akin to a world company law for the largest, globally-operated multinationals would reduce or eliminate the divergent legal structures in different nations. Further study of the managerial/legal structure may reveal ways to make the two more compatible. Certainly there is an aspect of the legal structure which must, by virtue of its external control goals, come into conflict with the managerial structure. But other aspects of the legal structure ought to be working toward the coincidence of internal managerial and legal control goals.

The Coming Integrative Role of Law

The past role of law is not inaccurately described by Kaplan: "During the past half century, the state corporation statute has in large measure been transformed from a device to control, restrict, and govern the corporations chartered under it into an enabling act granting to enterprises the relatively unrestricted opportunity to devise the type of

entity which they desire. " (218)   Others confirm this view that the law

of corporate structure was put at the service of management, and that

control for community and social purposes was left to ad hoc rules and

agencies outside the corporation. (219)

The central question that is now emerging is whether political

entities which wield the legal structure are going to dominate economic

entities. The truth of the matter is that private and public interests are

converging, as is private law and public law. And the same evolution

should take place with respect to company law.

The indication of a beginning at the national level is found in the

progressive attitude of some leaders in the legal profession. For the

United Kingdom and Europe Professor Schmitthoff has been a

spokesman and advocate of reform. (220)

Hadden's recent assessment of national company law is in the

right direction: "... the largest multi-national companies are free to

concentrate their operations in the most favorable economic and

political climate, and the balance of power is thus appreciably shifted

away from governments to the companies themselves as powerful, independent

and international organisations... To this extent the multinationals do

constitute a genuine threat to the controls which have been built up

against the power of capital in relation to that of organized labor and the

state, and pose new problems in the development of an acceptable legal

framework for the modern corporation.......

The ideal solution is the development of international legal controls

over the operation of what are in effect international companies, and

similarly the development of trade union organization on an international level, so that the power of   multi-national capital may be met by

that of multi-national labor and multi-national government. " (221)

The proposals for harmonization of European company law and

for a European Company are moves in this direction. (222) "Society,

as at present constituted in the West, seems determined to bring private

enterprise under closer control. This tendency is reflected in

Professor Saunders Societas Europa constitution, ... which presupposes

a firm framework of law within which the company may operate and which

divides power between three bodies - the general meeting, the

supervisory board, and the management board - in one of which the

workers must be represented. These trends of opinion suggest that

even wider representation may follow in the next decade or two. In the

case of the international company, this is foreshadowed by the necessity,

social if not legal, to include foreign nationals in key positions.

Compulsory worker representation is also becoming more common.

But if workers are represented on the main board, why not consumers,

also? If a major part of the state's economy is involved, why not

government representation, too? The British Petroleum example shows

that this is practicable. Existing board members may not like these

developments, may complain that they will interfere with efficient management.

Nevertheless, when the mass of people have made up their minds they

are irrestible.   Moreover, wider internal representation, whatever

its drawbacks, has advantages, too. When a company runs into trouble,

the reason in most cases is a breakdown in communications - between the

company and its workers, its customers, its government, or the

government of countries in which it operates. If all these are

represented on the board, such a breakdown is less likely ......

Thus, in addition to its external expansion, the international company will have to expand internally, to become more truly representative of the society in which it operates, if it is to face successfully the challenging tasks that lie ahead. " (223)

Although part of the solution does lie in the construction of some new form of supra-national controls, the responsibility and power of nations is still a factor, and may even develop a solution from within. "The ideal of world controls is attractive, but it can easily become an excuse for postponing more realistic action. Even if it were attainable, it would not be sufficient; for the great part of the welfare of individuals must continue to reside with the nations, around which the whole apparatus of taxation and the welfare state has been constructed. Nationalism, in this function, is far from outdated; .... The nation, in fact, has become much more a protective organisation, and must less an aggressive one; and its citizens will not readily entrust this protection to any larger unit. " (224)

It is possible that the idea of supra-national control is premature or even unrealistic as it would require the delegation of powers presently in the nation-state. The crucial recognition here, however, is that there is no international corporate law. (225) As a beginning it is possible that key nation-states could arrive at a mutual recognition of uniform corporate law for giant multinations. This would be in the nature of an international minimum standard and could be supervised by joint commissions as has been done with joint claims commissions. In other words, an international corporate legal structure can be constructed without absolute infringement on sovereignty.

What could accelerate this is the assessment by some that
such an international legal framework, although involving loss of
flexibility for MNEs, would in the long run, work to their advantage.
(226) Such a legal framework would provide a stable environment for
long range corporate planning.

Demand for a new legal framework also comes from the
problem of distributive justice inherent in the present international
economic system and practices. "These international capital
movements also create distributive problems, in determining how the
global gains should be shared between the investing country, which
permits the export of capital, the host country by whose labor and on
whose land the increased output is generated, and the owners of the
capital, whose mobility makes the increased output possible. Exactly
the same kind of gains arise from the movement of capital within a
country. The savings made in one part of Canada can be readily
transferred, through the mechanisms of the banking system and the
capital market, and put to work where they are most productive, perhaps
a thousand miles from the point where they were accummulated. How
the increased product is to be divided is settled peacefully, by a complex
of bargaining processes between borrowers and lenders, between buyers
and sellers, and between employers and employees. But the rules
under which the bargaining is conducted are laid down by a system of
law, and if the rules become unfair or unworkable they can be changed.
If any of the participants becomes unduly enriched, much of his gain
is expropriated through taxation, and used for the general benefit
of society - a fact which not only aids distributive justice, but also

discourages extortionate bargaining. It is precisely this framework

of law which is lacking, so far as international capital movements

are concerned." (227) What is overlooked in the international arena

is the almost universally recognized concept that 'ownership' is a

grant made by the law to achieve common social purposes. (228)

As things now stand, there is no system of 'rights' and

'non-rights' governing the relationships between MNE and nation-

states. Government policy toward the separate functions and

elements of MNE stem from its foreign economic and political

policies, and are not focused on the enterprises themselves.

Friedmann gives an accurate and balanced summation.

"The multinational corporation is no more immune from the rule

of law than its constituent elements or the state itself, and the law

must therefore be so developed as to embrace effectively the com-

plexity and range of its structure and transactions. . . . .

No international status for multinational corporations is

conceivable unless it represents a nice balance of advantages

and responsibilities for governments and corporations alike.

Corporations will not seek or willingly accept such a status unless

the obligations of registration, audit, disclosure and respect for

law which it involves are reasonable, and the general effect of the

status is to enhance the public position and facilitate their operations

rather than subject them to tiresome restraints inconsistent with

efficient and economical operation. Governments will not recognize

or concede such a status unless it permits them to protect the
public interest more effectively than is possible in the present
legal jungle. ...

The initial decision creating such a status could be taken
by the United Nations or OECD without recourse to an international
convention, which it might be difficult to get sufficiently widely
ratified to make its provisions effective; but the status would
become a significant reality only in so far as corporations sought
it and governments recognised it. In course of time, it might
become a requirement for and confer a right to the enjoyment of
valuable privileges and facilities under international conventions
and national laws." (229)

7   ANTITRUST

7. 1   IN GENERAL

In some respects this chapter is a continuation of the
'control' aspects of the previous chapter, since antitrust or
competition law is one method of controlling multinational
enterprises.

The advent of MNE has changed the environment of com -
petition in the world. In turn, the new environment has accelerated
the formation of additional MNE's. At the national and international
level enterprises have increased in size and competition in markets
has become more concentrated. Increases in size and concentration
have always been key factors in antitrust.

Size

The evolution of business organization has been such that
there has in fact been a steady drive towards bigness. As national
boundaries are more and more ignored new size potentials have
unfolded. The large get larger (1) and the small enterprises drop
out of the competition. (2)

Size of enterprises is said to be a major determinant of
overseas investment. (3) If a nation is to gain a share in expanding
world business by foreign investment than it must encourage the

growth of its enterprises by one means or another. It has even
been suggested that the number of large companies in a country
over a period of time is one of the indications of economic growth. (4)

In theory the antitrust laws and various company laws were
intended to check the size and power of business. In practice they
have not presented any serious or continuious obstacle to bigness.(5)
Consequently more mergers are coming and multinationalization of
enterprises thunders on. (6) In spite of the existence of antitrust
concepts in the European Common Market, its general policy is to
encourage mergers. And some of its leaders are especially keen
advocates of cross-border mergers. (7) In many European countries,
including England, there are national plans and institutions to foster
industrial concentration. In Italy, the state-owned holding company,
IRI, already controls 15 percent of the nation's total industrial output. Sweden has also been conglomerating its nationalized
companies. (8)

The days of international cartels are not gone either.
Recently Japan's Fair Trade Commission advised 14 Japanese fibre
manufacturers to break up what it says are illegal cartels with
certain European producers. It charged that the 14 firms, including
Mitsubishi Rayon, agreed with Western European fibre makers to
divide world fibre markets and set minimum prices. (9)

In recent years even new technology alleged to liberate,
has been employed to heighten the advantages of big producers. In

the research-intensive industries patent monopolies have provided

the basis for a division of markets. European participants in

restrictive agreements have assigned their legally acquired

monopoly position in the United States market to leading US companies;

and in turn, US leaders in that industry assigned their monopolies

in the European market to European leaders. (10)

Size has not been controlled at the national level and:

"Similarly, the battle against size on the international plane is being

lost in the current international merger movement, and international

antitrust is not likely to challenge the resulting size structures in

any serious way, indeed it is supporting them." (11) Nevertheless

worldwide competition has increased in spite of the growing con-

centration in many industries. (12)

In spite of overall growth in concentration the theory behind

the American antitrust policy has generally resulted in legal rulings

which prevent the elimination of competitors by merger or acquisition.

It is obvious that international mergers may run counter to national

competition policy. The merger of two foreign companies, each

with subsidiaries in a particular country may reduce competition

in that country. (13) This may have been the reason why certain

Pirelli interests (Pirelli Limited) became Dunlop majority-owned in

the Dunlop Pirelli Union. (14) In the case of an acquisition of a

national company by a foreign competitor what may follow is a

cessation of exports by the acquired subsidiary or of imports by

the acquiring firm.

There are several American cases involving international mergers or acquisitions. In the Schlitz case (15) the American company, Schlitz Brewing Company, acquired a substantial interest in the large Canadian brewer, John Labatt Limited. The acquisition was held illegal under Section 7 of the Clayton Act primarily because it eliminated actual direct competition in the domestic market between Schlitz and a United States subsidiary of Labatt. In addition there was the question of potential competition between Schlitz and Labott itself. The Labatt competition might have been by way of exports into the US. The court pointed to the concentrated state of the beer market in the US and stated that Canadian companies offered the greatest source of potential competition. (16)

A better known international case is that of BP Sohio. (17) BP first entered the US market by acquiring the East Coast properties of Sinclair Oil Company. Later BP and Sohio proposed to merge. Since Sohio had 30 percent of the market and BP, now operating on the East Coast, was a leading potential entrant into Ohio, this violated Section 7 of the Clayton Act. The case was settled by a consent decree providing for a divestiture of part of Sohio's holdings in Ohio. The case occasioned criticism in the British press which took the position that since the UK had allowed giant US companies to come into Britain, the US should not have wimpered when UK companies invested in the US. (18) It appears that the response of the US law would have been the same if the East Coast

properties involved were still held by Sinclair, an American company.
The legal reaction was not based on national ownership discrimination.
Like the Schlitz case it illustrates a dominant theme in the US antitrust policy - not to reduce the number of competitors or potential
competitors. However, it also demonstrates the potential for conflict
in the international arena. British and European laws have not been
as strict as the American - hence giving the American enterprises
an edge in their acquisitions in Europe. This will be discussed in
detail later.

Enterprise International Dispersion

Originally an enterprises' production took place all in its home
country. Now it is directed from home country headquarters but
produces in foreign subsidiaries dispersed throughout the globe. It
first presented competition only in its home market, then in export
markets served from the home country. Now local foreign subsidiaries
serve the former export markets as well as adjacent country markets.
The pattern of export or international trade competition is changing
each time production locations shift.

Formerly the bulk of benefits (employment, taxes, etc)
from increased production served the home country exclusively. Now
when production takes place largely in non-home countries, the
interests of the enterprise and its home country are not coincident,
but increasingly discordant. (19) Whereas the competition policy
of the home country only affected home enterprises, now its policy

affects all foreign enterprises present as well as those outside.

Taking a broader view of global competition, the underlying reality may not be competition between enterprises but economic competition between nations. The aggregate of one nation's enterprises against another's. This was formerly on the basis of export competition but has now become confused and complicated because each nation's enterprises are quickly dispersing among other nations. Although this may in the long term dilute nationalism, the short term result is that national competition continues. It continues partly in the backyards of competitor nations, and in the grounds of the relatively helpless and poorer third world.

A just global competition policy could set this in a right and equitable direction, but that is a long way off.

The fact that enterprise from one country can join with enterprises from another country as in the case of transnationals or in the joint venture subsidiaries of national multinationals presents additional complications for antitrust policy makers. Enterprise blocks from pairs or groups of nations may develop. Ultimately the communist monopoly block may be pitted against the non-communist, competition-oriented block. The finale may determine which type of economic organization and philosophy is superior or preferable. It may be a playing out of what Marx predicted or it may take us into an altogether unanticipated state of affairs.

If we assumed that all presently existing national and regional antitrust rules and competition barriers, including tariffs

and the like, were eliminated, what would happen. The likelihood
is that existing dominant economic enterprises and nations would
quickly gain more dominant positions and the small enterprises and
nations would be swallowed. In the long run nations with the least
economic resources might be left for tourism or retirement or if
occupied by productive facilities, they would be controlled by other
nations or enterprises.

In one respect the enterprises within each Communist
country can be viewed as one giant conglomerate enterprise directed
at the top by political-economic unity of command. In Russia it
could be called the USSR enterprise. And it is multinational in that
its joint activities dovetail with other Communist country enterprises
and, increasingly with Japanese, Arab, African and other national
enterprises.

In Europe cross-national mergers have taken place and are
being encouraged. In time that will result in European type conglomerate
enterprises. Nations and regional groups will tend more and more
to function as dominant enterprises.

No Uniformity among National Laws

In their drive toward efficiency and growth the multinationals
are impeded by diversity of antitrust regulations in different
countries and regional groupings. Likewise antitrust law makers in
each country are in a difficult position because the effectiveness of

what they do is also dependent upon the antitrust laws of other
countries. Indeed, the absence of such laws in some countries
means that new investment may go there rather than face restrictions
elsewhere.

Conflict between US and European laws has already been
mentioned in the BP Sohio case. US enterprises have been allowed
to buy-in locally in Europe, but the US laws may resist the reverse.
Recently Matsushita, the Japanese producer of Panasonic brand name
television sets, offered to buy the $100 million dollar television
business of America's Motorola Inc. Because Matsushita already
sells TV sets to the US, the US Department of Justice says that the
transaction could violate American antitrust regulations. If so,
the Japanese will have little to complain about. With very few
exceptions, their policy has been to exclude foreign investment
without even evaluating its affect on competition.

Lack of uniformity is understandable because each nation's
economy and enterprises are at different stages of growth. The
difference in value systems and economic philosophy only add to
that. The EEC antitrust policy makers have to decide whether to
have a discriminatory policy in favor of EEC enterprises. This
would be primarily aimed at the generally larger American
enterprises. Such a policy, if adopted is believed by some experts
to be a mistake. Professor Schmitthoff has observed: "It would,
however, be short-sighted and inward-looking if the Community
discriminated against multinationals based outside its territory and

in its legal arrangements distinguished between multinationals controlled from an EEC country and those controlled from outside. "(20)

It has also been argued that the size advantage of American enterprise has been overstated. Many non-US corporations, though operationally separate from each other, are linked through banks and financial institutions and form a corporate group not unlike the large US corporations. (21) This is the same suggestion that is made about the Mitsubishi Group companies.

Obtaining jurisdiction over enterprises outside a country, and the general clash of one country's laws with another, also presents a problem. Conduct of enterprises outside the US have come into conflict with the extraterritorial application of US antitrust laws. However, enforcement has required co-operation with the law courts and enforcements authorities of other countries which is generally not forthcoming. Not forthcoming, often because the request is in direct conflict with the laws of the other country. This was the situation in the well known case involving the English company Imperial Chemical Industries. The English view of this is that national antitrust laws should have no extraterritorial effect. The affront caused by the US view has met with considerable resistance. Legislation prohibiting compliance with foreign antitrust measures has now been enacted in Denmark, Finland, India, Holland and other countries. (22)

Another perplexity is the question of whether intra-enterprise practices should be subject to antitrust laws. The multinational firm in respect of its internal actions within the family is generally immune. (23) EEC and German rules do not apply. (24) However, American laws do. (25)

The crucial aspect according to Professor Corwin Edwards is that: "Within a relatively short time, an increase in the number of national laws and further hardening of the peculiarities of each law may make diversity less tolerable, yet incapable of being harmonized." (26)

Policy Dilemmas for Enterprises and Nations

The result of a diversity of antitrust laws among nations is that multinationals gravitate to those nations allowing the anti-competitive practices. This puts pressure on other nations to become more lenient. It also influences enterprises to adopt strategies based on non-economic considerations.

Multinationals govern themselves by world-wide profit results. Unlike smaller, national enterprises they can undertake anti-competitive practices in one part of the world for a limited time. For example, a multinational enterprise with a wide product and geographical diversification may employ massive price cuts in one country in order to eliminate domestic competition in a particular product. It thereby assures itself of a monopoly position in that market. (27)

The fact that subsidiary companies in one country are connected to subsidiaries in other countries and to a parent corporation

presents a major policy problem for each nation. A nation cannot
realistically establish its competition policy on the premise that
the local subsidiary is an independent entity unable to rely on the
resources of the others. Also the policy of the parent's country will
affect or even contradict the subsidiary country policy. (28)

Formerly, the growth of an enterprise was directly dependent
upon the economic health and growth of its home country. Now widely
dispersed multinationals will not be completely dependent upon any
one country. This scramble for international diversification means
that countries or continents without its own multinational corporations
will run the risk of becoming colonies or subservient nations. The
Japanese wisely excluded foreign investment, reserving their
domestic market for themselves, and creating the basis for large
domestic corporations to themselves go multi-national. Enterprises
must now decide how much they should produce at home and export,
and how much should be produced in the export market countries.
Those decisions seriously affect the balance of payments of all
countries concerned. Whereas countries formerly protected
domestic enterprise with tariffs, now they may give them financial
assistance to produce abroad to more ably themselves penetrate
foreign markets. (29)

What is brought into conflict is the policy to expand a
corporation's share of world market, and its home country's share.
Multinationalization of domestic firms has been found to reduce the
country's share. Purely national firms export more from the home
country. (30)

On the other hand, mergers or multinationalization does accelerate the world wide market penetration and growth in size of domestic enterprises and provides a nation with enterprises able to withstand world competition. (31)

The types of laws a nation or region enacts must be tied to its long range industrial strategy. The EEC countries are yet uncertain as to what to do. Concentration into large national enterprise units faces Europe with a difficult choice between an industry divided up into separate national monopolies or a single European monopoly. The better solution says Christopher Layton is to move toward international mergers of companies that do not represent the whole of a given national industry. For example, the creation of three nuclear-power equipment groups each containing what were formerly British, German and other national companies. (32)

The trend in Europe is clearly towards larger enterprises and towards additional inter-enterprise collaboration. Recent agreements between Japanese and European fibre producers, and similar incidents involving American firms verifies that the day of international cartels is not gone. These are fundamental dangers in this accelerating atmosphere of concentration.

International cartels render national concentration policy ineffectual. A liberal import policy cannot change the external situation. And no institution exists to deal with the external, international situation. Exporting countries have the power but do not use it. They are reluctant to harm their own national interests by proceeding against domestic export enterprises. (33)

Looking at the positive side economists generally believe that multinationals will be a powerful force in allocating world wide capital and resources efficiently and spreading technology. They welcome large firms spanning the entire world producing each component in the country where costs are lowest. It is also suggested that the exchange of national home markets by multi-nationals creates a better, less national, environment. (34)

At the philosophical level nations have taken different attitudes towards multinationalizations impact on individual freedom. This will influence the ultimate antitrust policies. The philosophy of Western antitrust rests, in theory, upon a preference for diversity, free choice, and ease of new entrants. In many respects a conflict is developing between individual freedom and economic efficiency. While the highly industrial nations now appear willing to sacrifice some economic progress for individual freedom, the less-developed nations appear convinced that the problems of subsistence come first. (35) Socialist economics also stresses the advantages of scale and political control over economic decision makers. This suggests that economic enterprises should not extend beyond political boundaries permitting their control. (36) Hyman and Rowthorn sum it up: "In short, there is a conflict at a funda-mental level between national planning by political units and international planning by corporations as direct investment grows." They also foresee the need for oligopoly equilibrium as between American and European enterprises. (37)

Servan-Schreiber's overview also goes to the heart of the matter. "So at the risk of over-simplifying the question, I would say the problem is not any more the American challenge because the Americans have the same problem. It is political power as opposed to industrial power." (38) This is the challenge of antitrust.

Resolution at the International Level

There is ample evidence that the matters to be addressed and resolved cannot be effectively dealt with at the national level. One excellent example is given in the Canadian context. Assume there is a price-fixing conspiracy between two foreign international parent firms. They agree not to cut prices against each other when trading into the Canadian market. Each foreign parent exports to its Canadian subsidiary and charges its subsidiary the price agreed by the two parents. The Canadian subsidiaries carry out the price policy dictated by the parents with the result that there is no price competition between them in Canada. Yet they have done nothing to violate Canadian law. (39)

A recent study by the Committee of Experts on Restrictive Business Practices of the OECD has shed light on another facet. They reported that the majority of national laws studied expressly limited the 'relevant geographical market' to the area of applicability of the laws - the national boundaries. The Committee also said that there was no need for an extra-nation extension of the 'relevant geographic market', since the countries took into question foreign

product alternatives (imports). (40)

Only a few countries have had truly effective antitrust laws

for a long period and there is scepticism whether those laws or their

influence on others will be successful in the global context. "It does

not seem likely that the movement of business involvements across

national boundaries and the expansion of business multinationalism,

will be visibly slowed by 'exportation' of domestic antitrust law by

the United States, the EEC or other authorities". (41) Adding to

this Professor Raymond Vernon has stated that the law has not

generally kept pace with the extensive qualitative and quantative

changes in the international business environment. (42) Others agree

that the international market has obsoleted the concept of monopolies

(43) The Common Market countries have the limitation that EEC

rules do not reach restrictions upon imports into the Common Market

that are imposed by cartels or monopolies in non-member states. (44)

The late Professor Kronstein's brilliant review of antitrust

also suggests scepticism. "Do actual economic units, integrated by

different devices and extending over political borders, exercise power

of a governmental character by enacting rules and regulations of

their own, and enforcing them? This chapter suggests that the study

in its entirety raises very substantial doubts whether antitrust or

other governmental rules on unfair 'competition' continue to be

practical, or if they ever have been. In our enquiry, the power

of multinational corporations, working in conjunction with many

national domestic economic entities, to set effective regulatory rules
and even to regulate governmental activities and economics, nationally
and internationally, is not only the result of the political and economic
power as well as the will of the managements of these enterprises,
but it is also deeply embodied in the integration of the economic phases
in an objective meaning. Nothing shows this point better than the
relationship between consumer countries and nationalizing countries
in which governments come in control of raw material, whether they
have a liberal or Communist economy. How the United States
Government or other governments shall deal with the new situation
remains to be seen. " (45)

The solution submitted by some is the establishment of rules
and enforcement machinery on an international basis against international restrictive business practices whether undertaken by
independent firms or internally within multinational enterprises. (46)

Bringing about an international solution, however applied,
faces the difficulty of accommodating a variety of antitrust philosophies
between nationals of unequal bargaining power. (47)

7.2   LAWS AFFECTING THE FORMATION OF MULTINATIONAL

ENTERPRISES

Broadly speaking, antitrust law may be divided into two

categories. The first is the 'structural' approach and the second is the

'conduct' approach. The first is concerned with the number, size, legal

structure and market power of the enterprises in a particular market.

The second approach ignores the formation and evolution of the market

structure and regulates the business practices of powerful or dominant

enterprises only if those practices have a detrimental effect.

The laws of any particular country or region generally take

one approach or the other or a combination of the two. The 'structural'

approach is preventative in nature; the 'conduct' is corrective. The

latter only concerns itself with the abuse of power; the former is con-

cerned with the power itself or its formation. (48) This chapter treats the

'structure' approach as it particularly relates to the formation of

multinational enterprises. The coverage is generally limited to the

laws in the two leading antitrust camps - the United States and the EEC.

Intra-Enterprise

Present antitrust laws in the world have not generally been

applied to practices between constituent parts of an enterprise. In

effect, multinational enterprises have been treated as one legal entity

even though they consist of many domestic and foreign subsidiaries

which are technically separate legal entities. If and when such giant

enterprises were felt to have become too powerful or detrimental, then

anticompetitive 'internal' practices could be attacked just like those

between completely separate corporate enterprises. Such a policy
would have a clear affect upon the formation and future legal structure
of multinational enterprises. What follows is an assessment of the
present applicability of the intra-enterprise doctrine. It is limited to
the two major antitrust camps - the United States and the European
Economic Community.

In the United States the wording of section one of the Sherman
Act is sufficiently broad to embrace intra-enterprise actions. The
pertinent language is "every person who shall make any contract or
engage in any combination or conspiracy hereby declared to be illegal."
The 'rule of reason' philosophy permits this to be interpreted either
way. The problem is that a combination or conspiracy requires, at
least, two legal persons. Viewed one way such a conspiracy could
exist between the parent and its wholly owned subsidiary, or between
two of its wholly subsidiaries. The word 'person' refers to legal
persons, including corporations.

If one views the legislative purpose of the Act, another
interpretation can be made. The Act intended to protect competition.
But there is no competition between or among a parent and its subsidiary
corporations and the subsidiaries are not, in fact, independent
competitors. There has been disagreement over which view American
courts have taken and should take. (49)

A case cited for its applicability states: "It is now settled
law that if a corporation chooses to conduct parts of its business through
subsidiary or affiliated corporations, and conspires with them to do

something that independent entities cannot conspire to do under
Section one of the Sherman Act, it is no defense that the corporations
are in reality a single economic entity." (50)

A case cited for the inapplicability of the doctrine states:
The basis of the rule that a corporation cannot conspire with its
unincorporated divisions is that there must be, at least, two persons
or entities to constitute a conspiracy, and a corporation cannot conspire
with itself any more than a person can." (51)

One difficulty with applying the doctrine is that certain conduct
would be illegal if done by a subsidiary and legal if done by a branch or
division. This would put undue emphasis on legal form. It would also
work a discrimination against multinational enterprises which must, for
practical reasons, function through separately incorporated foreign
subsidiaries. (52)

As a general proposition, I do not believe that the intra-
enterprise doctrine is applicable in the United States or should be
applicable. However, there is ample room for the courts to apply it
should unfolding circumstances require it.

The situation seems somewhat the same in the EEC. There
are indications both ways on the doctrine's applicability. To start
with, it should be noted that the language of Article 85 (1) of the Rome
Treaty refers to agreements between 'enterprises'. At first glance,
this would appear to exclude the application of the intra-enterprise
doctrine.

The first reinforcement of this came in the case of Christiani
and Nielsen. (53) At issue was an agreement between a Danish parent

company and its wholly owned subsidiary at The Hague. The agreement contained a territorial division and obliged the subsidiary to follow the directives emanating from Christiani and Nielsen in Copenhagen. Subsidiaries had also been set up in other Common Market countries and it appeared that all of them had to abstain from activities in countries where other subsidiaries were situated. The EEC Commission was concerned because apparently numerous other enterprises engage in similar activities.

The Commission took the attitude that Article 85 (1) pre-supposes that the concerned enterprises are competitors. Whether or not this is the case depends upon the subsidiary being capable of independent economic action with respect to the parent. The Commission concluded that the division of the market agreed upon by contract is nothing but a working division within one and the same economic entity.

The Commission made a pronouncement some time afterwards which points the matter in another direction. This concerned an agree-ment under which the American company, Sperry Rand, transferred its trade-mark 'Remington' for electric razors to its subsidiary Remington Rand Italia. (54) The subsidiary had used this trademark for the purpose of opposing the import of Remington products from other Common Market countries. The agreement did guarantee to Remington Rand Italia complete territorial protection and hence worked a restriction on third parties. In consequence, the Commission informed the parties that the agreement should probably be regarded as infringing Article 85 (1).

In 1971, a matter involving the Belgian Company, Beguelin, came before the Court of Justice of the European Communities. (55) Beguelin had been granted the exclusive right to sell the products of a Japanese manufacturer. Beguelin's French rights were ceded to its French subsidiary. Regarding this, the Court said that "in the case of a contract conceding exclusive rights of sale that condition is not met when such a concession is, in fact, partially transferred by a parent company to a subsidiary which, although enjoying a distinct legal personality, does not have any economic autonomy. (56)

Although there are more indications against the application of the intra-enterprise doctrine in the EEC, the door appears to be still open for its application.

A proper interpretation would seem to come from concentrating on the economic meaning rather than the legal form in which the situations present themselves. In the final analysis, the applicability of the doctrine really depends upon the factual determination of whether or not subsidiary companies are autonomous. (57)

Joint Venture Subsidiaries

In the United States, both Section 7 of the Clayton Act and Section 1 of the Sherman Act have been applied to joint venture subsidiaries where there has been a finding that there is a reasonable probability of lessening competition or a tendency toward monopoly. If the parent companies are compeitiors or potential competitors, then there is a likelihood that the joint venture will be unlawful. However, such joint ventures are not unlawful 'per se'. The outcome depends on an individual examination of the competition in the market concerned. (58)

One of the most prominent cases on the subject dealt with a joint venture by four American manufacturers to establish factories overseas. (59) Invoking Section 1 of the Sherman Act, the court determined that the joint venture would eliminate or reduce competition in the American domestic market.

The first joint venture case decided under Section 7 of the Clayton Act involved the American companies Pennsalt and Olin Matthieson. (60) They had formed a joint subsidiary for the manufacture and marketing of sodium chlorate. The United States Supreme Court established the applicable criteria as whether or not, absent the joint venture, either parent would have become independent competitors or were potential competitors for the market in question. The case was remanded to the lower court which was directed to apply the above criteria. The lower court found that neither parent would have entered the particular market and the joint subsidiary was allowed.

The joint venture company, Mobay, involved American and German parent companies. Monsanto and Bayer had joined together for the joint manufacture of some chemical products. The United States Justice Department claimed that Monsanto could have entered the market and that there was sufficient evidence that they might have been an independent competitor without the joint venture. By consent decree, the venture company, Mobay, became 100% German owned. (61)

In the EEC, the joint venture subsidiary is in an altogether different competitive economic environment and the law's attitude

toward it is likely to be liberal for the forseeable future. The
primary reason for this is that the EEC is desirous of accelerating
the formation of larger, more competitive enterprises in comparison
with American and Japanese enterprises. In addition, in those
instances where EEC joint ventures are created they seldom hold a
very large percentage of the market and do not present anticompetitive
effects.

Where one of the joint venture partners already has a
'dominant' position, it could take improper advantage of the venture
and hence come in violation of Article 86. (62)

It is also possible for an EEC joint venture to be unlawful
under Article 85. However, it would be necessary to prove not only
that the venture produced a restraint on competition, but that the
restraint was noticeable. To be noticeable, according to the
Commission, the venture must have more than 5 per cent of the
relevant market and the turnover of the firms concerned must be more
than 15-20 million units of account. Even then an appraisal of the
competitive structure of the market and the 'adverse affects' would
have to be made. And it could also be determined that the venture
strengthened the position of the firms involved in the international
market. (63)

Before going on to the subject of mergers, it is worth noting
that the joint venture may be viewed as a quasi-merger. The difference
is that a merger is a non-recurring event. In consequence of the
execution of a merger, it ceases to be an agreement between the enterprises. With a joint venture, there is an ongoing relationship between

two separate enterprises. And as the parent enterprises grow and
evolve, they may become competitors in other fields which may be
affected by the existing partial combination in the joint venture. (64)

Mergers

American antitrust laws may render certain mergers
unlawful on the same basis as joint venture subsidiaries. The criteria
applied would be whether or not the merger will restrain competition
in the American domestic or import market. The law would apply to
the merger of two American firms, either in the United States or
overseas, or to an American firm and a non-American firm. In
theory, it even applies to the merger of two European firms selling
to the United States market. In practice, however such an application
is unlikely, especially if the firms do not have American subsidiaries
over which jurisdiction could be had. When the American laws are
applied to mergers in Europe, they stand in obvious contrast to the
general passive attitude of European merger laws. Since the
European laws have not generally blocked American mergers and
acquisitions, there is resentment when American laws stop European
acquisitions or mergers in the United States. In contrast , the blocking
of American mergers in Europe by United States law is often favorably
received. These incongruities tend to favor multinationalization in
certain directions. The justified European policy of encouraging
mergers would apparently prefer to encourage European mergers and
discriminate against non-European firms, especially the larger American
firms. This may curtail the design of a uniform policy. (65)

The European attitude towards mergers and monopolies is entirely different than the American. Monopolies are considered as neither good nor bad in themselves, but are judged on the results and on their behavior. With such an attitude, it appears logical that no law would affect mergers. Until recently, it was generally assumed that neither Article 85 nor Article 86 provided a check on mergers. With, but few exceptions, no European statute has seriously attempted to regulate mergers. The English Monopolies and Mergers Act of 1965 is the most serious attempt to do so. It empowers a regulatory body to investigate and report whether any proposed or recently completed merger resulting in the control of one-third of the market or increasing the power of an existing monopoly may be expected to operate against the public interest. (66)

The EEC Commission and a few legal writers have advocated that mergers accomplished by dominant firms could be regarded as abusive under Article 86 when those mergers create undue market power. Joliet is one other writer that effectively argues the contrary. The Commission itself admits, he says, that Article 86 does permit the existence and creation of dominant positions. Therefore, the creation of a dominant position by way of mergers is lawful. He asserts that Article 86 is not directed against a probability of abuse, but against actual exploitation of market power. (67)

It appears now that the EEC is moving in the direction of the policy adopted in the 1965 English Statute on mergers. (68) The latest EEC proposal moves toward the prevention of concentrations. (69) The proposed regulation affects transactions which bring about a concentration between undertakings or groups of undertakings, at least one of which is established in the Common Market, whereby they acquire or enhance the power to hinder effective competition in the Common Market or in a substantial part thereof in so far as the concentration may affect trade between Member States. The regulation does not apply where the aggregate turnover of the participating under-takings is less than 200 million units of account and the goods and services concerned do not account in any Member State for more than 25 per cent of the turnover in the relevant market.

The proposed regulation, however, may be declared inapplicable to concentrations which are indispensable to the attainment of an objective which is given priority treatment in the common interest of the Community. It is the provision which could be used to favor EEC mergers, but not mergers involving non-EEC enterprises. It is noteworthy that the regulation's definition of concentrations carefully includes four separate categories of contractual arrangements. This properly recognizes that mergers other than by ownership, are increasingly important.

Dominant Enterprises, Monopolies, Market Power

Most enterprises considered to be multinationals are also large. Size and economic power can almost be viewed as coincidental with multinationality. Consequently, multinationals are especially subject to antitrust laws concerning dominance, market power or monopolization.

Another, and possibly conflicting outlook, is that enterprises become multi-national partly in attempt to expand without dominating any one particular national market. This might suggest the need for revised national antitrust laws or coordinated or international regulatory schemes.

In the United States, the Sherman Act was intended to deal with monopolies. Cases under it have resulted in the dissolution of some enterprises considered monopolies. However, some of the cases have become tangled in the confusion over so called 'good' or 'bad' monopolies. Partly because the Sherman Act was not especially successful, the Clayton Act was passed to deal with mergers and acquisitions in a monopoly-preventative fashion.

The idea of the Sherman Act was to preserve compeition in favor of the self-regulating mechanism of the market. In contrast, the EEC approach does not oppose the achievement or existence of monopoly or market power. But once an enterprise reaches a dominant position, it then becomes subject to regulation for abusive conduct. Until recently, the EEC has not been concerned with the achievement of dominant position whether by internal growth or external acquisition or merger.

The American approach is concerned more with preserving the number of competitors and a competitive environment. Whereas, the EEC's Article 86 seems preoccupied with the treatment of suppliers and purchasers instead of competitors and with the effect on consumers. One assumption inherent in Article 86 is that monopolistic structure

does not lead inevitably to monopostic performance. Some American
observers have expressed the fear that the 'conduct' or 'abuse'
approach could ultimately turn dominant firms into public utilities. (70)

One difficulty with the Sherman Act is that it does not define
the concept of monopolization. The courts have consistently emphasized,
however, that mere size is not a sufficient criteria. In some cases it
has appeared that size relative to that of competitors is significant.
The finding of excessive market power must, however, be accompanied
by the additional element of 'deliberateness' to constitute monopolization.
It is the wilful acquisition or maintenance of power, as distinguished from
growth or development as a consequence of superior product, business
tactics or historic accident. (71) Size alone is not enough. Monopoly
power has been defined primarily in terms of market percentages. The
percentage required to establish monopoly power has been relatively
high, in no case under 75 per cent. (72) It is significant to note that
the market power, which may be deliberately acquired by a single firm,
is substantially higher than that which may be achieved by a merger of
two or more firms. (73) This appears to favor existing multinationals
which have the financial resources and international borrowing power
to expand from within or to merge in selective nations and markets
avoiding the critical market percentages. Another important facet
of this is that the percentage where mergers are considered to be
against the public interest is, in most cases, lower in the United States
than in other countries. (74) This makes it easier for American

multinationals to merge outside the United States and conversely more difficult for non-American multinations to merge within the United States. Similar national disparities affect the overall pattern of multinationalization of firms.

The EEC attitude toward antitrust is to eliminate or control restrictive practices of dominant firms. This is a 'conduct' control system in which a determination of market power is prerequisite to intervention against adverse effects. The focus here is not on the abusive practices or adverse effects, but on the criteria by which market power or dominant enterprises are identified.

The EEC law and that of other countries with a 'conduct' approach defines the degree of market power deemed significant. (75) The extent to which that degree varies among nations and regions will, of course, have some influence on the location of new plants and expansion of existing ones.

The first step in the process is the identification of the relevant market or line of commerce. The second is the determination of the competition within that market. The latter can be done using a formal criteria such as percentage share in the market, or on an actual assessment of each situation at a particular point in time. In some countries, this is done by appraising whether a particular enterprise exerts a substantial influence on price, production or distribution, and its size and financial power relative to other competitors (76)

One aspect of market definition is especially significant for multinational enterprises and for nations formulating policies toward them. That is the question of whether or not foreign product alternatives (imports) are taken into account in determining percentage of market or market power. And whether or not the relevant geographical market should extend outside the national or regional boundaries where the law is in effect.

It appears that most present laws do take into account imports or foreign product alternatives. It is noted, however, that market power has still been found to exist even in small countries with a relatively high share of foreign trade in the particular product. An OECD study has concluded that since competing imports are taken into account, there is no need for an extra-national extension of the relevant geographical market. This may be an incorrect conclusion. In any event, the OECD study did not uncover any rulings where the relevant geographic market has been extended beyond the area in which the respective law applies. It concludes: "It can, therefore, not be generally said that with the increasing opening of markets, the issue of market power has lost its importance on the national level. Whether the removal of public trade barriers will reduce existing positions of market power in particular countries will essentially depend on whether increased imports, in fact, take place and present equivalent product alternatives to national buyers." (77)

More needs to be said about extension of the relevant geographical market beyond national or regional boundaries. Experience in the United States has shown that anticompetitive effects of a proposed merger can be demonstrated or not depending on whether or not the relevant geographical market is defined as that in a city, state, or national region. In some instances, a merger will reduce competition

in a narrow geographical area, but increase it in a wider regional
area. (78) The present American view appears to be that if
competition is reduced in any relevant market, then a merger can
be forbidden. The courts have, so far, rejected the concept of
'countervailing power'. Anticompetitive effect in one market cannot
be justified by procompetitive consequences in another. It is my
contention that every merger ruling or lack of a ruling makes that
decision. It cannot be avoided. The problem and value choice that
this suggests can be raised to the international level. A national
firm can be declared to be dominant if only the national market and
present imports are considered. Based on that, a national firm could
be ordered to make itself smaller or be regulated in some way. This
ignores the fact that potential competitors in other countries could
commence competition in that market at any time. It also ignores the
fact that the national enterprise in question is also in competition with
foreign enterprises in other national markets. The national enterprise
may be restricted in some way to preserve present competition in the
national market at the expense of the ability of the national enterprise
to compete overseas or to compete nationally in the future. Resolving
this matter requires assessment of present and future trade barriers
in relevant nations, assessment of competitors, as well as potential
foreign competitors, multinationality of enterprises concerned and
relevant time frames.

Some critics question whether the present concepts of
market power are adequate to cover the modern forms of business

power. Professor Edwards believes that size, financial power and diversification have become of primary significance. His concern lies in the fact that these factors are not taken into account in the present concepts. (79) The OECD study concluded that absolute size has never been an applied criteria for determining the existence of market dominance. (80)

Another criticism is the failure of the law to deal with existing monopolies and olgopolies. The United States merger law, and likely the EEC merger law of the future, will deal with those attempting to gain such positions of power. But it fails to deal with those who have it, especially olgopolies resulting from internal growth. Professor Galbraith is particularly critical of this. Professor Rahl likewise. (81)

The OECD study judged that, in the long term, an abuse or conduct control system could not guarantee the economic benefits expected from competition. This suggests that the concept of monopoly or dominance has a growing future. (82)The multinationals are the possessors of size, financial power, and diversification. They have grown partly because present concepts do not strike at those characteristics. The future may not be the same.

8.   LABOR

Although much has been said and written about the multinational corporation, little attention has been given to the labor and industrial relations aspect. (1) Nevertheless, the impact on the future of industrial relations will be fundamental.

In 1966, United States-controlled foreign subsidiaries in manufacturing and extraction industries employed 5.5 million local workers. (2) That number added to the figures for European and Japanese enterprises may not account for a very large portion of world employment. But it is likely that the pattern of labor relations that takes place in those segments will set the pattern for the others.

At the present time, the legal and managerial structures of MNE have advanced to meet changing global conditions. In contrast, the labor unions have not kept up with the integrating world economic structure. (3) Unless unions adapt their organizational structures and techniques there will be an increasing imbalance of power as between labor and management.

The conflicts that are developing on the international level are not altogether different than those that have existed at the national level especially in federal nations. Large multi-plant, national enterprises inititally gained advantages over purely local labor organizations.

Since labor organizations can be a balancing force against MNE management, they do serve as a 'control' device, like antitrust.

Many unions are, in fact closely aligned with the government. Unions
and government have a common interest in maintaining stability in
national employment and in similar areas in which MNE may have a
conflict of interest. On the other hand, future global labor strikes or
sympathy strikes may adversely affect national economic stability.
Nonetheless, the labor movement probably represents the major
political force in Europe and it's influence will reflect in government
regulation of MNE. (4) Increasingly, national governments will be put
in between the contending forces of MN labor and management. In the
past, priority given to economic objectives over social objectives may
have favored government alliances with the MN enterprises, at least,
in the developing countries. (5)

There is bound to be 'heat' in the forthcoming union efforts
to cope with MNE. The following is a statement taken from an American
union brochure. It is the quotation of an American businessman who
apparently decided to manufacture a particular product outside the
United States. It is an extreme example, but its quotation in the
brochure is intended to communicate the threat of multinationalization
as perceived by labor. "I am making the same product under the same
brand name, selling .... to the same customer, with the same equipment,
for one reason. The labor ... is fifty cents an hour, as compared to the
three dollars I was paying. I took everything except the labor and that
is exactly why I did it." (6) This, of course, is not a balanced
description of the motivation of home country multinationals, American
or others. But it is the view of labor in a home country. The attitude of
labor in host countries is something else.

The Dilemmas of Labor

The fundamental problems for labor are the impediments to international unity. As the internationalization of production continues, some nations gain jobs and some lose. There is a built-in conflict of interest between national unions. Added to this are the basic differences in economic and political ideologies. American unions favor free enterprise and a conflict model of labor-management relations within a defined legal framework. European unions adhere to a socialist line of philosophy and are moving towards a participatory role with management. (7) In contrast, Communist unions will not accept a participatory role in internal company management. (8) And unlike unions in Western nations, most unions in Japan are organized on a company level. This type of union, the company or enterprise union, accounts for 80% of Japanese unions. (9) Some multinational managers hold the view that the self-interest of local and national unions prevents any meaningful co-operation across national boundaries. (10)

Unions have other obstacles to cope with. Generally, they lack the overall technical and organizational sophistication possessed by international management. And the size of their international staffs are infinitesimal by comparison. And in negotiating with MN subsidiaries it is always unclear where the enterprise decision-making power is located - at the subsidiary, the regional headquarters or at the very top of the parent company. To this is added the inadequacy of published data about individual subsidiaries. Another obstacle

is variation in national labor laws. This means that labor tactics
such as sympathy strikes and secondary boycotts may be lawful
in one country and illegal in others. In some countries such
as England there is a philosopy against over-judicialization of
labor relations. Whether labor relations laws favor the unions,
nationally or internationally, depends, of course, on the particular
laws. The 1971 Industrial Relations Act is claimed to have weakened
labor's position in the UK, but is likely to be repealed. British company law
has also been said to make it difficult for U.K. unions to obtain
financial data about some MNEs operating in the U.K. This is
because many of those companies do not trade publicly on the stock
exchange. This situation is being corrected. There is the additional
problem that many MN companies like IBM and Kodak have a world wide
policy of non-recognition of unions. (11)

Problems of union recognition are also present with purely
national companies. As to this and other issues there is the question
of whether companies, national and multinational, can or should be treated
legally different. (12) Professor Wedderburn has put it this way: "Why
is foreign control of a local enterprise any different in quality from
control by a large domestic corporation which may in real terms be as
remote from the ordinary people over which its decisions hold sway." (13)
There is an analogy to the federal situation in the United States which
sheds some light on this question. The relationship between local, state
companies and national or interstate companies can be compared to
national companies and multinational companies. The commerce clause

in the United States Constitution has resulted in different treatment of interstate or national companies from purely local, state companies. A host of minimum legal standards, including wages and labor conditions, apply only to the national companies. The entire national labor relations laws in the U.S. are only applicable to them. This attitude presents a precedent for going a step further and having special national or international laws applied to multinational companies. No doubt this is what labor would prefer. In 1968 the British Trades Union Council urged the government to make union recognition a condition for foreign investment in the U.K., a condition not imposed on large British firms. (14)

Unions' Global Counterforce

The trade union movement envisions a three step process towards the creation of an international global counterforce to meet these problems. (15) First, union disputes in one country with one segment of a MNE is to be supported by actions by other national unions against other segments of the MNE. Parent company unions will support subsidiary country unions and vice versa. The final goal being MNE - wide union solidarity in all countries where the enterprise is present. Second, multiple negotiation with a MNE in several countries at the same time. This is to be accompanied by strikes, information and consumer campaigns and actions preventing transfer of production. Third, integrated negotiation for common demands in all segments of a MNE. As this may be complicated by varying national labor standards, the common demands may be in the form of uniform proportionate increases in various categories of benefits.

Diversity in Collective Bargaining Levels

Collective bargaining now takes place at so many different levels both within and among nations, and differently among enterprises and industries, as to make the process of international or global negotiation very difficult.

Some MNEs will retain basic labor policy-making at the parent headquarters while others such as Philips will leave labor relations as a matter for its national subsidiaries. Meanwhile enterprises like the French, German, Belgian Boussois - Souchon - Neuvesel have voluntarily taken some progressive steps to avoid labor-management confrontation. It is a commission uniting union and management representatives from all three countries. It does not yet include salary negotiation but is moving toward guaranteeing employment and equal growth in the three countries. (16)

In the UK the level of collective bargaining is industry rather than the individual company as it generally is in the U.S. The UK situation is complicated by the fact that some MNEs such as Kodak do not join the employer's association. Furthermore U.S. labor-managment contracts are legally binding whereas UK contracts generally are not. Varying national minimum wage and working condition laws complicate global bargaining. In some countries those national laws determine minimum contract terms and terms above that are negotiated at the company level. In others, minimum terms are determined by industry by a national union, and terms above that by plant negotiations by the local plant representative of the union. Another impediment to global negotiation is that some

national customs favor fixed contract termination dates while others do
not.   In any event lack of uniform contract dates throughout the
national subsidiaries of any MNE presents a definite roadblock.   There
is some movement to promote collective bargaining within regional
groupings such as the EEC and LAFTA.   These meet resistance
because of conflict with the legal frameworks of national member nations.
There is now some regional collective bargaining in the EEC in the field
of agriculture. (17)   Labor's prime advantage in regional negotiation
systems is that there is little threat of company unionism. (18)

International Trade Unions and Global Bargaining

There are a limited number of international trade union
confederations that now exist and are leading the multinationalization of
the trade unions. (19)   These unions are responsible for a number of
recent examples of co-ordinated international union successes in
negotiations with MNEs. (20)   In the United States the AFL-C10
has co-ordinated enterprise bargaining with MNEs, like General Electric
and Westinghouse, for all plants within the U.S.   This is a complex
process because of the multi-product, multi-plant variations. (21)   The
same organizational tactics can be extended overseas.   There are recent
examples of both U.S. and European unions working successfully with
unions abroad. (22)

The most successful international union actions have taken place
in the automobile industry.   The International Metalworkers Federation
has created company councils for selected MNs including General Motors
Chrysler, Fiat, Renault and Volkswagen.   They collect worldwide financial
data for each company and co-ordinate negotiations.   In 1971 the IMF
auto councils agreed to establish common contract termination dates.

A similar auto council in the United Automobile Workers Union
achieved U.S. and Canadian wage parity in the automobile plants of
General Motors, Ford, and Chrysler in 1967. The International Chemical
Federation plans to have twenty-five multinational company councils
established in the chemical, rubber paper and glass industries. (23)

In terms of global tactics the unions must decide between
regional or global agreements involving all companies of a given industry,
or enterprise bargaining across all national boundaries. It appears that
industry-wide bargaining is a dominant pattern in many countries. If
bargaining takes place at both the industry and enterprise levels in the
same country, difficulties could arise. National laws might bind
multinational corporations to industry agreements whether they consented
or not. This would conflict with enterprise-wide bargaining elsewhere.
This could be solved where centralized MNE bargaining dealt with issues
distinct from those dealt with in industry bargaining in a given country.
Or accommodation could come about where an agreement reached at one
level improves on the provisions of the minimum agreement reached at
another level. However if, for example, a MNE agreement improved on
industry-agreed terms, there could be a conflict with other industry
companies. Centralized MN-bargained terms could also differ with
some national income policies. Labor bargaining pressure tactics
such as strikes, secondary boycotts and lockouts could be lawful in
some countries and illegal in others. (24) In Germany, for example,
sympathetic strikes and secondary boycotts are normally unlawful, and
it would be difficult for local workers to join an internationally

co-ordinated industrial action. (25)   The union view towards such laws directed in respect of MNE is given by international labor leader, Charles Levinson: "If it is legally permissible for a foreign parent company directly to control and decide management policy from abroad, then it should be equally permissible for workers to act together with other workers of the same company abroad in their common interests without its being held to be an illegal sympathy strike or secondary boycott. " (26)

An issue has been made of labors' difficulty in finding the true locus of MNE decision making authority in labor relations, with inuendoes that the power should be at the subsidiary level.   It has been asserted, however, that it does not make any difference where the decisions are made since the interest of the enterprise is the same whether it comes from the centre or the subsidiary. (27)   Either way, there is much skepticism about the prospect for multinational collective nargaining since there are no international rules to govern the process. (28)

Impact on MNE Strategy

In response to labor's growing global tactics multinationals will have to give additional consideration to their international production strategies.   MNEs in natural resource extraction industries and service industries have limited choices open to them.   But manufacturing MNEs are more flexible.   Each enterprise must decide whether its subsidiary in each country should produce the same product mix, in which case a production stopage in one country may affect sales from that subsidiary only, and lost sales may be replaced through imports from subsidiaries in other countries.   Or an enterprise may choose to be vertically

integrated.   The output of one subsidiary is the input of another.
In that event a stopage in one country stops all production output.
Another alternative is international specialization.   Each subsidiary
produces a unique product or products for sale both domestically and
worldwide.   This avoids the loss of all enterprise production mentioned
in the previous strategy but it does not permit the replacement of lost
production in one country with production from others.   The MNE choice
of production organization not only affects its relationship with unions,
but also has implications for the host countries.   Imports. exports,
employment, research activities are obviously affected. (29)

Labor Participation. the European Company

      Recently, there have evolved a number of schemes for worker
participation in the management of enterprises.   This is broadly
referred to as worker co-determination and is accomplished through
unions or through non-union employee works or plant councils.   Germany
has made the most progress in this direction. (30)   There are some who
believe that this will bring about a new era of co-operative relations between
management and labor. (31)   If true, this would tend to simplify the coming
raising of labor-management relations to the regional and global level.
However, there are others who believe that labor-management conflict
is inevitable and healthy and that laws are needed to provide a framework
for the relationship. (32)   Whether or not co-determination will aid labor
when dealing with MNE is also questioned: "How far does it profit a
German worker to have a representative on the board of a German company
if the soul of the group to which that company is subject is to be found in
Tokyo or Detroit ?" (33)

The proposed European Company structure does recognise the
possibility of multinational collective bargaining but says little about
how it will actually function. (34)   The other deficiency not remedied
by the proposal or any portion of the EEC Treaty or its Commission is the
right of multinational labor organization and labor actions.   "The true
correlative to any international agreement securing to capital the right
to move and, therefore, organise across the boundaries of nation states
would be an agreement securing to collective organisations of workpeople
the right to take 'common' action in negotiating, bargaining with and,
if need be, striking against the multinational enterprises to which that
right is accorded.   It is not free movement of labor but free international
trade union action which is the true counterpart to free movement of
capital.   Neither in the text of the Rome Treaty nor in any of the
activities of the Community's Commission or other bodies is there to be
found the faintest echo of any such right. " (35)   It is generally conceded
by multinational companies that the prospect for multinational strikes is
the thorniest aspect of the European Company proposal. (36)   One clear
advantage of the proposal is that it recognizes the workers' right to information
and consultation in enterprise decision-making.   The need for 'disclosure'
in successful collective bargaining should not be overlooked. (37)

The Role of the International Labor Office

The ILO should play a big role in the internationalization of labor-
management relations.   It has the advantage of a tripartite structure
uniting representatives from labor, management and governments from
virtually every nation in the world.   The International Metalworkers
Federation advocates that fut ure international laws and agreements

on the subject should include provisions for adherence to all the provisions of ILO Conventions whether or not ratified by the country in which the multination corporations are operating. (38) There has been some demand by trade unions that the ILO draft separate labor standards for MNE. MNE agrument against this is that it would discriminate between multinational subsidiaries and other firms within a country as well as creating two sets of ILO standards. (39) A labor response to this is that there is no question of double standards because national and multinational companies are not the same; and furthermore, that progress has to be made and standards should be levelled up, not down. The MNE rebuttal is that there is no proof that multinationals have given rise to more problems or criticism than national companies. (40) Employers have also complained that increasing concentration of trade union power also represents a threat but there has been little suggestion of supervision of their activities. (41)

The main problems in raising world labor standards by global collective bargaining is that there is no legal enforceability of international collective agreements and upward harmonization of world standards may conflict with employment objectives in developing countries. (42)

The Future

It is doubtful that labor negotiations on a global basis will occur for a number of years. In a decade, however, it will be hard to defend differences of salary and working conditions between say, France, Belgium and Germany. (43)

In the past 'labor' has not been considered to be a mobile production factor. However rising educational attainments, skills and income expectations will encourage the mobility of labor. The result may not be on a scale comparable to the mobility of capital, but it will be a significant factor. (44) At the present time West Germany employs 2.6 million immigrant workers, approximately 10% of the West German workforce. (45) Similar mobility on a wider scale would seriously affect the strategies of both labor and management in the international arena.

At the present time MNE has brought about extensive mobility of jobs or employment. In capital exporting countries this has resulted in labor pressure for government - financial, manpower retraining, and adjustment benefits, as well as legal restriction of MNE foreign investment. (46)

There will be increasing pressure for special laws applicable to MNE. Whether this is justified or not it will bring a demand for more objective, comparative studies of MNE. It has been suggested, for example, that there are fewer strikes in foreign-owned firms in the UK. (47) This is the kind of issue that should be carefully studied. The truth may be that MNE are generally better corporate citizens than local enterprises, in so far as labor standards are concerned. Some believe that MNEs have spread favourable and progressive innovations in the field of labor relations while others assert adverse affects. MNEs in the UK have been criticized for setting patterns of wage settlements contributing to inflation and are therefore a cost to the British economy. (48) An American union economist has critically asserted the contrary - that

MNEs keep wages down, as a result of their pursuit of comparative advantages. (49)

It is hard to avoid the proposition that labor-management relations is a power struggle and that the balance of power favors MNE. Since there are numerous obstacles to effective global union organization, it is likely that labor will rely increasingly on legal assistance at all levels.

9   TAXATION

If there were no taxes in any nations of the world, and if there
were freedom and stability in currency exchange, it would be of little
importance to multinational corporations or to governments where in a
MNE system, profits were shown. (1) The incentive to arrange transactions among different countries for tax advantages would only be
removed if all income tax systems were identical, or if related corporations were taxed as parts of the same entity and subject to worldwide
taxation.

First, it is important to make clear that tax planning does not
play a preemptive role in overall enterprise strategy. Other considerations
predominate. However, once strategic decisions have been made,
management prefers to operate in a way that avoids taxes where possible.
(2) MNE management co-ordinate the work of legally separate entities
and in doing so attempt optimize the international tax environment.

It should not be forgotten that MNE is not the only form of multi-
company enterprise. Operating solely within the boundaries of a single
nation there are multi-company enterprises that we can call,
'uninationals'. If one understands the tax ramifications peculiar to them,
then one is on the road to comprehending taxation of multinationals. The
immediate complication of the latter stems from the fact that many national
taxing authorities are interested parties. However, in the federally-
organized nations there is some analogy to the conflict between one state
and another, and between states and the federal government.

National governments and MNE's pose certain unique problems
for each other not found in the relationship between governments and
purely national corporations. The problems arise primarily in the area
of income taxation. The value-added tax (VAT) is also significant. Since
the sources of profit of MNE are worldwide, questions always arise as
to which part of the total profit should be attributed to a particular enterprise or taxed by a particular authority. The conflict is between the tax-
minimizing practices of MNEs and the tax-maximizing policies of national
governments.

There are many tax-minimizing devices that can be employed by
MNE. All of them have an impact on the managerial and legal structure.
In response to the MNE tactics, national tax laws have been modified.
This interacting process is yet in its infancy. Within MNE's the process
is exceedingly complex. There is no such thing as simple tax manipulation.
A structural a tactical change for tax purposes also has an effect upon
other critical variables such as cash flow, accounts receivable, inventories
and effects on other subsidiaries in the MNE system. (3)

Uninationals are vulnerable to the arbitrary or onerous taxation of
one particular nation. The advantage of multinationals, if any, is in
flexibility. Their 'eggs' are not all in one national basket.

Variations in the International Tax Environment

National taxing systems can be classified and sub-classified in
many different ways. (4) Even the revenue raising aspect has been
approached with widely dissimilar methods. Added to that are the various

ways and degrees in which taxation is employed as an economic regulator.
Then there are differences in types of taxes, rates, definitions of income
and expenses, extraterritorial jurisdictorial principles and allowances for
foreign taxes paid.

Income tax rates do not vary greatly among the main industrial
countries. But with accelerating world competition even a few percentage
points can be significant. The advanced industrial country rates run
around 50%. But in countries such as Peru and Brazil the rates are 30%
and 35% respectively. (5) Compounding those income tax rate differentials
is the fact that some nations rely heavily on other types of taxes. The
United States, the major home country for MNE, places heavy reliance
on income taxes as its main source of federal revenue. Most other
countries rely proportionately more on indirect taxes such as value added
tax (VAT), turnover tax and excise taxes. For example, West Germany
derives more than 40% of its federal tax revenues from the VAT, whereas
the US derives more than 65% of its from income taxes, and only about
10% from indirect taxes. (6) The ratio of direct to indirect taxes contrasts
widely from nation to nation.

Taxing jurisdictional policies also differ. Under the US policy
the place of incorporation generally determines the tax jurisdiction.
The general European attitude is that corporate profits should be taxed
in the 'source' country where the profits are generated and the management
and control is located. In this respect the US has placed domestic
neutrality ahead of foreign neutrality as the desired goal. (7)

International Double Taxation

In the case of multi-company uninational enterprises dividends paid by one corporate body to another within the group are free of taxation. The parent is generally taxed for consolidated income. There is no double taxation. (8)

However, as soon as intercorporate company activity extends beyond the boundaries of a single nation, the situation changes. Few, if any, nations allow a local subsidiary to pay dividends to a parent company in another nation without first taxing those dividends. Otherwise the profits are lost as a tax source.

The double taxation enters where the country of the parent company taxes foreign-source income or has what is called a 'worldwide' tax policy. The United States follows this policy. Where this double taxation takes place it may mean that host country competition will take place under different tax rates if the connected home countries of the competing MNS's have different rax rates or principles of taxation. Although most countries presently follow the territorial or source principle, there is a trend in the direction of the worldwide attitude of home country taxation of profits, at least when repatriated. (9)

This international double taxation is generally avoided by several mechanisms - some established by nations and others by the MNE's themselves. Usually the home country grants a tax credit for the foreign taxes paid up to the level of the home country tax rate. There are problems in differences in definitions between home and host countries. MNE management must exercise care not to be caught in a double taxation situation at least to some extent. This is not a concern of uninationals.

In the US the credit provision is very broad, encompassing both withholding taxes and corporate income taxes, and extending down through three tiers of foreign subsidiaries.

The granting of tax credit by 'worldwide' taxing countries has not eliminated double taxation altogether. Bilateral tax treaties have aided the goal. But these have not been feasible between developed and less-developed countries because the flow of dividends is generally one way only. Consequently some less-developed countries have been prone to make individual agreements with MNE's concerning specific projects.

Double Taxation Deferral and Tax Havens

Few industrial 'home' countries do subject their MNE's to current taxation of earnings generated by their overseas subsidiaries. Some do not even tax those earnings when they are repatriated. (10)

The deferral of home country taxation is accomplished by home country tax laws which do not tax foreign subsidiary profits until such time as they are actually remitted to the parent company. A number of non-US MNE's have special foreign subsidiaries which act as tax havens for these foreign subsidiary profits. The tax haven subsidiary, located in a favourable national tax country, acts as a funnel for redistribution to other subsidiaries and for ultimate transmittal to the parent company. Since 1962 changes in the US tax law US multinational use of the device has been limited to situations involving actual economic rather than tax motives. (11)

The use of the tax haven subsidiary is particularly important where home country exchange controls make it difficult for the parent company to fulfil the function of redistributing system profits for new foreign investment or expansion. In a uninational company group the function of central reservoir can be played by the parent company without such complications. (12)

Although the idea of a tax haven subsidiary conjures up sinister visions, it may not have any unfair effect on any of the entities concerned. The taxing position of the host country is unaffected. If the home country taxes, it only means that its taxes will be received at a latter time. The only tax forgone is that of the base company's country, but that is by deliberate choice to encourage local commerce. (13) There is an opinion in the US that its multinations enjoyed an advantage over its national companies because they could retain overseas profits in foreign base companies when domestic profits were high, and declare them when low. Thus MNE total tax liability in the long run may be lower than equivalent domestic earnings would have caused. (14)

In the early years of a new foreign investment where losses are likely, a foreign subsidiary may not be the best legal structure. If the plant is merely an unincorporated branch, overseas losses may be deducted from parent profits. In 'worldwide' home countries this may not be possible if the structure is a foreign subsidiary. (15)

Dividend - Avoiding Procedures

The object of dividend -avoiding procedures is to transfer resources of the foreign subsidiary to the parent in a form that does not attract the taxation of the host and home country. These transfers can take the form of royalties, interest on loan capital, management fees, and similar expense items of the subsidiary which reduce its profits. A related method of reducing subsidiary profits is called transfer pricing. Inter-corporate pricing flexibility permits raising the cost of goods sold to the subsidiary by the parent. Either way, avoidance of subsidiary dividend payments is advantageous only when the income tax rate of the subsidiary is below that of the parent.

In the multinational oil industry transfer pricing is apparently readily employed, but in the reverse - profits are built-up in the subsidiary, and reduced in the parent. This results because of the preference of the host governments for large taxable revenues within their territories, and the tacit acceptance by downstream governments of high-priced crude oil imports for reasons of overall fuel policy. (16) Outside of the oil industry, the use of dividend-manipulating techniques is probably exaggerated. In the first place there must be a significant level of trade, in the right direction between parents and subsidiaries, or within MNE systems. This is not generally present except where there is a high degree of vertical integration. Where there are minority shareholders in the foreign subsidiary, there will be a conflict of interest in these matters. Also, by reason of their separate legal structure subsidiaries are generally required by company law to submit their accounts to independent auditors.

It should be remembered that all multi-company groups having an internal circulation of goods and services, whether uninational or multinational, could attempt these practices. There are national laws which have dealt with this, within the national framework, for a number of years, and their application has been extended to scrutinize these matters in both instances. (17) The operation of arbitrary displacement of profit from one company to another obscures judgment of the true return on capital in any one company and may be counterproductive.

If this type of manipulation were prevalent in MNE's then it would be expected that the dividend payment from subsidiary to parent would be greater in the multinationals than in uninational company enterprises. This has been demonstrated not to be so in at least one study. (18)

There is no question, however, but that the variations in the international tax environment give the multinationals an advantage of flexibility in these matter. And that any wrongdoing is less easily subject to scrutiny.

In the overall picture the multinational tax bill is eventually paid. Unlike the uninational enterprise there is a question as to which taxing nation gets the tax revenue, or should get it. It has been said that this question is wholly political, as between nations, and not ethical. (19)

Value-Added Tax (VAT)

The fact that some nations rely heavily on VAT and others on income taxes introduces unique implications for multinationals. The special character of VAT adds to it. VAT is essentially a national sales tax collected at each stage of production or sale of consumption goods in proportion to the value-added during that stage.

One advantage of VAT over the income tax is that it makes transfer-pricing difficult. It cannot be avoided by book writeoffs, accelerated depreciation, loss carry-forwards, loose expensing practices, interest on debt, or artifical transfer prices, and the like. All firms are taxed alike. Even state corporations pay VAT. (20) In the long run this equality should favor MNE. VAT did, however, eliminate an advantage that vertically-organized MNE's had under the earlier sales or turnover taxes that prevailed in Europe.

European MNE's exporting to overseas customers or to foreign subsidiaries avoid VAT by rebate payments given at the time of export. GATT regulations do not allow direct taxes such as income tax on which the United States relies, to be rebated on export sales. On the surface it appears that American MNE's are disadvantaged to some extent. (21)

The US multinationals are similarly disadvantaged in so far as US parent income tax is concerned. If its foreign subsidiary has paid extensive foreign VAT taxes rather than foreign income tax, it cannot obtain a tax credit because credit is only given for foreign income taxes. In consequence there can be effective double taxation of European affiliates. (22)

The Developing Environment

Tax treaties have begun to level the difference between national tax systems or at least to make accommodations so that there is more equality and fairness in the taxation of all enterprises. Most of the treaties are bilateral and not the most expedient method of harmonizing the international tax environment. Many of them merely accommodate the taxing differences between 'worldwide' taxing jurisdictions such as the US and host countries.

Of the various approaches to taxation of foreign investment it has been suggested that the tax credit approach is superior because it is neutral as to capital location and e; itable as to tax burden. (23) This has been criticized, however, as having caused a steady increase in the income tax rates in less-developed countries. (24) At a time when there is recognition of those countries' needs for additional revenues, the criticism is not especially valid. In fact, there has been an attempt to resolve this across the board. A United Nations ad hoc expert group on tax treaties, between developed and developing countries, has prepared several reports with a notable degree of consensus on specific points in respect to revenue division. (25) A futuristic suggestion has been made for the overall taxation of multinationals. It recommends a factor-formula technique similar to that employed in the US to apportion the tax revenue of interstate or national businesses among the states in which they operate. Under this approach a taxing nation would allocate to itself a share of MNE's aggregate profits, in proportion of such factors as the percentage of the MNE's worldwide payroll, sales or assets in the taxing country. (26)

What developments take place within the EEC will be some

indication of what might be achieved in other regions or on a global

scale. Considerable effort has already begun in the harmonization

of direct taxes. (27) National tax hindrances are one of the impediments

to the EEC's desired crossborder enterprise concentration. (28)

However, even full tax harmonization may not be enough. Having the

tax systems and rates the same may be insufficient if there are

completely different uses of the revenue collected and the national

economic policies. (29)

The need of both multinationals and nation states is certainty

and stabily in taxation. In their development efforts many developing

nations continue to forego revenues to which they should be entitled,

while MNE's sometimes use inefficient methods of doing

business in order to minimize their total tax bill. (30) To accomplish

this the MNE's are beginning to employ computerized tax simulation

models to find the optimal system for minimizing its global tax bill.

These models take into account factors such as the legal structure of

the parent and subsidiaries, policies on the movement of funds within

the MNE system, home and host tax rates, tax treaties, currency

convertibility and devaluation probabilities. (31)

10   DISCLOSURE

The changes brought about by the organization of legal and managerial structures on a multinational basis have been discussed in previous chapters. Changes within multinational enterprise and between it an national and international bodies have brought new problems, conflicts and policy issues which must be resolved. As with all such matters, the first step is to assemble the facts. Hence, the importance of the subject of disclosure by multinational enterprise.

In fact, Professor Vagts believes that there is no consensus for MNE regulation on a grand international scale and that information gathering should be the immediate goal. (1)

The information that is needed is not only the traditional data required by stockholders and creditors. Nations themselves need to know about the flow of money, materials and jobs in and out of their borders.

In the United States the irony is that it has spent enormous sums to support intelligence agencies for global political information systems. But, in contrast, has expended little for economic information systems necessary to regulate a vast national and global business enterprise. (2)

The objectionable feature of the limited existing disclosure systems is that information goes only to a limited scope of recipients and for limited purposes. We need more facts given a wider distribution.

Much of the present debate for and against multinationals is based on assumptions and prejudices, rather than facts. A satisfactory legal regime for MNE cannot be evolved without the facts. (3) No nation can develop an effective policy towards trade, foreign exchange, and other matters without a knowledge of the actors playing an increasing role in the process - the multinationals. As things are developing the decision - making unit is the enterprise and not the nation. (4)

The additional kind of MNE disclosure required has been divided into two types - capital and operational. On the capital side the needed data is the size and source of ownership, financing and profits, and location of assets. On the operational side the minimum would be the size, location and destination of production, materials and monies. (5) More detailed information is also required by labor groups. (6)

In General

Disclosure of information to 'outside' parties may be done wholly voluntarily, to comply with industry customs, or to comply with the requirements of law. The reasons for not disclosing data are that it is costly to compile and publish, and it may be harmful competitively. Ideas about what should or should not be disclosed vary greatly from one nation to another. The most widely found requirement demands that management report annually on the company. In some countries certain financial disclosure is required if the company is to be listed on a stock exchange or if securities are to be sold to the public. Some nations also permit stockholders to examine corporate records. Early European practice called for the filing of certain data at official depositories. (7)

The consensus of experts is that if companies were to be ranked in order of the forthrightness of their reporting, the American, British and German firms and the big Dutch and Swedish international companies would be first. The French, Belgian, Swiss and Japanese, Italian and Spanish firms would be a distant second. (8)

In the global framework, fully disclosed and freely available corporate reporting is the exception rather than the rule. European tradition has in the past favored an attitude of secrecy. Within the last decade experts, including Eurofinance, estimated that firms like Hoffman - La Roche were not unusual in reporting earnings which may represent merely 15 per cent of their true consolidated earnings.

Michelin did not publish true consolidated figures either, and funneled

remittances and dividends of its foreign subsidiaries through a Swiss

financial holding company about which nothing was revealed. This

contrasts with the better disclosure posture of companies such as

Unilever and Royal Dutch Shell. (9)

During the past decade, however, major changes have been

made in the laws relating to public disclosure, especially in England

and Germany. The English, in fact, may have been the first to intro-

duce the disclosure concept. Professor Schmitthoff has observed:

"The greatest - but not the only - contribution which British Company

Law has made to the science of Company Law is the discovery and

evolution of the principle of public accountability of the company which

is briefly called the disclosure philosophy." (10)

The Companies Act in England, as recently amended in 1967,

provides that every limited company, whether public or private, must

publish its accounts. The most progressive portions of the 1967 Act

are those relating to companies composed of a group of companies.

The holding or parent company is required to disclose various infor-

mation about its subsidiary companies, including those in another

country. This has provided a beginning for the United Kingdom to

ascertain the worldwide ramifications of multinational enterprises

governed by British Law. Experts in this area believe that future

amendments should require further information. Agreements between

various companies regarding managerial control should be disclosed.

Presently, the disclosure requirement for inter-connected companies is based only on ownership connections. Contractual connections are essentially ignored. Major transactions and capital movements between member companies of a multinational group should generally be disclosed. It may be that exceptions should be made if the disclosure might harm the enterprise. Such determinations should have to be made by the proper governmental body. (11)

The British Companies Act requires that the Directors' Report indicate the proportion of turnover (sales) and pre-tax profit contributed by each substantially different class of business carried on by the enterprise. (12) The thinking behind this type of provision could lead to more realistic MNE disclosure requirements. It recognizes economic units as well as legal units. The same breakdown by product lines is required in Japan. (13)

The United States has enjoyed a relatively advanced disclosure system since the 1930's when the Securities and Exchange Commission (SEC) was created. Before 1964, however, disclosure was principally required for those companies listed on the national stock exchange. Since 1966, coverage has been extended to all corporations with more than $U.S 1 million in assets and more than five hundred shareholders. The french decrees of 1959 and 1965 follow a similar approach by imposing special disclosure requirements on companies which are listed on a stock exchange and which have balance sheet assets of more than $U.S. 2 million equivalent. (14)

The EEC holds out the most promise for a disclosure system cutting across national borders. Formerly, the attitude of Continental countries was one of secrecy. This was founded on tradition, lack of pressure from creditor groups or banking groups, no need for public equity financing and a tax avoidment atmosphere. (15) However, in recent years, there has been a growing awareness among European countries that secrecy is self defeating and that its elimination could foster confidence for new equity capital from the public. (16) The EEC First Company Law directive does require that the balance sheet and profit and loss statement of companies be subject to man-datory publicity under the domestic laws of member states. Prior to its issuance there was disagreement over the inclusion of limited liability or 'private' companies, which were argued generally to be family-owned enterprises or enterprises not seeking capital from the public. Such a provision would have excluded many multi-national companies wholly owned and financed by foreign parent companies. To avoid that, a proposed draft directive provided that only limited liability companies with a total capital balance of $U.S 1 million or more had to publish financial reports. However, the directive as issued omitted this dividing line and instead provided that the mandatory publicity requirement as to financial statements would be deferred for limited liability companies, pending a further directive. (17) With British entry into the EEC likelihood of pro-gressive disclosure regulation is increased.

Needed Public Financing Forces Disclosure

It has become evident first in England and the United States and then in Continental Europe that creation of a general public capital market necessarily entails the disclosure to sustain general public confidence. (18) In the United States in general, financial information is disclosed to stockholders and to the public in large part because of the practical and membership requirements of stock market exchange listing. Prior to the time that public security markets existed, there was little need for disclosure. (19)

Competition for funds in world capital markets is the major force pushing companies toward full disclosure. Over 90 per cent of American investments in Europe are financed locally. Many American corporations have listed their shares on European exchanges and published annual reports in several languages. The discrepancy in reliability between American and British reports, and those of European Companies has, in turn, pressured the European firms into fuller and more accurate disclosure. (20)

Relationship to Accountancy and Financial Analysts

There is an interrelationship between disclosure and the advances and uniformity of accounting standards and practices. Professor Tunc has put it this way: 'Since disclosure is misleading if it is not based on reliable accounting and since it is well known substantial differences exist between accountancy practices within countries and among them, one of the most important tasks of such a commission (EEC) could also be the promotion of uniform rules of accountancy. " (21) United Kingdom entry into the EEC has already brought forward the announcement by the London Stock Exchange that it will not accept accounts audited by French accountants or commissaires aux comptes. (22)

Although effective disclosure is partly dependent on enlightened and understandable accounting, it appears that it is much easier, internationally, to evolve standards of financial disclosure than it is to evolve accounting principles that are in harmony with one another. It is believed that international standards of dis-closure in international financing will come first and that such a movement will accelerate uniformity and quality in accounting. (23)

The presence and usefulness of disclosure is also related to the existence of professional financial analysts. There are a variety of intermediaries whose primary purpose is to interpret and digest data for the public and for other special needs. This is done by the financial press, newsletters, advisory services and other bodies. Inthe absence of such institutions and professionals to operate them disclosure reports cannot be regularly judged and digested by the public. The presence of competent and independent auditors is also indispensable, especially in dealing with foreign financial statements. (24)

There appears to be a direct relationship between the quality of financial statements produced in areas where their preparation is guided by legal requirements and areas where their preparation is guided by pronouncements of a developed and organized accountancy profession. In its absence, governments have stepped in and prescribed minimum standards. (25) This does not imply that legal requirements are an impediment, but that a quality accountancy profession is crucial. In every country financial reporting is governed by a different mix of legal, administrative, stock exchange and professional association factors.

There is no question but that difference in accounting practices in various parts of the world are of such magnitude as to inhibit severely the communications function that financial statements are meant to perform. Unfortunately, the development of accounting has had a decidedly nationalistic flavor. There are no transnational accounting standards nor is there any specific organization which could persuade adherence to any such standards. Accounting principles have flowed from one country to another in two general circumstances, first, when the second country has no such principles to begin with and, second, when large amounts of capital from the first country to the second country enable investors to impose their own accounting principles.   (26)

There are a number of underlying factors which explain
accounting variations.   In some countries like the United States,
the income statement is regarded as the financial statement of
prime interest.   Most large United States corporations are publicly
owned with stockholder wealth dependent primarily on stock market
prices which, in turn, are influenced to a large extent by reported
earnings per share.   In most European and Latin American
countries, the balance sheet is the most important, reflecting concern over the ownership of wealth, as distinct from the generation
of income, and the strength of the firm relative to creditors.   The
latter are more concerned with dividends than with price apprecia-
tion.   (27)

While accountants in the United States have taken some
steps in the direction of uniformity in recent years in restricting
the definition of generally accepted accounting principles, the idea
of overall uniformity in the derivation and presentation of financial
information, including standard formats for statements, is said to
be unlikely. The same is, no doubt, true of many other countries,
especially those federally organized. Adding these domestic com -
plications to the international perplexities makes global accounting
harmonization a dismal prospect. This state of affairs came about
when international investment was on a scale much lower than that
which is probable in the future. As the uneven development of
accounting is one factor that obviously diminishes the mobility of

capital, efforts should be made to reduce the negative effects of
that unevenness. Harmonization should be approached without com-
promising the high standards existing in some areas. There is
some debate as to whether uniformity or harmonization should be
pursued on a worldwide scale or by nation or region. A negative
view of uniformity is that it seeks to treat dissimilar matters in
a similar way, thereby causing distortion and less meaningful disclosure. Uniformity may be costly as evidenced by the experience
of Germany and France, where acceptance of uniform charts of
accounts has generally been limited to larger companies. (28)

To minimize the effects of accounting differences, accountants prepare financial statements destined for use in another country
on the basis of the principles of the country of use rather than origin.
When the report is destined for many countries, this process
becomes costly, if not impractical. Nevertheless, this is what is
presently necessary when MNEs borrow or seek equity financing in
the money markets of several countries.

Internal Practices of MNE

Accounting and disclosure developments outside of enterprises presents one picture. Within multinational enterprises
accounting and reporting problems of the international environment
must be dealt with now. Their internal practices may accelerate
improvement of the external environment.

Financial operations of multi-national subsidiaries must

be translated or adjusted to one common denominator, usually
the principles of the parent country. This is necessary in order
to control and manage the enterprise as a single economic entity.
It is done by parent headquarters personnel adjusting local
reports or by local reports conforming to parent company
accounting principles. (29)

The emphasis of accounting in many countries has been
and still is on fulfilling external information requirements and
tax determination. This has shifted attention unduly away from
internal firm considerations. For overall control purposes MNEs
need one type of report. For comparison with local competition,
they need another. For taxation, legal matters, government aid,
loans and new financing, they need many more. (30)

A large proportion of MNEs have made some formal
effort to standardize accounting practices and systems to facilitate
financial reporting between parent headquarters and foreign subsidiaries. (31)

Worldwide Consolidated Accounts

The consolidation of enterprise or groups of companies'
accounts is not obligatory in the EEC and is rarely practiced outside Germany, England and the United States. (32) Failure to
consolidate the subsidiaries with parents is one procedure that
makes the reports of enterprises less meaningful. This is particularly true when the parent companies are holding companies
as well as operating companies which is the case for many
European multinationals. (33)

A beginning approach to this is the multiple statement system requiring that reports of the subsidiaries accompany that of the parent. This enables the reader to draw his own conclusions about the condition of the overall enterprise. However, it does not eliminate double counting of inter-company transactions, as does consolidation.

When consolidation is undertaken it should not ignore the doctrine of accounting separateness which may lead a court in the United States, for example, to rule that the subsidiary cannot serve to insulate the parent from liability. Where consolidation is practiced, it is also necessary to establish the percentage of subsidiary ownership requiring or allowing it. Accounts are not normally consolidated when ownership is less than 50 per cent.

Although consolidation is practiced on a national basis in Great Britain, Germany and the United States, foreign subsidiaries are not normally eligible for consolidation. (34) In moving forward to worldwide consolidation, there exists the question whether traditional national procedures will be valid. Professor Mueller asserts that financial statements have a domicile in terms of an underlying set of accounting principles and such domicile cannot be changed at will through restatements or adjustments of the statements themselves. When consolidated worldwide reports are distributed to many countries, it must be decided whether the reporting practices should be those of the countries of distribution or only those of the home country. The same question exists as to the language of the reports. (35)

It is likely that worldwide consolidation will develop out
of the need for MNE to supply meaningful financial statements
for the raising of capital in several national jurisdictions. The
requirement for consolidation and minimum disclosure in such
circumstances is feasible. The leader of one international auditing
firm believes that such a scheme could be incorporated in some
form of international companies act. (36)

Difficulties in cross-border consolidation are partly being
resolved by its achievement in increasing cross-border mergers.

MNE as a Legal Unit

The relationship between holding company and subsidiaries
has always caused obscurity of group accounts and has been the
foundation of many of the most notorious commercial frauds. (37)
This is especially dangerous in the case of multinational corporations.
As a general rule, they operate in specific foreign countries under
cover of a closed local corporation which are often exempt from the
more stringent rules of disclosure. (38) Consequently, the entire
question of what should be the reporting entities within MNE systems
needs attention. (39) Professor Schmitthoff has been an early
advocate of some reform within the EEC. "Further, in the area
Community Law will have to strike a careful balance between the
circumstances in which the companies constituting the groups are
treated as separate legal persons and those in which that fiction
must be abandoned and the group is deemed to be a legal, and not

merely an economic unit. The least that may be expected is that Community Law will impose obligations on the member states to demand far-reaching disclosure of the affairs of groups of companies and inter-connected companies. That disclosure should relate not only to the constitution of the group, but also to major inter group transactions." (40) Recognition must also be given to the fact that a company can be an affiliate of another through contract as well as stock ownership, as is now recognized in Germany. (41)

One approach to initiating these views may be to do so with respect to the very largest MNEs headquartered in developed countries. Disclosure requirements are already divided in some countries by size of enterprise and in the United States more stringent regulation is given to interstate commerce. At least agreement might be reached among capital exporting nations for worldwide consolidation and minimum disclosure in all cases where capital is sought outside of the home country. In time, that could be expanded to include a form of social responsibility accounting so much in need. A United Nations Committee has recently recommended that a permanent commission be established within UNESCO to begin data gathering on MNEs on a continuing basis, and to move in the regulatory direction. (42)

APPENDIX

UNITED NATIONS
Prospects for Disclosure and Control

In 1972 the Economic and Social Council of the United Nations
requested the Secretary-General to appoint a "group of eminent persons
... to study the role of multinational corporations and their impact
on the process of development, especially that of the developing countries, and also their implications for international relations, to
formulate conclusions which may possibly be used by Governments in making
their sovereign decisions regarding national policy in this respect, and
to submit recommendations for appropriate international action."

Such a group was formed and its recommendations have been adopted
and are in the process of implementation by the Council.

On January 28, 1975, the Council elected the nations to be represented
by experts on the newly established Commission on Transnational Corporations. It is to serve as an advisory body to the Council and to assist
it in dealing with the issues relating to such corporations.

The Commission consists of 48 members which are elected according
to the following geographical pattern: 12 from African States; 11 from
Asian States; 10 from Latin American States; 10 from Western European
and other States; and 5 from the socialist States of Eastern Europe.
Each member's term of office is for three years.

The initial members of the Commission include the U.S., U.S.S.R.,
United Kingdon, France, Japan, Federal Republic of Germany and the
Netherlands. However, the majority of the members are not the home
country of multinational enterprises, but are host developing countries.
The consequence of this is that, for better or worse, the attitude of the
Commission is likely to reflect the viewpoint of the host developing States.

Overall, the Commission reflects a balanced geographical distribution of States. Since the problems confronting the Commission stem
from the tensions between home and host institutions and policies, it
might have been preferable to strike a balance between those two groups
of nations.

The responsibilities of the Commission are to: act as a forum in
dealing with problems; conduct inquiries on the activities of transnations; assist in evolving a code of conduct for transnations; guide
and oversee the work of the newly created Information and Research Centre
on Transnational Corporations.

The Centre which will be constituted during 1975, is charged with
the responsibility of: developing a comprehensive information system
on the activities of transnational corporations; organizing programs to
strengthen the capacity of host countries in dealings with transnationals;
conducting research on various political, legal, economic and social
aspects relating to transnationals.

It is too soon to predict what the influence of these new United
Nations units will be. However, machinery has been set in motion which
may some day lead to enforceable international regulation. The first
priority is for the collection of facts and this function can be
commenced as soon as the personnel are selected for the Information and
Research Centre.

The successful operation of the Centre will in the final analysis
depend upon disclosure requirements backed by law, national or otherwise.
Whether such legal support is forthcoming remains to be seen.

References

1. United Nations, Department of Economic and Social Affairs, The Impact of Multinational Corporations on Development and on International Relations, (E/5500/Rev. 1, St/ ESA/6, 1974).

2. United Nations, Department of Economic and Social Affairs, Summary of the Hearings Before the Group of Eminent Persons to Study the Impact of Multinational Corporations on Development and on International Relations, (ST/ESA/15, 1975).

3. United Nations, Economic and Social Council, Resolution Adopted by the Economic and Social Council on "The Impact of Transnational Corporations on the Development Process and on International Relations," /E/RES/1913(LVII) 11 December 1974/

4. United Nations, Economic and Social Council, Election of Members to the Commission on Transnational Corporations, 28 January 1975.

OVERVIEW

The basic conflict in the world today is between the rich and the poor. The struggle is played-out within nations and between nations. At the international level the evolving multinational enterprise structures play an important role in this process. Economically and politically they have the power to reduce the gap between rich and poor nations, or to magnify it.

Like individual persons, MNEs have done some good and are responsible for some evils. It is not easy to produce an overall 'balance sheet' showing the net gain or loss within each developing nation.

Recent Congressional hearings in the United States have shown that foreign operations of American-based MNEs have actually produced net gains in the U.S. in terms of balance of payments, domestic U.S. employment and other factors. In so far as balance of payments are concerned this may suggest that a net loss was reflected in the foreign host countries in the long term.

The unknown factor in all of this is that we do not know what would have happened, both in home and host countries, had the foreign invest-ments not been made. In other words, what would the situation be if MNEs had not come into being? Would the rich be richer and the poor even poorer, or not.

The truth appears to be that too much criticism has been heaped upon the MNEs to cover up the real issue - the failure of States to fulfill their responsibilities toward themselves. In general, no nation has to accept foreign investment and is free to nationalize existing foreign investments. It is the States responsibility to plan and control its own economic and social future.

What the developed nations fail to accept, however, is that there is a legitimate and just need on the part of the developing nations for effective assistance.

Within the United States it has been accepted that the labor unions, the minorities, consumers, and others require and deserve special economic and legal assistance. This same recognition must be extended to the developing nations.

All too often the Western industrialized nations stand by the international legal and economic norms of the colonial period in their current dealings with developing States. They assume that a 'contract' is a 'contract and ignore that the contracting parties do not have equal bargaining power or skill. In the field of labor - management relations in the U.S., the problem of unequal bargaining power was remedied decades ago. Similar action in the form of laws or minimum standards are necessary at the global level.

The United Nations Commission on Transnational Corporations is a possible forum for the resolution of this. The danger is that the developing nations will establish excessive and unreasonable standards and that the multinationals will invest in the developed States and not elsewhere.

Reasonable minimum investment standards should be established. If all multinationals based in the capital exporting nations are subject to such standards, then they will be competing on an equal basis. This is something that cannot easily be done by developing nations acting alone. Like the individual worker of years ago, they compete against each other to their own detriment.

Nearly all nations have taken steps within their borders to equalize the economic status of their citizens. Led by the multinationals, a way must be found to do the same thing between nations.

304.

Reference Notes for Chapter I - Historical Perspective and Definitions

1. James Willard Hurst. The Legitimacy of the Business Corporation in the Law of the United States 1780-1970 (The Charlottesville University Press of Virginia, 1970), 2 .

2. G. H. Plumb, The Growth of Political Stability in England, 1675-1725 (London: Macmillan, 1967), 36-42.

3. Joseph H. Smith, Cases and Materials on the Development of Legal Institutions (St. Paul: West Publishing, 1965), 664 .

4. Hurst, op. cit. (note 1), 4.

5. Paul J. Mc Nulty,"Predecessors of the Multinational Corporation", Columbia Journal of World Business (May-June 1972), 73.

6. Mc Nulty, 77.

7. Mc Nulty, 79 quoting from K. N. Chaudhuri, The English East India Company (London: Frank Cass, 1965) .

8. Hurst op. cit. (note 1), 4.

9. Stewart A. Kyd, A Treatise on the Law of Corporations (London: J. Butterworth, 1794).

    Hurst. 7.

10. Joseph K. Angell and Samuel Ames, Treatise on the Law of Private Corporative Aggregate (Boston: Little and Brown, 1832), v.

11. Hurst. op. cit. (note 1), 8, 10, 11.

Reference Notes for Chapter 1 - Historial Perspective and Definitions (contd)

12.   Hurst, 9.

13.   Peter F. Drucker, The Practice of Management (New York: Harper and Bros., 1954). 2-14.

      Wilbert E. Moore, The Conduct of the Corporation (New York: Random House, 1962) 193-4.

14.   Adolph A. Berle, Jr. and Gardiner C. Means, The Modern Corporation and Private Property (New York: Macmillan, 1933) 130-137

15.   Hurst op. cit. (note 1), 69, 84 147.

16.   Christopher Tugenhat, The Multinationals (London: Eyre and Spottiswoode 1971), 12-13.

17.   Endel J. Kolde International Business Enterprise (Englewood Cliffs, N.J.: Prentice-Hall, 1973), 141.

      Tugenhat, 14-15

      See also Mira Wilkins The Emergence of Multinational Enterprise: American Business Abroad from the Colonial Era to 1914 (Cambridge Mass.: Harvard University Press, 1970).

18.   Tugenhat, 18-23.

19.   Kolde, op. cit. (note 17) 145-6

20.   Kolde, 146-9,

      John H. Dunning, ed., The Multi-National Enterprise (London: George Allen and Unwin, 1971), 19-21.

Reference Notes for Chapter 1 - Historical Perpsective and Definitions (contd)

20.   (contd)

Stephan H. Robock and Kenneth Simmonds "International Business:
How Big Is It - The Missing Measurements", Columbia Journal of
World Business (May-June 1970), 6.

Lester R. Brown, World Without Borders (New York: Random House,
1972), 210-217.

21.   See:

Donald F. Mulvihill, "Terminology in International Business Studies
- Order out of Chaos", Journal of International Business Studies
(Spring 1973) 87.

Yair Aharoni, "On the Definition of a Multinational Corporation",
The Quarterly Review of Economics and Business (Autumn 1971), 27.

Charles De Houghton ed. The Company (London: The Macmillan
Company, 1969), 252-262.

22.   Clive M. Schmitthoff, Chapter 20, The Role of the Multinational
Enterprise in an Enlarged European Community Legal Problems
of an Enlarged European Community, British Institute Studies in
International and Comparative Law, No. 6, eds., M. E. Bathurst,
K. R. Simmonds N. March Hunnings, Jane Welch (London:
Stevens and Sons, 1972), 211.

Clive M. Schmitthoff, "Multi-National Enterprises" The New Law
Journal (1971), 1953.

23.   Schmitthoff.

Reference Notes for Chapter 2 - National Multinationals

1. The 500 Largest Industrial Corporations, Fortune
    (May 1970) 190.

    Ford Annual Report 1972, 2.

    David L. Lewis, "Ford: A Global Corporation", Booklet
    (Dearborn Michigan: Ford Motor Company, 1972) 3, 7

2. Mira Wilkins and Frank Ernest Hill, American Business Abroad -
    Ford on Six Continents (Detroit: Wayne State University Press,
    (1964), 8-10.

3. Wilkins 8-11.

    Alfred D. Chandler, Jr., Giant Enterprise - Ford, General Motors
    and the Automobile Industry (Harcourt, Brace and World, 1964), 25.

4. Wilkins, 4-6.

5. Wilkins, 14-19.

6. Wilkins, 18-19, 59.

7. Wilkins, 42-44, 120

8. Wilkins 119-123.

9. Wilkins, 124-127.

10. Wilkins, 130-133

11. Wilkins, 130-1

12. Wilkins, 325-6

13.   Wilkins, 398.

14.   Wilkins, 399.

15.   Wilkins, 400.

16.   Wilkins, 426.

17.   Wilkins, 23 -6.

18.   Wilkins, 39

19.   Wilkins 47, 51

20.   Wilkins, 142.

21.   Wilkins, 98 -100, 139 -140

22.   Wilkins, 193 -6.

23.   Wilkins, 196 -7, 307.

24.   Wilkins, 91 -95 147 473.

25.   Wilkins, 414 -420.

26.   Wilkins, 55, 139, 160, 204, 401.

27.   Wilkins 247 -8, 272, 277, 280 -1.

28.   Wilkins 284, 409.

29.   Lewis, op. cit. (note 1), 8.

        Ford Annual Report 1972. 32.

        Wilkins, 412.

30.   Lewis, op. cit. (note 1) 6.

        Wilkins, 339, 341 358, 376.

Reference Notes for Chapter 2 - National Multinationals (contd)

31.   Wilkins, 423.

32.   Wilkins, 370.

33.   Wilkins, 377-8.

34.   Wilkins, 380-386 398, 403 406-9.

35.   Wilkins, 378, 421-24.

36.   Wilkins, 404, 421.

37.   Wilkins 406-409.

38.   Wilkins 406, 409.

39.   Lewis, op. cit. (note 1), 7.

       Wilkins, 410-413.

40.   Wilkins, 421-22.

41   John M. Stopford and Louis T. Wells, Jr., Managing the Multinational Enterprise - Organization of the Firm and Ownership of the Subsidiaries (London: Longman, 1972), 114.

       H. Peter Gray, The Economics of Business Investment Abroad (London: Macmillan, 1972), 226-7, 236.

42.   Wilkins, 423.

43.   Wilkins, 424,

44.   Lewis, op. cit. (note 1), 3.

45.   Lewis, 10.

Reference Notes for Chapter 2 - National Multinationals (contd)

46.   Christopher Tugenhat, The Multinationals (london: Eyre and
       Spottiswoode 1971), 109-110.

       Lewis, 10.

47.   Lester R. Brown, World Without Borders (New York: Random
       House, 1972), 218.

48.   Ford Annual Report, 1972.

       Lewis.

       Wilkins, 434-5.

49.   "Ford in Europe", booklet (Nottingham: Ford of Europe Incorporated).

       Ford Motor Company Organizational Manual, April, 1973.

50.   Noritake Koyayashi, "Problems of International Business Management
       in Japan", International Studies of Management and Organization
       (Winter 1971-72), 372.

50.1   The substance of this Mitsubishi Group material was previously
       published by the author in "Mitsubishi Group: World's Largest
       Multinational Enterprise?", MSU Business Topics (Spring 1974), 27.

51.   Yusaku Furuhashi, "Foreign Capital in Japan", Columbia Journal
       of World Business (March-April, 1972), 52

52.   Business International S.A. in conjunction with the Centre d'Etudes
       Industrielles Geneva, Managing the Multinationals: Preparing for
       Tomorrow (London: George Allen and Unwin Ltd., 1972) 51.

       Stephan H. Robock and Kenneth Simmonds, "How Big Is It -
       The missing Measurements", Columbia Journal of World Business
       (May-June, 1970), 11.

Reference Notes for Chapter 2 - National Multinationals (contd)

53.   Yoshi Tsurumi, "Japanese Multinational Firms", Journal of World
      Trade Law (Jan/Feb 1973), 74.

      Business Week (March 24, 1973), 56.

      Newsweek (September 3, 1973), 44.

      Oriental Economist (January, 1973), 20

54.   Newsweek (September 3, 1973), 44.

55.   "Japan's Mitsubishi: A Giant Reborn", Newsweek (International
      Edition, April 23, 1973), 32.

      The 500 Largest Industrial Corporations, Fortune (May 1970), 190.

      The 200 Industrial Corporations Outside the US, Fortune
      (August 1972), 161.

56.   Charles De Houghton, ed., The Company (London: The Macmillan
      Company, 1969), 287.

57.   M Y Yoshino, Japan's Managerial System (Cambridge, Mass.
      The MIT Press, 1968), 133.

58.   John C Lobb, "Japan Inc - The Total Conglomerate", Columbia
      Journal of World Business (March-April 1971), 41.

59.   T F Adams and N Kobayashi, The World of Japanese Business
      (Tokyo: Kodansha International Ltd, 1969), 123

60   Business International, op. cit (note 52), 55, 58.

Reference Notes for Chapter 2 - National Multinationals (contd)

61.   De Houghton, op. cit. (note 56), 286.

62.   Business International, 57-8.

63.   Furahashi, op. cit. (note 51), 53.

64.   Kitoshi Misono, Nihon no Dokusen (Monopoly in Japan) (Tokyo:
        Shiseido, 1965), 37-38.

65.   "Mitsubishi Group", booklet (Tokyo: Mainchi Daily News, September
        1971), 20.

66.   Richard Fishbein, "Patterns of Conglomeration", Columbia Journal
        of World Business. (September-October 1970), 25-27.

67.   Misono, op. cit. (note 64), 72.

68.   Yoshino, op. cit. (note 57), 131.

69.   "Mitsubishi Shoji Kaisha, Ltd and Mitsubishi Group", booklet
        (Tokyo: Mitsubishi Shoji Kaisha Ltd, 1970), 27.

70.   Furahashi, op. cit. (note 51), 51.

71   "Mitsubishi Group", op. cit. (note 65), 33.

Reference Notes for Chapter 3 - International Multinationals (Transnationals)

1.   Information about the Royal Dutch/Shell Group is taken from the
        following sources:

        "The Royal Dutch/Shell Companies, What They Are -- What They
        Do", pamphlet (London: Shell Printing Limited, January 1972).

        "Royal Dutch/Shell Group of Companies", Addresses to the
        Financial Analysts Federation, Boston, 6 May 1968.

        "How Shell Works, Management Techniques in a Large International
        Group of Companies", pamphlet, Address by David Barran,
        Chairman, The 'Shell' Transport and Trading Company Limited
        to the British Institute of Management, 30 November 1967.

        Annual Report, The 'Shell' Transport and Trading Company
        Limited, 1971.

        "The Royal Dutch/Shell Group of Companies" Information
        Handbook 1971-2.

        Arvind V Phatak, Evolution of World Enterprise (New York:
        American Management Association, 1971), 191-202.

2.   Information about Unilever is taken from the following sources:

        E A Hofman, "The Dual Structure of the Unilever Group of
        Companies and the Equalisation Agreement" Journal of Companies,
        Associations and Foundations, Special Number on Groups of
        Companies translated from Dutch (September 1963).

Reference Notes for Chapter 3 - International Multinationals (Transnationals) contd

Carl-Arend Weingardt, "Organization Structure and Communication in the Unilever Company", International Studies of Management & Organization (Winter 1971-2), 377.

Arvind V Phatak Evolution of World Enterprise (New York: American Management Association 1971), 182-190.

Great Britain, The Monopolies Commission, "Unilever Limited and Allied Breweries Limited, a Report on the Proposed Merger" (London: Her Majesty's Stationery Office, 9 June 1969).

Unilever Report and Accounts 1971

3.   Information about the Dunlop Pirelli Union is taken from the following sources:

Special Report to stockholders entitled "Proposals to Effect the Union of the Operating Activities of the Dunlop Company Limited, and Pirelli SpA and Societe International Pirelli SA December 1970.

Annual Report, Dunlop Holdings Limited, Dunlop and Pirelli 1971.

"International Marriage", Forbes (November 15, 1970), 22.

"Marriage, Italian Style", The Economist (November 6, 1971), 94.

"Marital Trouble in Europe", Time (December 4, 1972), 50.

"Multinations: The Unhappy union of Dunlop-Pirelli", Business Week (November 4, 1972), 38.

Reference Notes for Chapter 3 - International Multinationals (Transnationals) contd

Note: Certain assets of Dunlop and Pirelli were initially excluded from the Union, but were not significant enough to alter the basic 50/50 concept.

4.   Endel J Kolde, International Business Enterprise (Englewood Cliffs, NJ; Prentice-Hall, 1968), 241.

5.   Christopher Tugenhat The Multinationals (London: Eyre & Spotteswoode, 1971) 206.

316.

Reference Notes for Chapter 4 - Legal Structure of Multinational Enterprise

1. Clive M Schmitthoff, "The Multinational Enterprise in the United
   Kingdom", Nationalism and the Multinational Enterprise, ed
   H R Hahlo, J Graham Smith, and Richard W Wright (Leiden:
   A W Sijthoff and Oceana Publications, 1973), 33.

2. Paul B Hannon, "Use of an International Consortium in a Major
   International Project", Private Investors Abroad - Problems and
   Solutions in International Business. (New York: Matthew Bender and
   The South Western Legal Foundation. 1970), 103.

   Christopher Layton, Cross-Frontier Mergers in Europe (Bath:
   Bath University Press, 1971), 21.

3. See Chapter 2. herein.

4. Michael B Stewart, "Transnational Enterprise: The European
   Challenge", Columbia Journal of World Business (July-August 1972), 9.

   Layton, op. cit. (note 2), 30 ; Francis M Goldmark, "Europe Catches
   the Merger Fever", Columbia Journal of World Business (March-
   April 1969), 54.

5. Renato Mazzolini, "The Obstacle Course for European Transnational
   Consolidations", Columbia Journal of World Business (Spring 1973) 55.

   Stewart, op. cit. (note 4), 9.

   Layton, op. cit. (note 2), 22.

6. See Chapter 2 herein.

Reference Notes for Chapter 4 - Legal Structure of Multinational Enterprise contd

7. Schmitthof, op. cit. (note 1), 33-4.

8. See chapter 3.2 herein.

9. Donald M. Barrett, "Multi-Flag Airlines: A New Breed in World
    Business", Columbia Journal of World Business (March-April 1969), 9

10. See chapter 3.3 herein.

    Schmitthoff, op. cit. (note 1), 34.

11. "Agfa-Gevaert - Model Merger", Business Week (July 5, 1969), 62.

    Michael Whitehead, The Multinationally-owned Company: a case
    Study", The Multinational Enterprise, ed. John H Dunning (London:
    George Allen & Unwin Ltd, 1971), 315-329.

    Layton, op. cit. (note 2), 24-6.

    Mazzolini, op. cit. (note 5), 56.

12. See chapter 3.1 herein.

13. Layton, op. cit. (note 2), 26-7.

    Stewart, op. cit. (note 4), 13.

    Mazzolini, op. cit. (note 5), 57.

    Schmitthoff, op. cit. (note 1), 34.

14. Clive M Schmitthoff, "Multi-National Companies", Journal of
    Business Law (1970), 177-8.

Reference Notes for Chapter 4 - Legal Structure of Multinational Enterprise contd

Clive M Schmitthoff, "The Role of the Multinational Enterprise in
an Enlarged European Community", Legal Problems of an
Enlarged European Community, British Institute Studies in International
and Comparative Law, No. 6, ed. M E Bathurst, K R Simmonds,
N March Hunnings, Jane Welch (London: Stevens and Sons, 1972), 212.

15.   Wolfgang Friedmann, Chapter 13, "Government (Public) Enterprises,"
Volume XIII Business and Private Organisations, under the auspices
of the International Association of Legal Science (Tubingen:
J C B Mohr (Paul Siebeck), 1972), 25-6.

16.   Friedmann, 26.

17.   Friedmann.

18.   John B Holt, "New Roles for Western Multinationals in Eastern
Europe", Columbia Journal of World Business (Fall 1973), 131.

19.   Charles Henry Alexandrowicz, The Law of Global Communications
(New York: Columbia University Press, 1971), 152.

Friedmann, 26-7.

20.   Barrett, op. cit. (note 9), 10-12.

21.   F A Mann, "International Corporations and National Law",
The British Yearbook of International Law (1967), 146.

22.   For a comparison with managerial organizational structures see:
Hans Schollhammer, "Organization Structures of Multinational
Corporations," Academy of Management Journal (September 1971), 345.

Reference Notes for Chapter 4 - Legal Structure of Multinational Enterprise contd

David P Rutenberg, "Organizational Archetypes of a Multi-National Company", Management Science (February 1970), 337.

Endel J Kolde, "Chapter 12 The Organization of Multinational Companies", International Business Enterprise (Englewood Cliffs, N.J. 1973), 173.

Reference Notes for Chapter 5 - Legal Structure of Future Enterprise,
Harmonization of European Company Law, European Company, World
Company.

1. Henry P de Vries, "Transnational Legal Trends - The Problem of
    Identity: Whose Law Determines Inc", Columbia Journal of World
    Business (March-April 1969), 76.

    Sam Scott Miller, "Access to do Business Across International
    Boundaries", Tulane Law Review (1968), 795.

2. Stanley A Kaplan, "Foreign Corporations and Local Corporate
    Policy", Vanderbilt Law Review (1968), 433.

3. Joel F Henning, "Federal Corporate Chartering for Big Business:
    An Idea Whose Time has Come?", De Paul Law Review (1972), 915.

4. James Willard Hurst, The Legitimacy of the Business Corporation
    in the Law of the US 1780-1970, (Charlottesville: The University
    Press of Virginia, 1970), 156-164).

5. Don Berger, "Harmonization of Company Law under the Common
    Market Treaty", Creighton Law Review (1971), 205-6.

6. Christopher Layton, Cross Frontier Mergers in Europe (Bath:
    Bath University Press, 1971), vii-4.

7. Clive M Schmitthoff, ed, The Harmonisation of European Company
    Law (London: The United Kingdom National Committee of Comparative
    Law, 1973), 3-10.

Reference Notes for Chapter 5 - Legal Structure of Future Enterprise,

Harmonization of European Company Law, European Company, World

Company contd

8.   For information about Mergers, see :

Alfred Conard, Chapter 6, "Fundamental Changes in Marketable

Share Companies", Volume XIII Business and Private Corporations,

under the auspices of the International Association of Legal Science

(Tubinger: J C Mohr (Paul Siebeck), 1972), 72-9.

Hans Claudius Ficker, Chapter 4, "The EEC Directives on Company

Law Harmonisation", op. cit. (note 7), 77-8.

Robert R Pennington, Companies in the Common Market (London

Oyez Publications, 1970), 103, 110-114, 136.

Clive M Schmitthoff, "The Role of the Multinational Enterprise in

an Enlarged European Community", Legal Problems of an Enlarged

European Community, British Institute Studies in International and

Comparative Law, No. 6, eds, M E Bathurst, K R Simmonds,

N March Hunnings, Jane Welch (London: Stevens & Sons, 1972),

222-224.

9.   For information about taxation in the formation of mergers and

combinations, see :

Conard, op. cit. (note 8), 81.

Berger, op. cit. (note 5), 225.

Layton, op. cit. (note 6), 13-18, 47-48, 57.

Reference Notes for Chapter 5 - Legal Structure of Future Enterprise, Harmonization of European Company Law, European Company, World Company contd

Samuel David Cheris and Eric Robert Fischer, "The European Company: Its Promise and Problems", Stanford Journal of International Studies (1971), 116-127.

10. For information about income taxation of multinational combinations, see:

Cheris and Fischer.

Layton, 16.

Endel J Kolde, Chapter 17, "Taxation of the Multinational Firm", International Business Enterprise (Englewood Cliffs, N.J. 1973), 247.

Conard, 76.

Ulrich Anschutz, "Harmonization of Direct Taxes in the European Economic Community", Havard International Law Journal (1972), 1.

11. For information about the European Company,

Pieter Sanders, "Structure and Progress of the European Company", op. cit. (note 7), 83 (Primary source).

Clive M Schmitthoff, "The Future of the European Company Law Scene", op. cit. (note 7), 3.

Clive M Schmitthoff, op. cit. (note 8(, 224-230.

Reference Notes for Chapter 5 - Legal Structure of Future Enterprise,

Harmonization of European Company Law, European Company, World

Company contd

Clive M Schmitthoff, "The Multinational Enterprise in the United

Kingdom", Nationalism and the Multinational Enterprise, ed.

H R Hahlo, J Graham Smith and Richard W Wright (Leiden:

A W Sijthoff and Oceana Publications, 1973), 36.

Clive M Schmitthoff, "Multi-National Companies", Journal of

Business Law (1970)   182-184.

Hans Claudius Ficker, "The Proposed Statute of a European

Corporation", Journal of Business Law (1971), 167.

Fritz Fabricius, "A Theory of Co-determination", op. cit. (note 7),

138.

Maurice Kay, "A Theory of Co-determination - A Comment",

op. cit. (note 7), 157.

F A Mann, "The European Company", International and Comparative

Law Quarterly (1970), 468.

Raffaello Fornasier, "Toward a European Company", Columbia

Journal of World Business (September-October 1969), 51.

Cheris and Fischer, op. cit. (note 9), 113.

Joseph Jude Norton, "A Cheshire Cat Affair: The European-type

Company and its meaning for the American Enterprise in the

European Community", Cornell International Law Journal (1973), 111.

Clive M Schmitthof, European Company Law Texts, (London: Stevens

& Sons, 1974).

Reference Notes for Chapter 5 - Legal Structure of Future Enterprise,

Harmonization of European Company Law, European Company, World

Company contd

12.   Sanders, op. cit. (note 11), 99.

13.   Mann, op. cit. (note 11).

14.   Norton op. cit. (note 11), 131-2.

        Pennington, op. cit. (note 8), 136-8.

15.   Volker Bringezu, "Parent-Subsidiary Relations under German Law",

        International Lawyer (1973), 138.

15a   Clive M Schmitthoff, 30 Trans. Grotius Society 172 (1944).

16.   George W Ball, "Cosmocorp: the Importance of Being Stateless",

        Columbia Journal of World Business (November-December 1967), 25.

17.   Charles Henry Alexandronicz, The Law of Global Communications

        (New York: Columbia University Press, 1971).

18.   Richard Eels, "Corporate Sovereignty: A Charter for the Seven

        Seas", Columbia Journal of World Business (July-August 1970), 66.

19.   Erich Jantsch, "The 'World Corporation': The Total Commitment"

        Columbia Journal of World Business (May-June 1971), 5.

20.   United Nations, Department of Economic and Social Affairs,

        Multinational Corporations in World Development (ST/ECA/190)

        (New York).

21.   Robert Rowthorn, International Big Business 1957-1967 - A Study of

        Corporate Growth (Cambridge: Cambridge University Press, 1971).

Reference Notes for Chater 5 - Legal Structure of Future Enterprise,
Harmonization of European Company Law, European Company, World
Company contd

    Francis M Goldmark, "Europe Catches the Merger Fever", Columbia
Journal of World Business (March-April 1969), 49.

    Johannes Semler, "The Prospect for Mergers and Acquisitions in
Europe", Conference Board Record (January 1972), 54.

22.   Ball, op. cit. (note 16).

23.   J N Behrman, "Sharing International Production through the
Multinational Enterprise and Sectoral Integration", Law & Policy
in International Business (1972/4:1), 1.

Reference Notes for Chapter 6 - Ownership and Control

1. C. S. Burchill, "The Multi-National Corporation: An Unresolved
    Problem in International Relations", Queens Quarterly (1970), 3.

2. Harry Johnson, "Economic Benefit of the Multinational Enterprise",
    Nationalism and the Multinational Enterprise, ed. H. R. Hahlo,
    J. Graham Smith and Richard W. Wright (Leiden: A. W. Sijthoff
    and Oceana Publications, 1973), 165.

3. Burton Teague, "Multinational Corporations: Profiles & Prospects",
    The Conference Board Record (September, 1971), 31.

4. The Multinational Firm and the Nation State , ed. Gilles Paguet
    (Collier-Macmillan Canada, Ltd. , 1972), 1.

5. Donald Kendall, "Corporate Ownership: The International Dimension",
    Columbia Journal of World Business (August 1969), 65.

6. Kendall.

7. Kendall.

8. Roy A. Matthews, "The Multinational Firm and the World of
    Tomorrow, " op. cit. (Note 4), 154.

9. Leland M. Wooton, "The Multinational Corporation: Administering
    Development in a Global Political System", Management International
    Review (1971/4-5), 13

10. J. N. Behrman, "Sharing International Production through the
    Multinational Enterprise and Sectoral Integration", Law and Policy
    in International Business (1972/4:1), 4

Reference Notes for Chapter 6 - Ownership and Control contd

11. Behrman, 2-3.

12. Behrman, 2,

13. Erich Jantsch, "The 'World Corporation': The Total Commitment",
     Columbia Journal of World Business (May-June 1971) 9.

14. George W. Ball, "Cosmocorp: The Importance of Being Stateless",
     Columbia Journal of World Business (Nov. -Dec. 1967), 28.

15. Kendall, op. cit. (Note 5), 64

     F. A. McKenzie, The American Invaders (Grant Richards, 1902).

16. I. A. Litvak and C. J. Maule, "The Multinational Firm: Some
     Perspectives", op. cit. (Note 4), 20.

17. Robert Warren Stevens, "Scanning the Multinational Firm",
     Business Horizons (June 1971), 47.

18. Richard Robinson, "Nationalism and Centralized Control", op. cit.
     (Note 2), 211.

19. Gene E. Bradley and Edward C. Bursk
     "Multinationalism and the 29th day", Harvard Business Review
     (Jan. -Feb. 1972), 46.

20. David W. Ewing, "MNCs on Trial", Harvard Business Review
     (May-June 1972), 138.

21. Ewing, 130.

22. Stephen Hymer, "The Efficiency Contradictions of Multinational
     Corporations", op. cit. (Note 4), 63.

328.

Reference Notes for Chapter 6 - Ownership and Control contd

23. Clive M. Schmitthoff. "The Multinational Enterprise in the United Kingdom", op. cit. (Note 2), 25.

24. Christopher Tugenhat, The Multinationals (London: Eyre & Spottiswoode, 1971), 204.

25. John Fayerweather, "Nationalistic Control Attitudes and the Multinational Enterprise", op. cit. (Note 2), 214.

26. United Nations, Department of Economic and Social Affairs, Multinational Corporations in World Development (ST/ECA/190) (New York, 1973), 34.

27. C. Vaitsos, Income Generation and Income Distribution in the Foreign Investment Model, (Oxford: Oxford University Press, forthcoming)

28. Wooton, op. cit. (Note 9), 6.

29. Burchill, op. cit. (Note 1), 9.

30. Frederick T. Knickerbocker, Oligopalistic Reaction and Multinational Enterprise, (Boston: Division of Research, Graduate School of Business Administration, Harvard University, 1973).

31. Business International S.A. in conjunction with the Centre d'Etudes Industrielles, Geneva, Managing the Multinationals: Preparing for Tomorrow (London: George Allen & Unwin Ltd., 1972), 11.

32. Burchill, op. cit. (Note 9), 9.

33. Howard Ross, "An Attempted Summing-Up", op. cit. (Note 2), 337.

34. United Nations, op. cit. (Note 26), 12.

Reference Notes for Chapter 6 - Ownership and Control contd

35   Richard D Robinson, "Ownership across National Frontiers",
      Industrial Management Review (Fall 1969), 41.

36   John M Stopford and Louis T Wells, Jr, Managing the Multinational
      Enterprise : Organization of the Firm and Ownership of the
      Subsidiaries (London : Longman, 1972). 165.

37   H PEter Gray, The Economics of Business Investment Abroad
      (London : Macmillan, 1972), 225.

38   Gray, 227.

39   Lawrence G Franko, Joint Venture Divorce in the Multinational
      Company, Columbia Journal of World Business (May-June 1971), 13.

40   Franko, 20.

41   Stopford, op. cit. (note 36).

42   Stopford, 5.

43   Jack N Behrman, US International Business and Governments (New
      York : McGraw-Hill, 1971), 113-114.

44   United Nations op.cit (note 26), 38.

45   John H Dunning, "The Multinational Enterprise : The Background"
      The Multinational Enterprise, ed. John H Dunning (London :
      George Allan & Unwin Ltd, 1971), 48.

46   Ivan R Feltham, and William R Ravenbusch, "Canada and the
      Multinational Enterprise", op. cit. (Note 2), 43.

47   "Nationalism sets Boundaries for Multinational Enterprise",
      Business Week (June 14 1969), 94.

330.

Reference Notes for Chapter 6 - Ownership and Control   contd

48. Ball, op. cit. (note 14), 28.

49. Ball.

50. Ball, 30.

51. Kendall, op. cit (note 5).

52. Arvind V. Phatak, Evolution of World Enterprise (New York: American Management Association, 1971), 105.

53. John C. McManus, "The Theory of the International Firm", op. cit. (note 4), 72.

54. Kendall, op. cit (note 5), 60.

55. Phatak, op. cit. (note 52), 102.

56. Burchill, op. cit (note 1), 6.

57. McManus, op. cit. (note 53), 70-71.

58. Raymond Vernon, Sovereignty at Bay (New York: Basic Books, Inc., 1971), 245.

59. Abraham Rotstein, "The Multinational Corporation in the Political Economy - A Matter of Survival", op. cit. (note 2), 184.

60. Daniel Jay Baum, "The Global Corporation: An American Challenge to the Nation-State", Iowa Law Review (1969), 430.

61. Feltham and Rauenbusch, op. cit. (note 46), 47-48.

62. Baum, op. cit. (note 60), 421.

63. Adolf A. Berle and Gardiner C. Means, The Modern Corporation and Private Property, (New York: Harcourt, Brace and World Inc., Revised Edition, 1967), 309.

64. Ross, op. cit. (note 33), 333.

331.

Reference Notes for Chapter 6 - Ownership and Control contd

65. Joel F. Henning, "Federal Corporate Chartering for Big
    Business: An Idea whose Time Has Come?", De Paul Law
    Review (1972), 925.

66. Bradley and Bursk (quoting Borch), op. cit. (note 19), 42.
    W. Friedmann. The State and the Rule of Law in a Mixed
    Economy (London: Stevens and Sons, 1971), 5.

67. Baum, op. cit. (note 60), 411-412.

68. John Kenneth Galbraith, Economics and the Public Purpose
    (Boston: Houghton Mifflin, 1973).

69. John B. Holt, "New Roles for Western Multinationals in Eastern
    Europe", Columbia Journal of World Business (Fall 1973), 132.

70. Eric Kierans, "The Cosmocorporation : An Unsympathetic View",
    op. cit. (note 2), 178.

71. John Kenneth Galbraith, The New Industrial State (New York :
    The New American Library, Inc. (paperback), 1967), 115.

72. Henning, op. cit. (note 65), 925.

73. Feltham and Rauenbusch, op. cit. (note 2), 48.

74. Henning, op. cit. (note 65), 925.

75. Berle and Means, op. cit. (note 63), 219.

76. Hymer, op. cit. (note 22), 51.

77. Hymer, 54.

78. Baum, op. cit. (note 60), 435.

79. M. Y. Yoshino, "Toward a Concept of Managerial Control
    for a World Enterprise", Michigan Business Review (March 1966),
    25.

Reference Notes for Chapter 6 - Ownership and Control contd

80. Michael Z Brooke and H. Lee Remmers, The Multinational
    Company in Europe (London : Longman, 1972), 165.

81. Ewing, op. cit. (note 20), 136.

82. Kenneth Simmonds, "Multinational? Well Not Quite", Columbia
    Journal of World Business (Fall 1966), 116.

83. Simmonds, 121.

84. Baum, op. cit. (note 60), 432.

85. Brooke and Remmers, op. cit. (note 80).

86. United Nations, op. cit. (note 26), 31.

87. Stopford and Wells, op. cit. (note 36), 21, 86.

88. Endel J. Kolde, International Business Enterprise (Englewood
    Cliffs, N. J. : Prentice-Hall, 1973), 184.

89. Howard V. Perlmutter, "Toward Research on and Development
    of Nations, Unions, and Firms as Worldwide Institutions",
    International Studies of Management and Organization (Winter
    1971-1972), 432.

90. Erich Jantsch, "World Corporation : The Total Commitment",
    Columbia Journal of World Business (May-June 1971), 6.

91. Frank H. Cassell, "The Corporation and the Community :
    Realities and Myths", MSU Business Topics (Autumn 1970), 14.

92. Cassell, 17.

93. Stevens, op. cit. (note 17), 49.

94. Cassell, 17, 20.

95. Richard Eells, "Corporate Sovereignty : A Charter for the
    Seven Seas", Columbia Journal of World Business (July-August 1970),
    68.

Reference Notes for Chapter 6 - Ownership and Control contd

96. Wooton, op. cit. (note 9), 6.

97. Hugh Stephenson, The Coming Clash : The Impact of the International Corporation on the Nation State (London : Weidenfeld and Nicolson, 1972), 175.

98. Richard Eells, "Multinational Corporations : The Intelligence Function", Columbia Journal of World Business (November-December, 1969), 24.

99. Perlmutter, op. cit. (note 89), 427.

100. Business Week, op. cit. (note 47).

    International Chamber of Commerce, Guidelines for International Investment (Paris, 1972).

101. D. H. W. Henry, "Anti-Monopoly Legislation in Canada", op. cit. (note 2), 312.

102. Business Week, op. cit. (note 47), 95.

103. Sidney M. Robbins and Robert B. Stobaugh, "The Profit Potential of Multinational Enterprises", Columbia Journal of World Business (Fall 1973), 140.

104. Burchill, op. cit. (note 1), 6.

105. J. S. Arpan, International Intercorporate Pricing (New York : Praeger, 1971).

106. Ball, op. cit. (note 14), 27.

107. Andre Tunc, "Multi-National Companies in French Law", Law and International Trade : Festschrift fur Clive M. Schmitthoff, ed. Fritz Fabricius (Frankfurt : Athenaum Verlag, 1973), 376.

334.

Reference Notes for Chapter 6 - Ownership and Control contd

108. Alfred Conard, "Chapter 6 Fundamental Changes in Marketable Share Companies", Volume XIII Business and Private Organizations, ed. Alfred Conard,International Association of Legal Science (Tubingen : J. C. B. Mohr (Paul Siebeck), 73.

109. Burchill, op. cit. (note 1), 8.

110. Burchill, 9.

111. Burchill, 13.

112. I. A. Litvak and C. J. Maule, "Foreign Subsidiaries an Instrument of Host Government Policy", op. cit. (note 2), 200

113. Stevens, op. cit. (note 17), 53.

114. Hymer, op. cit. (note 22), 59.

115. Perlmutter, op. cit. (note 89), 426.

116. Kierans, op. cit. (note 70), 174.

117. Hymer, op. cit. (note 22), 62.

118. Johnson, op. cit. (note 2), 169.

119. Bradley and Bursk (quoting Maisonrouge), op. cit. (note 19), 43.

120. Friedmann, op. cit. (note 66), 16, 19.

121. Hymer, op. cit. (note 22), 60.

122. Stevens, op. cit. (note 17), 51.

123. Henning (quoting Berle and Means) op. cit. (note 65), 918.

124. Kendall, op. cit. (note 5), 65.

125. Anthony Sampson, The Sovereign State - The Secret History of ITT (London : Holder and Stoughton, 1973), 270.

126. Charles Levinson Capital, Inflation and the Multinationals (London : George Allen and Unwin, 1971), 103-4.

Reference Notes for Chapter 6 - Ownership and Control contd

127. Sampson, op. cit. (note 125), 271.

128. Fayerweather, op. cit. (note 25).

129. Baum (referring to the Watkins Report), op. cit. (note 60), 420.

130. Behrman, op. cit. (note 10).

131. Hymer, op. cit. (note 22), 63.

132. Litvak and Maule, op. cit. (note 2), 205.

133. K. Simonds, "Is the World Going more Multinational", Internationalization of Business, Papers read at the Society of Business Economists Conference at Churchill College (Cambridge, April, 1971), 7.

134. Baum, op. cit. (note 60), 429.

135. Rostein, op. cit. (note 59), 190.

136. Charles P. Kindleberger, American Business Abroad (New Haven : Yale University Press, 1969), 210.

137. Feltham and Rauenbusch, op. cit. (note 46), 54-5.

138. Baum, op. cit. (note 60), 425-430.

139. Detlev Vagts, "The United States of America and the Multinational Enterprise", op. cit. (note 2).

140. Stevens, op. cit. (note 17), 54.

141. W. G. Friedmann and J. F. Garner (ed.), Government Enterprise - A Comparative Study (New York : Columbia University Press 1970), 325.

142. Teague, op. cit. (note 3), 31.

Reference Notes for Chapter 6 - Ownership and Control contd

143. Schmitthoff, op. cit. (note 23), 26.

144. Ewing, op. cit. (note 20), 130.

145. Jack N. Behrman, "Multinational Corporations, Transnational Interests and National Sovereignty", Columbia Journal of World Business (March-April 1969), 15.

146. Ross, op. cit. (note 33), 339.

147. Baum, op. cit. (note 60), 436.

148. Hymer, op. cit. (note 22), 62.

149. Hymer, 63.

150. Fayerweather, op. cit. (note 25), 215.

151. Lester R. Brown, World Without Borders (New York : Random House, 1972), 310.

152. Jantsch, op. cit. (note 13), 10.

153. Stopford and Wells, op. cit. (note 36), 181.

154. Tugenhat, op. cit. (note 24), 217-18.

155. Stanley Hyman, Management and World Development (London: Sir Isaac Pitman and Sons Limited, 1967), 105.

156. Brown, op. cit. (note 151), 311-12.

157. Hymer, Op. cit. (note 22), 54-5.

158. Stevens, op. cit. (note 17), 54 ; United Nations, op. cit. (note 26), 92.

159. Ewing, op. cit. (note 20), 138. United Nations, op. cit. (note 26), 77.

160. Behrman, op. cit. (note 10).

Reference Notes for Chapter 6 - Ownership and Control contd

161. Wooton, op. cit. (note 9), 6.

162. Perlmutter, op. cit. (note 89), 439.

163. Baum, op. cit. (note 60), 430.

164. Kendall, op. cit. (note 5), 65.

165. Roy A. Matthews, "The Multinational Firm and the World
     of Tomorrow", op. cit. (note 4), 165.

166. Matthews, 164.

167. Brown, op. cit. (note 151), 301.

168. Eells, op. cit. (note 98), 502.

169. Charles Henry Alexandrowicz, The Law of Global
     Communications (New York : Columbia University Press, 1971),
     144-5.

170. Ball, op. cit. (note 14), 28.

171. Wooton, op. cit. (note 9), 5. Max Mark, Beyond Sovereignty
     (Washington : Public Affairs Press, 1965), 130.

172. Business International, op. cit. (note 31), 27.

173. E. A. G. Robinson, The Structure of Competitive Industry
     (Cambridge : James Nisbet and Company and Cambridge
     University Press, 1958), 141.

174. Eells, op. cit. (note 95), 67.

175. United Nations, op. cit. (note 26), 87.

176. United Nations, 93.

177. Raymond Vernon, Sovereignty at Bay (London : Longman, 1971),
     284.

338.

Reference Notes for Chapter 6 - Ownership and Control contd

178. Fayerweather, op. cit. (note 25), 216.

179. Burchill, op. cit. (note 1), 15-16, 18.

180. Brown, op. cit. (note 151), 312.

181. Eells, op. cit. (note 95), 70.

182. Ball, op. cit. (note 14), 29-30.

183. Detler F. Vagts, "The Host Country Faces the Multinational
     Enterprise", Boston University Law Review (1973), 275-6

184. Behrman, op. cit. (note 10), 4-5.

185. Louis Turner, Invisible Empires : Multinational Companies and
     the Modern World (London : Hamish Hamilton. 1970), 207.

186. Kierans, op. cit. (note 70), 173.

187. Kierans, 174.

188. Berle and Means, op. cit. (note 63), 196, 207, 218.

189. A. B. Levy, Private Corporations and Their Control (London :
     Routledge and Kegan Paul Limited 1950), 817, 855-6.

190. Tom Hadden, Company Law and Capitalism (London : Weidenfeld
     and Nicolson, 1972), 133, 138, 288, 289, 436.

191. C. Wilfred Jenks, "Multinational Entities in the Law of Nations"
     Transnational Law in a Changing Society, ed. Wolfgang Friedmann,
     Louis Henkin and Oliver Lissitzyn (New York : Columbia University
     Press, 1972), 79, 80.

192. Ross, op. cit. (note 33), 338.

193. Paul Leleux, "France, Belgium, European Economic Community
     and the Multinational Enterprise," op. cit. (note 2), 103-4.

Reference Notes for Chapter 6 - Ownership and Control contd

194. Ball, op. cit. (note 14).

195. Philip Colebrook, Going International - a Handbook of British
     Direct Investment Overseas (London : McGraw - Hill, 1972),
     206.

196. Ross, op. cit. (note 33), 339.

197. Wolfgang Friedmann, Law in a Changing Society (Middlesex :
     Penguin Books, 1972), 333.

198. Ball, op. cit. (note 14).

199. Richard Eells, The Meaning of Modern Enterprise - An
     Introduction to the Philosophy of Large Corporate Enterprise
     (New York : Columbia University Press, 1960), 315.

200. Galbraith, op. cit. (note 68).

201. Friedmann, op. cit. (note 66), 19.

202. Richard Eells, The Government of Corporations (New York :
     The Free Press, 1962), V, 142.

203. Eells, 149.

204. Berle and Means, op. cit. (note 63), 313.

205. Scott Buchanan, The Corporation and the Republic (pamphlet)
     (New York : The Fund for the Republic, 1958), 20.

206. Eells, op. cit. (note 199), 323.

207. Eells, 332.

208. Henning, op. cit. (note 65), 918. Chayes, "The Modern
     Corporation and the Rule of Law", The Corpor-
     ation in Modern Society (E.S. Mason, ed., 1959),
     25-45.

340.

Reference Notes for Chapter 6 - Ownership and Control contd

209. Henning, op. cit. (note 65), 919, 920, 923.

210. Henning, 924.

211. David P. Rutenberg (quoting Clee and di Scipio), "Organizational
      Archetypes of a Multi-National Company", Management Science (B)
      (February 1970), 338.

212. Galbraith, op. cit. (note 71), 84, 98.

213. Alfred D. Chandler, Jr. Strategy and Structure : Chapters in
      the History of the American Industrial Enterprise (Cambridge,
      Mass : The M.I.T. Press (paperback), 1962), 30.

214. Chandler, 30, 31.

215. Chandler, 384.

216. Stopford and Wells, op. cit. (note 36), 10.

217. Kolde, op. cit. (note 88), 174, 187, 188, 190.

218. Stanley A. Kaplan, "Foreign Corporations and Local Corporate
      Policy", Vanderbilt Law Review (May 1968), 433.

219. James Willard Hurst, The Legitimacy of the Business Corporation
      in the Law of the United States 1780-1970 (Charlottesville, Va. :
      The University of Virginia, 1970.

220. Clive M. Schmitthoff, "New Concepts in Company Law", The
      Journal of Business Law (1973), 312.
      Clive M. Schmitthoff, "The Reform of Company Law", 93.
      See Also: D. A. Sarre, "The Lawyer in International Business"
      The Journal of Business Law (1972), 104.

221. Hadden, op. cit. (note 190), 451-2.

Reference Notes for Chapter 6 - Ownership and Control contd

222. Clive M. Schmitthoff, ed., The Harmonisation of European
Company Law (London : The United Kingdom National
Committee of Comparative Law, 1973).

223. Colebrook, op. cit. (note 195), 207.

224. Sampson, op. cit. (note 125).

225. Paquet, op. cit. (note 4), 11.

226. Ewing, op. cit. (note 20), 142.

227. Burchill, op. cit. (note 1), 9-10.

228. Baum, op. cit. (note 60), 437.

229. Jenks, op. cit. (note 191), 81, 82.

Reference Notes for Chapter 7 - Antitrust

1   Frederick T Knickerbocker, Oligopolistic Reaction and Multinational
    Enterprise (Boston: Division of Research, Graduate School of
    Business Administration, Harvard University, 1973) 192-206.

2   Stephen Hymer and Robert Rowthorn, "Multinational Corporations
    and International Oligopoly : The Non-American Challenge",
    The International Corporation, ed Charles P Kindleberger (Cambridge,
    Mass. : The MIT Press, 1970), 74.

3   Hymer and Rowthorn, 75.

4   Frederick L Pryor, "An International Comparison of Concentration
    Ratios", Review of Economics and Statistics (1972), 130-140.

5   Alfred Conard, "Chapter & Fundamental Changes in Marketable
    Share Companies", Volume XIII Business and Private Organizations,
    ed. Alfred Conard, International Association of Legal Science
    (Tubingen : J C B Mohr (Paul Siebeck), 73-74.

6   Nicholas A H Stacey, Mergers in Modern Business (London :
    Hutchinson & Co, 1970), 13-29.

    Hymer and Rowthorn, op. cit. (note 2), 81.

7   Christopher Layton, Cross Frontier Mergers in Europe (Bath :
    Bath University Press, 1971).

8   PhilipSiekman, "Europe's Love Affair with Bigness", Fortune
    (March 1970), 95-8.

343.

Reference Notes for Chapter 7 - Antitrust contd

9   "Japan Acts Against Fibre Cartel, Chemical Week (January 3, 1973) 29.

10   Raymond Vernon, "Antitrust and International Business", Harvard Business Review (Sept-Oct 1968), 82.

11   Hymer and Rowthorn, op. cit (note 2), 85.

12   Remarks of Ambassador Harold B Malmgren, Deputy Special Representative to the United States President for Trade Negotiations, delivered at Round Table discussion of The Multinational Corporation and World Economic Development April 27, 1972.

13   D H W Henry, "Anti-Monopoly Leglislation in Canada", Nationalism and the Multinational Enterprise, ed. H R Hahlo, J Graham Smith and Richard W Wright (Leiden : A W Sythoff and Oceana Publications, 1973), 310.

14   Special Report to stockholders entitled "Proposals to effect the Union of the Operating Activities of the Dunlop Company Limited and Pirelli SpA and Societe Internationale Pirelli SA, December 1970, p. 4.

15   United States v Schlitz Brewing Company.
253 F Supp. 129 (D. Cal. 1966), affirmed.
385 US 37 (1966), rehearing denied.
385 US 1021 (1967).

Reference Notes for Chapter 7   Antitrust contd

16   Wilbur L Fugate, "Anti Monopoly Leglislation in the United States",
      Nationalism and the Multinational Enterprise, op. cit. (note 13),
      275.

17   United States v Standard Oil Co CCH 1970 Trade Cas. 72,988
      (N.D. Ohio 1969), consent decree.

18   Edwin M Zimmerman, "Antitrust Problems in International
      Operations", Private Investors Abroad - Problems and Solutions
      in International Business in 1971, ed The Southwestern Legal
      Foundation (New York : Matthew Bender, 1971), 285-6.

      Op. cit. (Note 16), 276.

19   Op. cit. (note 2), 82-3.

20   Clive M Schmitthoff, "The Future of the European Company Law
      Scene", The Harmonisation of European Company Law, ed
      Clive M Schmitthoff (London : The United Kingdom National
      Committee of Comparative Law, 1973), 10.

21   Hymer and Rowthorn, op. cit. (note 2), 64.

22   G Philip Nowak, Note : "The Multinational Corporation as a
      Challenge to the Nation-State : A Need to Co-ordinate National
      Competition Policies", Vanderbilt Law Review (1969), 86.

23   Henry, op. cit. (note 13), 326.

24   Kurt Markert, "Anti-Monopoly Legislation in Europe" op. cit.
      (note 13), 282.

Reference Notes for Chapter 7 - Antitrust contd

25   A van Oven, "The Intra-Enterprise Conspiracy Paradox",

      European Competition Policy, ed. The Europa Institute of the

      University of Leiden (Leiden : Sijthoff, 1973), 105-9.

26   Corwin D Edwards, "The World of Antitrust", Columbia Journal

      of World Business (July-August 1969), 25.

27   Nowak, op. cit. (note 22), 79.

28   Nowak, 79-81.

29   Hyman and Rowthorn, op. cit. (note 2), 58, 73, 82-4.

30   Hyman and Rowthorn, 84.

31   Hyman and Rowthorn, 80.

32   Siekman, op. cit. (note 8), 168-9.

33   Helmut Arndt, "Basic Problems of Concentration Policy",

      The Antitrust Bulletin (1972), 1122-3.

34   Hyman and Rowthorn, op. cit. (note 2), 81, 86.

35   Nowak, op. cit. (note 22), 95.

36   Hyman and Rowthorn, op. cit. (note 2), 86.

37   Hyman and Rowthorn, 90-91.

38   J J Servan-Schreiber, "American Capitalism in Europe - A

      European Point of View", Antitrust Law Journal (1971), 964.

39   Henry, op. cit. (note 13), 316.

40   A Report of the Committee of Experts on Restrictive Practices,

      Market Power and the Law (Organization for Economic Co-operation

      and Development, 1970), 187.

346.

Reference Notes for Chapter 7 - Antitrust contd

41   Seymour J Rubin, "Multinational Enterprise and National
      Sovereignty : A Sleptic's Analysis", Law and Policy in
      International Business (1971), 14-15.

42   Vernon, op. cit. (note 10), 73.

43   Siekman, op. cit. (note 8), 98.

44   Corwin D Edwards, Control of Cartels and Monopolies An
      International Comparison (Dobbs Ferry, New York : Oceana
      Publications, Inc. 1967), 321.

45   Heinrick Kronstein, The Law of International Cartels (Ithaca,
      New York : Cornell University Press, 1973), 480.

46   Henry, op. cit. (note 13), 328.

47   Vernon, op. cit. (note 10), 86. See Chapter XVII "Possibilities
      and Problems of International Collaboration", op. cit. (note 44), 321.

48   OECD, op. cit. (note 40), 15-17.

49   Report of the Attorney Generals' National Commitee, The United
      States Department of Justice, 1955.

50   Joseph E Seagram & Sons, Inc v Hawaiian Oke Liquors Limited
      416 F2 71 (1969).

51   Cliff Food Stores, Inc v Kroger Inc. 417 F2 203 (1969).

52   See dissenting opinion in United States v Timken Roller Bearing Co.
      341 US 593 (1951).

53   Taken from van Oven, op. cit. (note 25), 111.
      Decision of the EEC Commission of June 18 1969, OJ. L. 165/12
      (1969) CMLR, D36.

Reference Notes for Chapter 7 - Antitrust - contd

54   Taken from van Oven, op. cit. (note 25), 112.

Bulletin E.G. 1969, No 8, 40/41.

55   Taken from van Oven, op. cit. (note 25), 113-4.

Judgment of November 25, 1971, Case No 22/71, (1972) CMLR,

81-102.

56   (1972) CMLR, 95.

57   van Oven, op. cit. (note 25), 117-8.

58   James A Rahl, Common Market and American Antitrust (New York :

McGraw-Hall 1970), 181-199.

59   United States v Minnesota Mining and Manufacturing, 92 F.S. 947

(1950).

60   United States v Penn-Olin, 378 US 158 (1964).

61   March 20, 1967, Trade Cases 72.001 (1967).

62   M R Mok, "The Jointly-Owned Subsidiary (Joint Venture) and

Article 85 of the EEC-Treaty", European Competition Policy,

ed. The Europa Institute of the University of Leiden (Leiden :

Sijthoff, 1973), 135.

63   Mok, 131, 136-139.

64   Mok, 132, 136.

65   Rahl, op. cit. (note 58), 174-180.

66   Rene Joliet, Monopolization and Abuse of Dominant Position

(Lay Haye : Faculte de Droit, Liege Martinus, 1970), 13-15.

348.

Reference Notes for Chapter 7 - Antitrust contd

67 Joliet, 290-293.

Note that the European Court of Justice in its decision of February 21, 1973 in the Continental Can case appears to have agreed with the Commissions views. See : Branches and Subsidiaries in the European Common Market (London _ Harrap Handbooks 1973), 26.

68 Joliet, 290-293.

69 Clive M Schmitthoff, ed, European Company Law Texts (London Stevens & Sons Limited, forthcoming 1974), See Text 9 "Proposal for a Regulation of the Council on the Control of Concentrations between Undertakings submitted by the Commission to the Council on July 18, 1973. "

70 Joliet, op. cit. (note 66), 11, 131, 247, 250.

71 Joliet, 10.
OECD, op. cit. (note 40), 97-8.

72 OECD, 103.

73 OECD.

74 OECD, 94

75 OECD, 17.

76 Edwards, op. cit. (note 44), 183.

77 OECD, 22, 47, 59-60.

78 See United States v Philadelphia National Bank, 347 U.S. 321(1963).

79 OECD, 194-5.

80 OECD, 60,98.

81 Joliet, op. cit. (note 66), 298-9.

82 OECD, 196.

Reference Notes for Chapter 8 - Labor

1. John Genrard, Multinational Corporation and British Labour.
    A Review of Attitudes and Responses (London: British-North
    American Research Association, 1972), 1.

2. International Labor Office, Multinantional Enterprises and Social
    Policy (Geneva, 1973), 46.

3. David H. Blake, "Corporate Structure and International Unionism",
    Columbia Journal of World Business (March-April 1972), 20.

4. John Allan James, "Multinational Trade Unions Muscle Their
    Strength", European Business (Autumn 1973), 36.

5. Hans Gunter, ed. , Transnational Industrial Relations (London:
    Macmillan, 1972), 438.

6. International Association of Machinists, "Multinational Corporations,
    A Threat to America's Future", pamphlet (Washington, D.C.), 3.

7. Stephen K. Smith, "National Labor Unions v. Multinational
    Companies: The Dilemma of Unequal Bargaining Power", Columbia
    Journal of Transnational Law (1972), 124-157

    Alfred Kamin, ed. , Western European Labor and the American
    Corporation (Washington, D.C.: The Bureau of National Affairs
    Inc. , 1970), 19.

8. I. A. Litvak and C. J. Maule, "The Union Response to International
    Corporations" Industrial Relations (February 1972), 64.

350.

Reference Notes for Chapter 8 - Labor contd

9. Japan Air Lines, "Business in Japan: The Labor Movement",
    pamphlet (Japan, 1972).

    See also T. F. Adams and N. Kobayashi, The World of
    Japanese Business (Tokyo: Kodansha International, Ltd., 1969).

10. James, op. cit. (Note 4), 36.

11. Gennard, op. cit. (Note 1), 5-6 10, 19, 25.

12. ILO, op. cit. (Note 2), 158.

13. K. W. Wedderburn, "Industrial Relations", Nationalism and the
    Multinational Enterprise, ed. H. R. Hahlo, J. Graham Smith, and
    Richard W. Wright (Leider: A. W. Sijthoff and Oceana Publications,
    1973), 253.

14. Gennard, op. cit. (Note 1), 15, 42.

15. Charles Levison, International Trade Unionism (London: George
    Allen & Unwin Ltd., 1972), 110-11.

16. James, op. cit. (Note 4), 45.

17. Gunter op. cit. (Note 5), 419, 443.

18. Levinson, op. cit. (Note 15), 102, 104.

19. See James , op. cit, (Note 4), 38.

20. See James, 41-43.

21. Levinson, op. cit. (Note 15), 104.

22. Regarding Dunlop Pirelli see The Economist (November 25, 1972), 117
    Chemical Week (July 5, 1972), 15.

351.

Note 22 (contd)

"Multinationals: A Step Toward Global Bargaining", Business Week (October 28, 1972), 52.

"U. S. Unions find Allies Abroad" Business Week (February 17, 1973), 66.

23.   Karl F. Treckel, "The World Auto Councils and Collective Bargaining", Industrial Relations (February 1972), 72.

Levinson, op. cit. (Note 15), 107.

James, op. cit. (Note 4) 42-3.

24.   ILO, op. cit. (Note 2), 103-4.

25.   Wedderburn op. cit. (Note 13), 252.

26.   Levinson, op. cit. (Note 15), 111.

27.   ILO, op. cit. (Note 2), 91.

28.   ILO, 102-3.

29.   Litvak and Maule, op. cit. (Note 8), 68-9.

30.   Otto A. Freidrich, "German Co-Determination: Parity is the Goal", Columbia Journal of World Business (Jan-Feb, 1970), 49.

31.   Fritz Fabricius, "A Theory of C-determination", The Harmonisation of European Company Law ed. Clive M. Schmitthoff (London: The United Kingdom National Committee of Comparative Law, 1973), 138.

352.

Reference Notes for Chapter 8 - Labour contd

32.   Maurice Kay, "A Theory of Co-determination - A Comment",
       op. cit. (Note 31), 157.

33.   Wedderburn, op. cit. (Note 13), 254.

34.   Wedderburn, 255.

       ILO, op. cit. (Note 2), 104.

35.   Wedderburn, 256.

36.   The Economist (June 12, 1971), 47.

37.   Maurice Kay, "Disclosure and Collective Bargaining", Journal of
       Business Law (1973),   126-134.

38.   ILO, op. cit. (Note 2), 115.

39.   ILO, 117.

40.   ILO, 155.

41.   ILO, 151.

42.   ILO, 155.

43.   James, op. cit. (Note 4), 42-45.

44.   David Banan, "Comment" The Multinational Enterprise, ed.
       John H. Dunning (London: George Allen & Unwin, 1971), 166.

45.   The Sunday Times Magazine (London, May 26, 1974).

46.   Nat Goldfinger, "The Case for Hartke-Burke", Columbia Journal of
       World Business (Spring 1973), 22-26.

       ILO, op. cit (Note 2), 36.

Reference Notes for Chapter 8 - Labor contd

47. Gennard, op. cit. (Note 1), 9.

48. Gennard, 11, 40.

49. Elizabeth Jager, "Multinationalism and Labor: For Whose Benefit",
Columbia Journal of World Business (Jan. -Feb. , 1970), 56.

Reference Notes for Chapter 9 - Taxation

1. James S. Shulman, The Tax Environment of Multinational Firms
(Boston: Bureau of Business and Economic Research, Northeastern
University, 1967), 173-4., Drawing from the thoughts of Professor
Edith Penrose of the University of London in a lecture entitled
"The Economic Neutrality of the Large International Firm",
delivered at Harvard University in 1966.

2. Raymond Vernon, The Economic Environment of International Business
(Englewood Cliffs, New Jersey: Prentice-Hall, 1972), 242.

3. Vernon, 243.

4. Ernst K. Briner, "International Tax Management", Management
Accounting (February, 1973), 48.

5. David K. Eiteman, Multinantional Business Finance (Reading,
Massachusettes: Addison-Wesley Publishing Company, 1973), 146.

6. Eiteman, 146,

7. Endel J. Kolde, International Business Enterprise (Englewood Cliffs,
New Jersey: Prentice-Hall, 1973), 255.

8. W. A. P. Manser, The Financial Role of Multinational Enterprises
(London: Cassell/Associated Business Programme Ltd., 1973), 84.

9. United Nations, Department of Economic and Social Affairs,
Multinational Corporations in World Development (ST/ECA/190)
(New York, 1973), 67-69.

Reference Notes for Chapter 9 - Taxation contd

10. Sanford Rose, "Multinational Corporations in a Tough New World",
     Fortune (August, 1973), 57.

11. Eiteman, op. cit. (Note 5), 150-51.

12. Manser, op. cit. (Note 8), 105-6.

13. Manser, 108.

14. Kolde, op. cit. (Note 7), 251.

15. Vernon, op. cit. (Note 2), 244.

16. Manser, op. cit. (Note 8), 98.

17. Adrian A. Krogen, "Avoidance of International Double Taxation
     Arising from Section 482 Reallocations", California Law Review
     (November, 1972), 14, 93.

18. Michael Z. Brooke and Lee Remmers, The Strategy of Multinational
     Enterprise (London: Longman, 1970), 309-10.

19. Manser, op. cit. (Note 8), 102.

20. Eiteman, op. cit. (Note 5), 148.

21. Eiteman.

22. Eiteman, 256-57.

23. Kolde, op. cit. (Note 7), 250.

24. Eiteman, 146.

25. U.N., op. cit. (Note 9) 89.

26. U.N., 91.

356.

Reference Notes for Chapter 9 - Taxation contd

27. Ulrich Anschutz, "Harmonization of Direct Taxes in the European
Economic Community", Harvard International Law Journal (1972), 1

28. Guido Brosio, "National Tax Hindrances to Crossborder Concentration
in the European Economic Community", Harvard International
Law Journal (1970), 311.

29. Clara K. Sullivan, The Search for Tax Principles in the European
Economic Community (Cambridge, Mass.: The Law School of
Harvard University, 1963), 24-5.

30. U.N., op. cit. (Note 9), 91.

31. Eiteman, op. cit. (Note 5), 145.

Reference Notes for Chapter 10 - Disclosure

1. Detlev F. Vagts, "The Host Country Faces the Multinational
    Enterprise", Boston University Law Review (1973), 276.

2. Joel F. Henning, "Federal Corporate Chartering for Big Business:
    An Idea Whose Time Has Come", De Paul Law Review (1972),
    920.

3. C. Wilfred Jenks, "Multinational Entities in the Law of Nations",
    Transnational Law in a Changing Society, ed. Wolfang Friedmann
    (New York: Columbia University Press, 1972), 81.

4. Stefan H. Robock and Kenneth Simmonds, "International Business:
    How Big Is It - The Missing Measurements", Columbia Journal of
    World Business (May-June 1970), 7-8.

5. Robock and Simmonds, 9, 10, 19.

6. See:

    Maurice Kay, "Disclosure and Collective Bargaining", Journal of
    Business Law (1973), 126-134.

    K. W. Wedderburn, "Industrial Relations", Nationalism and the
    Multinational Enterprise, ed. H. R. Hahlo, J. Graham Smith and
    Richard W. Wright (Leiden: A. W. Sythoff and Oceana Publications,
    1973), 249.

7. Detlev F. Vagts, Volume XIII, Chapter 12A Law and Accounting
    in Business Associations, International Encyclopedia of Comparative
    Law, (Tubingen: J. C. B. Mohr (Paul Siebeck), 11-14.

358.

Reference Notes for Chapter 10 - Disclosure contd

8. Jeffrey S. Arpan, "International Differences in Disclosure Practices", Business Horizons (October 1971), 69.

9. Robert Ball, "The Declining Art of Concealing the Figures", Fortune (September 1967).

10. Clive M. Schmitthoff, ed., The Harmonisation of European Company Law (London: The United Kingdom Committee of Comparative Law, 1973).

11. Clive M. Schmitthoff, "The Multinational Enterprise in the United Kingdom", Nationalism and the Multinational Enterprise, op. cit. (note 6), 27-8.

Clive M. Schmitthoff, "The Role of the Multinational Enterprise in an Enlarged European Community", Legal Problems of an Enlarged European Community (London: Stevens and Sons, 1972), 214-16.

Tom Hadden, Company Law and Capitalism (London: Weidenfeld and Nicholson, 1972), Chapter 7, "The Quoted Company: Legal Controls and the Disclosure System".

12. Theodore L. Wilkinson, "International Accounting: Harmony or Disharmony", Columbia Journal of World Business (March-April 1969), 32.

13. Vagts, op. cit. (note 7), 52.

14. Vagts, 12.

Paul Leleux, "France, Belgium and the EEC", Nationalism and the Multinational Enterprise, op. cit. (note 6), 111.

359.

Reference Notes for Chapter 10 - Disclosure contd

15. David K. E iteman, <u>Multinational Business Finance</u> (Reading,
    Masachusettes: Addison - Wesley Publishing Company, 1973),
    338.

16. Gerhard G. Mueller, "An International View of Accounting
    Disclosure", <u>The International Journal of Accounting</u> (1972-1973),
    122.

17. Don Berger, "Harmonization of Company Law under the Common
    Market Treaty", <u>Creighton Law Review</u> (1971), 214-216.

18. Vagts, op. cit. (note 7), 12.

19. Eiteman, op. cit. (note 15).
    Mueller, op. cit. (note 16), 121-22.

20. Mueller.
    Arpan, op. cit. (note 8), 70.

21. Andre Tunc, "A Comparison of European and British Company Law",
    <u>Harmonisation of European Company Law</u>, ed. Clive M. Schmitthoff,
    op. cit. (note 10), 44.

22. Schmitthoff, 22.

23. Wilkinson, op. cit. (note 12), 36.
    Mueller, op. cit. (note 8), 122-3.

24. Tunc, op. cit. (note 21), 43.
    Vagts, op. cit. (note 7), 15.
    Eiteman, op. cit. (note 15), 339.

25. Wilkinson, op. cit. (note 12), 32-33.

26. Wilkinson, 29-30.

27. Eiteman, op. cit. (note 15), 336-7.

28. Wilkinson, op. cit. (note 12), 34-5.

360.

Reference Notes for Chapter 10 - Disclosure contd

29. American Accounting Association, An Introduction to Financial Control and Reporting in Multinational Enterprises (Austin, Texas: Bureau of Business Research, The University of Texas at Austin, 1973), 46.

30. H. M. Schoenfeld, "Some Special Accounting Problems of Multinational Enterprises", Management International Review (4/5, 1969), 3-11.

31. J. M. McInnes, "Financial Control Systems for Multinational Operations: An Empirical Investigation", Journal of International Business Studies (Fall, 1971), 13-16.

32. Mueller, op. cit. (note 16), 118, quoting from Harold Rose, Disclosure in Company Accounts (London: Institute of Economic Affairs, Ltd., 1965), 24.
Vagts, op. cit. (note 7), 52.

33. Vagts, 50-52.
Arpan, op. cit. (note 8), 67 70.

34. Vagts.

35. AAA, op. cit. (note 29), 50-51.

36. Wilkinson, op. cit. (note 12), 35.

37. A. B. Levy, Private Corporations and Their Control (London: Routledge and Kegan Paul Limited, 1950), 819-20.
Hadden, op. cit. (note 11), 290-1.

38. Burton Teague "Multinational Corporations: Profiles and Prospects", Conference Board Record (September 1971), 31.

Reference Notes for Chapter 10 - Disclosure contd

39. AAA, op. cit. (note 29), 50.

40. Schmitthoff, Harmonisation of European Company Law, op. cit (note 10), 10.

41. Wilkinson, op. cit. (note 12), 35.

42. International Herald Tribune (June 11, 1974), 1.

INDEX